THE LAW AND THE NEW TESTAMENT

THE LAW AND THE NEW TESTAMENT

The Question of Continuity

F RANK T HIELMAN

A Herder & Herder Book
The Crossroad Publishing Company
New York

Quotations from the Old Testament and Deuterocanonical books, except where otherwise indicated, are from the New Revised Standard Version of the Bible, copyright 1989 by the Division of Christian Education of the National Council of the Churches of Christ in the USA. Used by permission. All rights reserved.

The Crossroad Publishing Company
370 Lexington Avenue, New York, NY 10017

Copyright © 1999 by Frank Thielman

Printed in the United States of America

Library of Congress Cataloging-in-Publication Data

Thielman, Frank.
    The law and the New Testament: the question of continuity / Frank
  S. Thielman.
        p.   cm.
    "A Herder & Herder book."
    Includes bibliographical references.
    ISBN 0-8245-1829-2 (pbk.)
    1. Bible. N.T.—Theology.   2. Law (Theology)—Biblical teaching.
  3. Jewish law.   I. Title.
  BS2545.L34T45   1999
  241'.2'09015—dc21   99-29119
                                                CIP

1   2   3   4   5   6   7   8   9   10   03   02   01   00   99

For Abby

Contents

Preface to the Series

THE COMPANIONS TO THE NEW TESTAMENT SERIES aims to unite New Testament study with theological concerns in a clear and concise manner. Each volume:

- engages the New Testament text directly.
- focuses on the religious (theological/ethical) content of the New Testament.
- is written out of respect for the integrity of the religious tradition being studied. This means that the New Testament is studied in terms of its own time and place. It is allowed to speak in its own terms, out of its own assumptions, espousing its own values.
- involves cutting-edge research, bringing the results of scholarly discussions to the general reader
- provides resources for the reader who wishes to enter more deeply into the scholarly discussion.

The contributors to the series are established scholars who have studied and taught the New Testament for many years and who can now reap a wide-ranging harvest from the fruits of their labors. Multiple theological perspectives and denominational identities are represented. Each author is free to address the issues from his or her own social and religious location, within the parameters set for the series.

It is our hope that these small volumes will make some contribution to the recovery of the vision of the New Testament world for our time.

Charles H. Talbert
Baylor University

Preface

THE ROLE OF THE MOSAIC LAW in Christian life and thought has been a point of dispute among Christians at least since that contentious meeting in Antioch when Peter refused to eat with Gentile believers and Paul "opposed him to his face." The reason for the prolonged debate is not far to seek: wherever the New Testament itself addresses the question, it provides a complex answer. Continuity with the Mosaic law is always mixed with elements of discontinuity, and plausible arguments can often be made for the dominance of either element.

In this book, I argue that the element of discontinuity consistently dominates the thinking of the five New Testament authors who explicitly address the question; but I try also to give due weight to, and an adequate explanation for, the elements of continuity. Not all will agree after turning the last page, but perhaps even some who beg to differ will find it convenient to have the principal passages relevant to the debate before them and some of the critical exegetical problems described. If in the process of working through these texts some readers come to understand better what Paul called "the depth of the richness of the wisdom and knowledge of God," the effort will have been worthwhile.

This already enjoyable task was made even more pleasant by the help of a number of friends. Among my professional colleagues, Brent Kinman, Eric Mason, Charles Talbert, and Ben Witherington read the manuscript in part or whole and through substantive discussions helped me to clarify my thinking at several key points. I deeply appre-

ciate the willingness of each of these productive scholars to take time
from his own labor to help me with this project. I am also grateful to
Robert Heller at Crossroad Publishing, who kindly urged me to trim
forty pages of prolixity from my original manuscript. The result is,
without question, more readable.

Samford University generously granted me a sabbatical leave during
the spring semester of 1997, when much of the book was written, and
a faculty development grant that enabled me to do a week of fruitful
bibliographical research at the Andover-Harvard Library in Cambridge,
Massachusetts.* For my parents, Calvin and Dorothy Thielman, whose
lively interest in my work has been a source of encouragement over the
years, I am deeply thankful. Most of all, I am indebted to my wife,
Abby, for her friendship, encouragement, and common labor in the service of Christ and his church. Without her help in practical ways too
numerous to recount, this book, like so much of my other work, would
not have been possible.

Frank Thielman
Epiphany 1998

---

*William R. G. Loader's substantial work *Jesus' Attitude towards the Law: A Study
of the Gospels*, WUNT 2.97 (Tübingen: J. C. B. Mohr [Paul Siebeck], 1997) unfortunately
appeared after my manuscript was complete.

Abbreviations

Abbreviations of the books of the Bible follow standard conventions. Other abbreviations and their meanings are listed below:

2 Apoc. Baruch	Syriac *Apocalypse of Baruch*
2 Enoch	Slavonic *Enoch*
AB	Anchor Bible
AGJU	Arbeiten zur Geschichte des antiken Judentums und des Urchristentums
AnBib	Analecta biblica
ANF	*The Ante-Nicene Fathers: The Writings of the Fathers Down to A.D. 325*, ed. Alexander Roberts, James Donaldson, Allan Menzies, and A. Cleveland Coxe, 10 vols. (Peabody, Mass.: Hendrickson, 1994; orig. ed. 1885–87).
AusBR	*Australian Biblical Review*
BAGD	Walter Bauer, *A Greek-English Lexicon of the New Testament and Other Early Christian Literature,* 2nd ed., translated, adapted, and augmented by William F. Arndt, F. Wilbur Gingrich, and Frederick W. Danker (Chicago: University of Chicago Press, 1979).
BECNT	Baker Exegetical Commentary on the New Testament
BETL	Bibliotheca Ephemeridum Theologicarum Lovaniensium
Bib	*Biblica*
BBR	*Bulletin for Biblical Research*
BNTC	Black's New Testament Commentary
CBQ	*Catholic Biblical Quarterly*
CEV	Contemporary English Version

Ebib	Études bibliques
EDNT	*Exegetical Dictionary of the New Testament*, ed. Horst Balz and Gerhard Schneider, 3 vols. (Grand Rapids, Mich.: Eerdmans, 1990-93).
EKK	Evangelisch-katholischer Kommentar zum Neuen Testament
Ep. Arist.	*Epistle of Aristeas*
ErIsr	Eretz Israel
HNTC	Harper's New Testament Commentaries
HTR	*Harvard Theological Review*
ICC	International Critical Commentary
IEJ	*Israel Exploration Journal*
JBL	*Journal of Biblical Literature*
JCS	*Journal of Cuneiform Studies*
JSNT	*Journal for the Study of the New Testament*
JSNTSup	Journal for the Study of the New Testament—Supplement Series
JTS	*Journal of Theological Studies*
Jub.	*Jubilees*
LCC	Library of Christian Classics
LXX	Septuagint
MNTC	Moffatt New Testament Commentary
MeyerK	H. A. W. Meyer, Kritisch-exegetischer Kommentar über das Neue Testament
NAS	New American Standard Bible
NICNT	New International Commentary on the New Testament
NIV	New International Version
NIGTC	New International Greek Testament Commentary
NovTSup	Novum Testamentum, Supplements
NPNF	*A Select Library of the Nicene and Post-Nicene Fathers of the Christian Church*, ed. Philip Schaff, 1st ser.; 14 vols. (Peabody, Mass.: Hendrickson, 1994; orig. ed. 1886–89).
NRSV	New Revised Standard Version
NTD	Das Neue Testament Deutsch
NTS	*New Testament Studies*
PTMS	Princeton Theological Monograph Series
QD	Quaestiones disputatae
REB	Revised English Bible
RSV	Revised Standard Version
SBLDS	Society of Biblical Literature Dissertation Series
SBS	Stuttgarter Bibelstudien
SBT	Studies in Biblical Theology
SEÅ	*Svensk exegetisk årsbok*

SFSHJ	South Florida Studies in the History of Judaism
Sib. Or.	*Sibylline Oracles*
SJT	*Scottish Journal of Theology*
SNTSMS	Society for New Testament Studies Monograph Series
SP	Sacra Pagina
SSEJC	Studies in Scripture in Early Judaism and Christianity
SUNT	Studien zur Umwelt des Neuen Testaments
Test. Jos.	*Testament of Joseph*
Test. Job	*Testament of Job*
TDNT	*Theological Dictionary of the New Testament,* ed. G. Kittel and G. Friedrich, 10 vols. (Grand Rapids, Mich.: Eerdmans, 1964–76; orig. ed. 1933–74).
TLNT	Celsas Spicq, *Theological Lexicon of the New Testament,* 3 vols. (Peabody, Mass.: Hendrickson, 1994).
TNTC	Tyndale New Testament Commentaries
TPINTC	Trinity Press International New Testament Commentaries
TynBul	*Tyndale Bulletin*
VTSup	Vetus Testamentum, Supplements
WBC	Word Biblical Commentary
WUNT	Wissenschaftliche Untersuchungen zum Neuen Testament
ZNW	*Zeitschrift für die neutestamentliche Wissenschaft*

1

The Mosaic Law
in the New Testament:
The Present Importance
of an Ancient Question

W HAT ROLE SHOULD THE MOSAIC LAW PLAY in Christian theology and practice? This is one of Christian theology's oldest and most persistent questions. Already in the mid-first century, it vexed the mother church in Jerusalem, its daughter church in Antioch, and Paul's mission to the Gentiles. In the second century, permutations of orthodox Christianity arose that alternately claimed that all believers should live by the Mosaic law and that the Mosaic law was the product of a pettifogging deity of secondary importance.[1]

Perhaps the clearest expression of the problem in the early history of the church is found in Justin Martyr's mid-second-century *Dialogue with Trypho the Jew*. The *Dialogue* purports to be the record of a debate between Justin and a Jewish skeptic named Trypho over the merits of Christianity. Early in the argument, Justin attempts to clarify with Trypho exactly what Trypho and his compatriots find objectionable about Christianity. This, says Trypho, is the surprising thing:

> You claim to be pious and to imagine yourselves to be different from others, but separate yourselves from them in no way nor make your manner of life different from that of the Gentiles. While keeping neither the feasts nor the sabbaths nor observing circumcision, you, at the same time, set your hope on a crucified man. You hope to receive some good thing from God although you do not keep his commandments. . . . If, then, you can offer some defense on these points and show how you hope for anything whatsoever even though you do not keep the law, this we would be especially happy to hear. (*Dialogue* 10.2–3)

Everywhere that Christianity and Judaism came into conflict or that

1

Marcionites and Gnostics pitted the God of the Mosaic law against Jesus these questions surfaced again. Everywhere that Christian thinkers such as Irenaeus, Origen, Augustine, Thomas Aquinas, Martin Luther, or John Calvin attempted to explain the entire Bible within a single, coherent theological system, it became essential to ask what role the Mosaic law played in the system.

Over the last two and a half centuries this ancient question has been raised again in two distinctive ways.[2] First, with the rise of the critical study of the Bible after the Enlightenment, the question of the place of the Mosaic law within Christian theology was caught up in the larger question of the theological unity of the Bible. In the view of many eighteenth- and nineteenth-century scholars, the Enlightenment had unshackled the Bible from the chains of official, ecclesiastical dogma, and without this official theological overlay the Bible could only be explained as a complex collection of religious traditions.[3] Because these traditions arose from a variety of cultural circumstances, they often expressed theological convictions that were incompatible with each other. By the early twentieth century the effort to find theological unity within the Christian scriptures was considered by many scholars to be the relic of a dogmatic past.[4] This distraction could now be set aside, and the task of writing a historical and scientific account of the biblical traditions could move forward. This understanding of the task of biblical scholarship still commands the assent of many biblical scholars today.[5]

Alongside this position, however, lies a position that appropriates the Enlightenment differently. Supporters of this approach celebrate with equal enthusiasm the rise of the critical age, but believe that the search for theological unity within the canonical scriptures is nevertheless scientifically defensible. The scriptures of the early Christians, they argue, were the Jewish scriptures, and writing a description of the theological indebtedness of early Christians to these scriptures seems, even from a strictly scientific point of view, not only possible but necessary.[6]

In the debate between these different appropriations of the Enlightenment heritage, the question of the early Christian understanding of the Mosaic law is critical.[7] Can we only speak of discontinuity between early Christian theology and the Jewish scriptures on this point? Or is it possible that the early Christians derived their new approaches to the Mosaic law from the Jewish scriptures themselves?

Another development of the Enlightenment—the Protestant Reformation—pushed the question of the Mosaic law's place in Christianity to the surface again in a second form. Luther and the Reformers protested against the view among Roman Catholic scholastics that human effort cooperated with God's grace to effect salvation. Standing upon Paul's own polemic against works of the law as a means of justification, Luther and the Reformers claimed that salvation was a result only of God's gracious acceptance of the sinner apart from any human effort. In many Protestant writings that make this point, Roman Catholics are paired with the Jews against whom Paul debated, and it seems to be assumed that the Jews of Paul's time believed, like the scholastics, that salvation could be achieved only by a combination of human effort and God's grace.[8]

This understanding of Judaism became common among many Christian scholars in subsequent centuries. It sometimes led to the notion that the Christian gospel, with its emphasis on God's grace, was incompatible with the supposedly legalistic Mosaic law.[9] The Enlightenment verdict that the Old Testament and the New Testament advocated incompatible understandings of the Mosaic law seemed to be a boon for these scholars. For them, the Mosaic law expressed a primitive form of religion over which the simple piety of Jesus was a profound advancement.[10]

Since the unspeakable tragedy of the Holocaust and the nauseating realization that church officials and scholars contributed to the atmosphere of anti-Semitism in Nazi Germany, however, some Christian scholars have undergone a sobering period of soul-searching.[11] This has resulted in a recognition that many Jews in the Second Temple period, even when they did not speak explicitly of the prior grace of God, assumed it, and that not every Jew of this period was mired in a degenerate legalism.[12] This reappraisal of Judaism has, in turn, produced a renewed attempt to clarify the precise nature of the quarrel between the earliest Christians and their unbelieving Jewish neighbors.[13] Since that quarrel often focused on the Mosaic law, the question of what the New Testament says about the validity of the Mosaic law has been critical to these efforts.

These two post-Enlightenment developments in biblical scholarship leave the student of the New Testament with two questions: (1) What do the New Testament texts that address the issue say about the continuing validity of the Mosaic law? (2) On this issue, are the voices within the New Testament harmonious, discordant, or some mixture of the two? In the following pages, we shall investigate these questions. We shall look only at texts in which the issue of continuity and discontinuity between the Mosaic law and the Christian gospel is an explicit and primary concern. This means the exclusion not only of some Pauline correspondence, the Petrine letters, the Johannine letters, Jude, and the Apocalypse, but, perhaps to the surprise of some, of James and Mark as well.

We shall not investigate the epistle of James because there the continuity between the Mosaic law and the gospel is not an issue. Instead, James accepts Jesus' distillations of the Mosaic law (2:8, 11, 19; 4:2, 11; 5:4) without argument or explanation as the "law of freedom" or "the royal law" (1:25; 2:8, 12) and makes no effort to show how they are related to the Mosaic law.[14] For him, and apparently for his readers, Jesus' teaching about the Mosaic law had already become the law itself, and no debate on the issue was necessary.

James has much to say about the relationship between "faith" and "works" in 2:14–26, and this might at first seem relevant. The issue in that passage, however, is not whether the Mosaic law is binding upon Christians. It is instead how intellectual assent to the Christian faith and obedience to an external ethical norm are related. That is an important theological question, and we shall address it occasionally, but it is a separate issue from the question of the Mosaic law's continuing validity.

Nor shall we look at Mark's Gospel. Mark never uses the term "law" (*nomos*), and although Jesus frequently engages in legal disputes with his opponents in the Gospel, the law is not a burning issue for him.[15] Mark's primary purpose in recording discussion over legal issues is not to clarify Jesus' position on the law but to portray him as a powerful figure, able to get the best of his opponents in debate (12:34) and to astonish those who hear him with the authority of his teaching (10:22, 26). The reason why Mark does not give the issue of the law's continuing authority more prominence is plain from his brief, parenthetical comment in 7:3–4. This aside explains to his readers in the most general terms the Jewish laws of purity, and such a comment would be necessary only if Mark were writing for a readership who knew little about the Mosaic law and for whom the issue of whether or not to observe it had long since been decided.[16]

In this study, then, we shall attempt to hear what Paul, Matthew, John, the author of Hebrews, and Luke say about the continuing validity of the Mosaic law. These New Testament voices raise the issue of continuity and discontinuity explicitly. Perhaps by listening to each voice individually and then comparing them, we shall be able to lay an exegetical foundation for further theological reflection.

NOTES

1. On second-century Jewish Christianity, see Hans Lietzmann, *The Beginnings of the Christian Church* (London: Lutterworth, 1937), 177–90; and on Marcion's antithetical approach to the Mosaic law, see Adolf von Harnack, *Marcion: The Gospel of the Alien God* (Durham, N.C.: Labyrinth, 1990; orig. ed. 1924), 73–77.

2. On the historical development of "biblical theology," see Brevard S. Childs, *Biblical Theology of the Old and New Testaments: Theological Reflection on the Christian Bible* (Minneapolis: Fortress, 1992), 3–10; and Charles H. H. Scobie, "The Challenge of Biblical Theology," *TynBul* 42 (1991): 31–61.

3. For the eighteenth century, see the translation of J. P. Gabler's seminal 1787 lecture on biblical theology in John Sandys-Wunsch and Laurence Eldredge, "J.P. Gabler and the Distinction between Biblical and Dogmatic Theology: Translation, Commentary, and Discussion of His Originality," *SJT* 33 (1980): 133–58. For the nineteenth century, see William Wrede, "The Task and Methods of 'New Testament Theology,'" in *The Nature of New Testament Theology*, ed. Robert Morgan, SBT 2.25 (London: SCM, 1973), 68–116.

4. See Hermann Gunkel, "Biblische Theologie und biblische Religionsgeschichte: I des AT," in *Die Religion in Geschichte und Gegenwart*, 2nd ed., 7 vols. (Tübingen: J. C. B. Mohr [Paul Siebeck], 1927–31), 1:1090–91, quoted in Childs, *Biblical Theology*, 6.

5. See, e.g., Heikki Räisänen, *Beyond New Testament Theology* (London: SCM; Philadelphia: Trinity Press International, 1990); and idem, "The Law as a Theme of 'New Testament Theology,'" in *Jesus, Paul and Torah: Collected Essays* (Sheffield: Sheffield Academic Press, 1992), 252–77.

6. See, e.g., C. H. Dodd, *According to the Scriptures: The Substructure of New Testament Theology* (London: Nisbet, 1952); and Peter Stuhlmacher, *How to Do Biblical Theology*, PTMS 38 (Allison Park, Penn.: Pickwick, 1995), 1–14; idem, *Biblische Theologie des Neuen Testaments*, 2 vols. (Göttingen: Vandenhoeck & Ruprecht, 1992–), 1:1–39.

7. On one side, see Hartmut Gese, "The Law," in *Essays on Biblical Theology* (Minneapolis: Augsburg, 1981), 60–92; Peter Stuhlmacher, "The Law as a Topic of Biblical Theology," in *Reconciliation, Law, and Righteousness: Essays in Biblical Theology* (Philadelphia: Fortress, 1986), 110–33; and Childs, *Biblical Theology*, 532–65, especially 550. On the other side, see Heikki Räi-

sänen, "Zion Torah and Biblical Theology: Thoughts on a Tübingen Theory," in *Jesus, Paul and Torah: Collected Essays* (Sheffield: Sheffield Academic Press, 1992), 225–51.

8. On this, see Frank Thielman, *Paul and the Law: A Contextual Approach* (Downers Grove, Ill.: InterVarsity, 1994), 14–27.

9. See, e.g., Harnack, *Marcion*, 133–45.

10. See, e.g., Gabler's comments in Sandys-Wunsch and Eldredge, "J.P. Gabler," 139.

11. On the involvement of Christian scholars in German National Socialism, see Robert P. Ericksen, *Theologians under Hitler: Gerhard Kittel, Paul Althaus and Emmanuel Hirsch* (New Haven, Conn.: Yale University Press, 1985).

12. See especially E. P. Sanders, *Paul and Palestinian Judaism: A Comparison of Patterns of Religion* (Philadelphia: Fortress, 1977).

13. See Thielman, *Paul and the Law*, 27–45.

14. See Räisänen, "The Law as a Theme of 'New Testament Theology,'" 273; and Douglas J. Moo, "The Law of Christ as the Fulfillment of the Law of Moses," in *Five Views on Law and Gospel*, ed. Greg L. Bahnsen, Walter C. Kaiser, Jr., Douglas J. Moo, Wayne G. Strickland, and Willem A. Van Gemeren (Grand Rapids, Mich.: Zondervan, 1996), 374–75.

15. On this, see Räisänen, "The Law as a Theme of 'New Testament Theology,'" 273; and Gerhard Dautzenberg, "Gesetzeskritik und Gesetzesgehorsam in der Jesustradition" in *Das Gesetz im Neuen Testament*, ed. Karl Kertelge, QD 108 (Freiburg: Herder, 1986), 54–61.

16. See Robert H. Gundry, *Mark: A Commentary on His Apology for the Cross* (Grand Rapids, Mich.: Eerdmans, 1993), 348.

2

The Mosaic Law
and the Law of Christ:
Law in Paul's Letters
to Galatia and Rome

ROM ANCIENT TIMES, Paul has been at the center of the church's debate over the Mosaic law. The reasons for this are clear. Over 60 percent of the New Testament's nearly two hundred references to the term "law" (*nomos*) belong to the Pauline letters. Yet because of the occasional nature of his letters, Paul's statements about the Mosaic law are often tolerant of more than one reading. Throughout Christian history advocates of various positions on the relationship between the Mosaic law and the Christian gospel have exploited this ambiguity to claim for their positions the authority of Paul.

Already in Paul's lifetime, some believed that his gospel implied the abrogation of the law, indeed, of any moral standard.[1] Later, Paul's statements about the law were tossed back and forth between Marcionites and various Gnostic sects on one side and the orthodox successors of the apostles on the other. One side hoped to use Paul to show that the Mosaic law was the product of an inferior God separate from the God revealed in the gospel; the other side hoped to show that the Mosaic law and the gospel both proceeded from the same gracious deity.[2]

Later still, in the swirl of theological activity around the time of the Protestant Reformation, Protestants called upon one set of Paul's statements about the law to show that salvation came through God's grace alone, while Catholics pointed to another set of statements as evidence that God's grace cooperated with human deeds to effect salvation.[3] Protestants soon became divided among themselves, some emphasizing the discontinuity between law and gospel, others emphasizing the continuity, and both appealing to Paul.[4]

In modern times, Paul's statements about the law have produced an intense debate over the nature of ancient Jewish religion. Some believe that when Paul spoke about the Jewish law he accurately targeted the legalistic tendencies of most first-century Jews. Others think that most Jews of Paul's time believed that membership in the people of God was a result of God's grace. For this second group, Paul's polemic against "works of the law" either misrepresents Judaism or is simply a denial that Gentiles must adhere to the Jewish law in order to belong to the people of God.

All this foment has also frequently brought the question of Paul's consistency to the surface. Is it possible, many inquire, that the responsibility for the confusion over Paul's view of the law lies not with Paul's interpreters or even with the incompleteness of Paul's account of the Mosaic law but with Paul himself? Perhaps the apostle's understanding of the law evolved over the years during which he wrote his letters, or, on a less sympathetic reading, is simply illogical.[5]

In two letters—Galatians and Romans—the pastoral situations that compelled Paul to write led him to discuss extensively the purpose and nature of the Mosaic law. In these letters, convictions that are expressed only briefly or subtly in other letters rise to the surface of the debate and form the focus of Paul's concern.

Although Paul discusses the Mosaic law directly and fully in these letters, the cultural, historical, and linguistic distance between these texts and the modern interpreter means that Paul's statements on the law in them are not easy to understand. Especially important for understanding Paul's comments on the law are his often unspoken eschatological convictions. These convictions were shaped by the Jewish scriptures, the writings to whose accurate interpretation Paul had devoted much of his life prior to his conversion (Acts 22:3; 23:6; 26:5; Gal. 1:14; Phil. 3:5) and which remained authoritative for him as a Christian (1 Cor. 10:6, 11; Rom. 4:23–24; 15:4; 2 Tim. 3:16). Before we attempt to understand Paul's convictions about the law in Galatians and Romans, therefore, we must first understand the biblical soil from which they grew. When we read Paul's statements about the law in Galatians and Romans in the light of these biblically shaped presuppositions we come to the following conclusions:

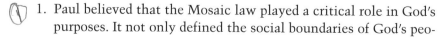

1. Paul believed that the Mosaic law played a critical role in God's purposes. It not only defined the social boundaries of God's peo-

ple, but it also defined sin as transgression of God's explicit commands and was used by sin to bring human rebellion against God to its fullest expression.

2. The death and resurrection of Jesus Christ rescued believers from this plight and brought the divinely appointed task of the Mosaic law to an end. Because the Mosaic law (is no longer in effect,) it no longer defines the boundaries of God's people. *FuLFILLED?*

3. Paul nevertheless believed that Christians are obligated to a concrete set of ethical standards, analogous to the Mosaic law and incorporating some of its precepts, but based on Jesus' ethical teaching. Paul called this new law "the law of Christ."

TRANSGRESSION, CURSE, AND HOPE IN PAUL'S BIBLE

Paul's eschatological convictions are indebted to a theological theme that appears in the Mosaic law itself and frequently throughout the Bible. This theme expresses the history of Israel as a story of the nation's failure to keep its covenant obligations to God. Although God graciously rescued his people from slavery in Egypt and called them to be his special possession at Sinai, they almost immediately forsook their commitment to follow the way of life God laid down for them in the law of Moses. Israel's downward spiral of rebellion ended in disaster when the Babylonians laid siege to Jerusalem, broke through its walls, destroyed the city and the temple, and deported all but the poorest of its citizens to Babylon. In the Mosaic law itself and frequently in the prophets, a note of hope follows the recitation of Israel's sin and its consequences.

The Theme in Leviticus and Deuteronomy

After God graciously redeemed his people from slavery in Egypt, he entered into a covenant with them in the wilderness of Sinai. The basis of the covenant was God's act of redemption (Exod. 19:4; 20:2; Deut. 5:6), and under the terms of the covenant, if Israel obeyed the laws that God revealed to Moses, God would bless them. If they disobeyed, however, they would be cursed. The covenant's blessings for obedience and curses for disobedience are specified in Leviticus and Deuteronomy.

The section of blessings in each book is brief and general, a relatively colorless recital of broad areas of life that will flourish if God's people follow his commands (Lev. 26:3–13; Deut. 28:1–14). Each book's section of curses, however, is lengthy and detailed. When examined closely, this section of each book summarizes the history of Israel as it appears in the historical books of the scriptures (Lev. 26:14–39; Deut. 28:15–68).[6]

Despite the subtle but clear message that Israel will not keep the law and will receive the law's curses for disobedience, the curse sections in both Leviticus and Deuteronomy end on a positive note. Both passages extend the hope that Israel, while experiencing the law's curses, will repent of its wickedness, turn back to God, and receive the covenant's blessings (Lev. 26:40–45; Deut. 30:1–10).[7] Deuteronomy, moreover, hints that God himself will initiate this period of repentance and restoration by circumcising the hearts of his people so that they will love him fully and live (30:6; cf. Lev. 26:41; Deut. 4:25–31).

The Theme in Jeremiah and Ezekiel

This understanding of Israel's history also appears, among other places, in Jeremiah and Ezekiel, and the notion that God must take the initiative in the restoration of Israel receives particular emphasis. Both prophets had seen firsthand Israel's disregard of the law and its willingness to mingle worship of God with worship of foreign deities. Jeremiah had seen his countrymen claim a magical immunity from harm, despite their flagrant violation of the law, because they were circumcised and because they offered sacrifice in God's temple (Jer. 4:4; 6:20; 7:4, 12–14; 9:25–26; 11:15; 14:12). He had also received the brunt of their angry rejection of God's word (11:21–23; 20:1–6; 26:7–11; 36:1–26; 38:6–13). It is therefore not surprising that he viewed the people among whom he prophesied as indelibly tainted with sin (4:22; 8:4–5; 13:23; 32:30).

The source of this trouble, according to Jeremiah, lies in the hearts of the people. Although circumcised physically, they have uncircumcised hearts (4:4; 9:26) that need to be washed to remove their wickedness (4:14) and that are both stubborn and rebellious (5:23; 9:14). Like their polluted worship, their hearts are deeply etched with evil (17:1). The result of this condition is rebellion against the Mosaic law and punishment according to the curses that the law pronounces against the disobedient (9:12–16).

Ezekiel is equally pessimistic about the tendency of God's people to rebel against the law. Their history was tainted by profound ingratitude toward the God who had rescued them from the desperate conditions of Egyptian bondage. It was marred by rebellion against the covenant that God had graciously made with them to separate them from all the nations of the earth as his special people (16:1–52; 20:1–31; 23:1–49). God had given them the law so that they might obey it and live (20:11), but not only had they violated it (20:21, 24), they had used it perversely as an instrument of disobedience (20:25).[8] The result, as in Leviticus, Deuteronomy, and Jeremiah, was destruction (16:35–52). Like Deuteronomy and Jeremiah, Ezekiel identified the source of the problem as the people's heart. It was stubborn (3:7), wanton (6:9), hard as stone (11:19), attracted to detestable things (11:21), devoted to idols (14:5; 20:16), sick (16:30), and greedy (33:31).

Perhaps because of this intensely pessimistic perspective on Israel's ability to obey God's law, both Jeremiah and Ezekiel claimed that Israel's future restoration must come at God's initiative. At its center must be God's recreation of the hearts of his people to take away their entrenched tendency toward disobedience. This would happen, according to Jeremiah, when God entered into a new covenant with his people, a covenant analogous to but greater than the covenant God made with his people at Sinai:

> The days are surely coming, says the LORD, when I will make a new covenant with the house of Israel and the house of Judah. It will not be like the covenant that I made with their ancestors when I took them out of the land of Egypt—a covenant that they broke, though I was their husband, says the LORD. But this is the covenant that I will make with the house of Israel after those days, says the LORD: I will put my law within them, and I will write it on their hearts; and I will be their God, and they shall be my people. No longer shall they teach one another, or say to each other, "Know the LORD," for they shall all know me, from the least of them to the greatest, says the LORD; for I will forgive their iniquity, and remember their sin no more. (Jer. 31:31–34; cf. 23:7–8; 24:7; 32:40; 50:5; Ezek. 11:19–20; 20:33–38; 34:25; 36:25–28; 37:26)

When Ezekiel expresses this vision, he not only speaks of a renewed covenant (Ezek. 20:30–33; 34:25; 37:26) and recreated hearts (Ezek 11:19–20; 36:25–27) but also of the presence of God's Spirit among his people. During the time of Israel's restoration, he says, God will give his Spirit to his people so that they might do his will:

I will sprinkle clean water upon you, and you shall be clean from all your uncleannesses, and from all your idols I will cleanse you. A new heart I will give you, and a new spirit I will put within you; and I will remove from your body the heart of stone and give you a heart of flesh. I will put my spirit within you and make you follow my statutes and be careful to observe my ordinances. (Ezek. 36:25–27; cf. 11:19–20; 37:1–14; 39:29)

The Theme in Paul's Time

Both the notion that Israel lived in a state of exile because of its disobedience to the law and the idea that God would one day intervene in this situation to provide its permanent remedy enjoyed wide currency during the time of Paul. The prayer of confession in Baruch 1:15–3:8, for example, begins with an account of Israel's tendency to follow "the intent of our own wicked hearts" (1:22; 2:8) and to disobey "the statutes of the Lord" (1:18; 2:10). As a result, "to this day there have clung to us the calamities and the curse that the Lord declared through his servant Moses" (cf. 2:6). Toward its conclusion, however, the prayer paraphrases Deut. 30:1–10 to express the hope that in exile God's people will turn from their seemingly indelible wickedness when God gives them obedient hearts, attentive ears, and makes "an everlasting covenant with them to be their God and they . . . [his] people" (2:29–35).

This prayer was probably composed in the second century B.C. and, since it occurs in a liturgical setting in Baruch, was probably used in the worship of the synagogue. It may still have been in use during the time of Paul and is an example that could easily be multiplied of the prominence of these themes during Judaism's Second Temple period.[9] It is not surprising, then, that these presuppositions also lie beneath Paul's understanding of the law in Romans and Galatians.

THE LAW OF MOSES, THE LAW OF CHRIST, AND PAUL'S GALATIAN CHURCHES

Paul's letter to the Galatians attempts to rescue several of his churches in south-central Asia Minor from a group of unorthodox Jewish Christian missionaries. In Paul's eyes these "agitators" (1:7) have misunderstood the relationship between the Mosaic law and the gospel of Jesus

Christ. Claiming that the covenant of circumcision God made with Abraham was eternal (Gen. 17:9–14), they have told the Gentile Christians in Galatia that in order to belong to the people of God they must not only believe in Christ Jesus but also accept circumcision and the entire Mosaic law (Gal. 4:21; 5:2; 6:12–13).

In addition, they have mounted an attack on Paul himself, who, they say, has conveniently claimed that membership in the people of God comes through faith in Jesus Christ alone. Such a "gospel," they claim, is a renegade truncation of the authentic message of the Jerusalem apostles (2:6–10). It panders to those who are unwilling to submit to the yoke of the Mosaic law and is tailored to produce easy, if unauthentic, conversions (1:10).

The Incident at Antioch
and Its Theological Implications (Gal. 2:11–21)

Paul knew when he dictated Galatians that before he addressed his opponents' understanding of the relationship between the Mosaic law and the gospel, he had to repair the damage they had done to his character.[10] He devotes the first section of the epistle, therefore, to the refutation of his opponents' claims that he had no authority to preach the gospel except as it was kindly dispensed to him by the Jerusalem apostles—apostles who, his opponents say, agree with them (1:11–2:21).

Paul concludes his self-defense by telling the story of his encounter with Peter, one of the Jerusalem apostles, at the church in Antioch. The Christians in Antioch included both Jews and uncircumcised Gentiles, and the two groups met together for the common meals that formed an important part of Christian fellowship in the early church. Peter had come to visit Antioch and at first had eaten with the Gentile believers. Later, however, under pressure from a group of Jews claiming to be messengers from the Jerusalem church, Peter, Barnabas, and all the other Jewish Christians except Paul withdrew from fellowship with the Gentile believers.[11] This withdrawal, at least as Paul saw it, was an attempt to force the Gentiles to accept the Jewish way of life (2:11–14). Paul's theological commentary on this episode (2:15–21) provides a transition from the portion of the letter in which he defends himself to the part in which he defends his understanding of the gospel. This dense paragraph encapsulates the argument of the rest of the letter.[12]

Paul begins the paragraph by observing something that every Jew who had read Deuteronomy and Jeremiah, Leviticus and Ezekiel should know: no one has kept the terms of the covenant that Moses mediated to God's people at Mount Sinai:

> We are Jews by nature and not Gentile "sinners." But since we know that a person is not justified by works of the law but only through faith in Jesus Christ, even we have believed in Christ Jesus in order that we might be justified by faith in Christ and not by works of the law, because no flesh shall be justified before him by works of the law. (2:15–16)

The last phrase is reminiscent of Ps. 143:2 ("Do not enter into judgment with your servant, for no one living is righteous before you") and therefore underlines the Jewishness of Paul's conviction that no one has kept the law. If this is true, Paul says, then all believing Jews should know that their only hope for acquittal before God's tribunal on the final day rests with Messiah Jesus and not in accepting the yoke of the Mosaic law. Obedience to the Mosaic covenant had been unsuccessful, and God's people had received the promised punishment of exile and foreign domination. Now, however, God had initiated the period of restoration with the coming of the Messiah. The people from James and the other Jews in Antioch, along with Paul's opponents in Galatia, by making conformity to the Mosaic law a requirement for salvation, have implied that the law can justify. This, Paul says, is something that Jews who have read their scriptures know not to be true.[13]

Now that the Messiah has come, Paul continues, the covenant that God made with Israel at Sinai in some instances no longer defines sin. This is probably the significance of Paul's statement in 2:17:

> But if, while seeking to be justified by Christ we ourselves were also found to be sinners, is Christ then a servant of sin? Surely not!

The statement is notoriously obscure, but within its broad context it is probably best understood as a reference to the Antioch incident. At that time, the people from James, Peter, Barnabas, and the rest of the Jews found Paul to be out of conformity with the Jewish law, and therefore to be a sinner. Thus, while Paul attempted to live out the implications of justification by faith in Christ ("while seeking to be justified by Christ"), the others viewed him as no better than a Gentile sinner ("we ourselves were also found to be sinners"; cf. 2:15).

The trouble lay in two different definitions of sin. Those who gathered under the banner of the Jerusalem church believed that eating with uncircumcised Gentiles, presumably without asking questions about the origin and purity of the food, was a violation of the Mosaic dietary laws and therefore sin. Paul believed that the dietary require-ments of the Mosaic law were no longer binding on the people of God, now composed of both Jews and Gentiles. Violating those require-ments was therefore not sin, and so Christ, as proclaimed in Paul's gospel, is not the servant of sin.[14] To the contrary, Paul goes on to say, one becomes a transgressor by reasserting the binding authority of the Mosaic dietary laws and therefore rebuilding the walls of division between Jew and Gentile (2:18). "For through the law I died to the law, that I might live to God" (2:19).

Paul appears to be saying that the covenant God made with Israel at Mount Sinai is no longer in effect. Not only have Jews and Gentiles been rescued by faith in Christ from the law's just penalty for disobe-dience, but the law itself no longer defines who is inside and who is outside the people of God. Now a new principle appears to guide God's people, and following the law's dietary regulations, if those regulations are interpreted to forbid eating a meal with Gentile believers, entails "transgression" of that principle.[15]

Paul Supports His Position
from Experience and Scripture (Gal. 3:1–5:1)

This opening salvo has, however, left important questions unan-swered. On the basis of the Jewish scriptures alone, it is difficult to see how Paul can conclude that Gentiles should become part of God's peo-ple without accepting the Mosaic law. After all, Ezekiel's prophetic vision appears to exclude uncircumcised Gentiles from the restored Jerusalem (Ezek. 44:7, 9). What evidence can Paul offer for his claim that the dividing wall of the Mosaic covenant has been removed? Is not the solution to disobedience, as in the time of Ezra and Nehemiah, greater conformity to the law rather than abandonment of it?[16] Why should this be incompatible with the belief that the prophetic prom-ises of restoration were being fulfilled in Messiah Jesus? Perhaps most important of all, if Paul is correct that the Mosaic covenant no longer governs the conduct of God's people, then where can the believer find ethical guidance?

Paul fills much of the rest of the letter with arguments that answer these questions. In this part of the letter, he produces two kinds of evidence that, despite expectations to the contrary, God has included Gentiles among his people without requiring their conformity to the Mosaic law. First, he briefly reminds the Galatian readers of their own experience of God's eschatological Spirit: God had included them in the eschatological outpouring of his Spirit promised by the prophets merely through their passive hearing of the gospel, not through any active acceptance of the yoke of the Mosaic law (3:1–5; cf. 3:14). Second, and at much greater length, Paul supplies biblical evidence that the inclusion of Gentiles apart from the Mosaic law had always been God's design and that, in light of this, the Galatians must reject the agitators (3:6–5:1). In order to understand Paul's approach to the law in Galatians, we must look at this second point carefully.

Paul's goal in 3:6–5:1 is to answer the question, Who are the children of Abraham? The agitators had probably first raised this issue with the Galatians and pointed out that, according to Genesis, the distinguishing mark of Abraham's people, whether born from him or purchased from foreigners as slaves, was circumcision (Gen. 17:13a). Moreover, the rite of circumcision (Gen. 17:10) was to be an "everlasting covenant" (Gen. 17:7, 13b), and anyone who remained uncircumcised would be "cut off from his people" (Gen. 17:14). Although Abraham was at first an uncircumcised believer (Gen. 15:6), he obediently accepted circumcision as a divinely ordered second step in becoming the father of God's people (Gen. 17:23–27). If the Galatians want to be Abraham's spiritual descendants, the agitators probably said, then they must accept the law. Otherwise they will become like Ishmael, who was driven away because he was not the rightful heir of Abraham (Gen. 21:8–14).

Paul understands the Genesis account of Abraham, his descendants, and their relationship to the Mosaic law differently. His argument takes three steps and ends with a forceful series of admonitions based on his conclusions. The first two steps examine, in turn, the positive benefits of faith and the negative consequences of life under the law. The third step contrasts two biblical narratives, one that is important to Paul and another that is important to his opponents.

First, Paul makes the positive point that Gentiles who define themselves by faith are the offspring of Abraham and the recipients of scripture's blessing (3:6–9). His text is Gen. 15:6, which, according to Paul's rendering, says that Abraham "believed God and it was reckoned to him as righteousness." Paul takes this statement as an affirmation that God justifies those who have faith, and concludes from it that those who have faith are offspring of faithful Abraham (3:7, 9). Since uncircumcised Gentiles can have faith, they can qualify as Abraham's offspring and consequently represent the fulfillment of scripture's proclamation to Abraham, "all the Gentiles shall be blessed in you" (Gen 12:3; 18:18). Gentiles who only have faith and cannot claim allegiance to the law, then, nevertheless belong to Abraham's family because of their faith, and they too stand under the scripture's benediction.

Second, Paul turns to the negative side of his argument from scripture and focuses on scripture's approach to those who define themselves by means of the law (3:10–14). Paul reminds his readers that according to scripture, those who do not keep the law fall under a curse and those who succeed in keeping it receive life (3:10, 12). The agitators, however, by their efforts to enforce the law among the Galatian Gentiles, have made a serious blunder in time-keeping. Every biblically literate Jew should know that "those who define themselves by means of the law are under a curse" (3:10) because Israel has broken the Mosaic law and has received the law's penalty of destruction and exile. Now, however, the Messiah himself has absorbed the law's curse and initiated the time of redemption (3:13; cf. 4:5), when, as God promised to Abraham and the prophets, the Gentiles will be blessed and God's Spirit will dwell among his people (3:14).[17]

Third, Paul contrasts the biblical narrative most critical to those who define themselves by faith with the biblical narrative most important to those who define themselves by the law. The founding narrative for believers, Paul assumes, is the record of God's covenant, made directly with Abraham "and with his seed" (3:15–16). The corresponding narrative for Paul's judaizing opponents is the record of God's mediation of the law through Moses to his people (3:17–18). The path of Paul's argument in 3:15–5:1 is sometimes obscure, and interpreters have mapped it in several different ways over the centuries, but six points of contrast between the two narratives seem clear.

1. Christ and those who belong to Christ (3:29) are linked with the Abrahamic covenant, not with the Mosaic covenant (3:15–16).
2. The arrival of the Mosaic covenant 430 years after God's covenant with Abraham could not invalidate or amend God's original covenant with Abraham (3:15, 17).[18]
3. God made the covenant with Abraham directly (3:16, 17, 18), but the Mosaic covenant required a mediator (3:19).[19]
4. The direct nature of the covenant with Abraham demonstrates

more clearly the oneness of God (Deut. 6:4) than the mediated nature of the Mosaic covenant (3:20).[20]

5. The Mosaic covenant served the temporal purpose of revealing sinful human conduct as transgression of God's will (3:19, 22), but the covenant with Abraham was eternal, since it incorporated a promise that would be eschatologically fulfilled (3:22, 29; 4:7).[21]

6. Those who represent the fulfillment of God's promise to Abraham should expel from their midst those who attempt to reintroduce the outmoded Mosaic law (4:21–5:1).[22]

The Galatians and the judaizers in their midst may have been more interested, however, in a difference Paul does not mention: the Abrahamic covenant contains no guidance for ethical behavior, but the Mosaic covenant is filled with detailed directives for behaving as the people of God. After their conversion, the Galatians may have felt ethically adrift. Cut off from their own traditions (4:8–10), Paul's ethical teaching may have seemed too vague and untested to provide them with a sufficient ethical anchor. The agitators' gospel, however, possessed all the needed qualities: the Mosaic law that they advocated was ancient and held in high regard among many Gentiles. Moreover, it provided the detailed guidance and ethnic identity that the Galatians had lost when they had turned away from their own religious traditions.[23]

The Law of Christ (Gal. 5:2–6:18)

For Paul's argument to carry conviction in such a situation, it needed to answer the critical question of how, apart from accepting the Mosaic law, one can live in a way that is pleasing to God. Paul's attempt to address this issue (5:2–6:10) emphasizes the advent of two new realities in the eschatological age: the Spirit's presence within believers and the concrete ethical teaching of "the law of Christ."

The Spirit, Paul says, has come to believers in fulfillment of God's biblical promise (5:5, 16–25; cf. 3:2–5, 14; 4:6), and this means that believers have the inner guidance of the Spirit in ethical matters. Their most fundamental ethical "rule" is to live in a way that is consistent with their status as God's eschatological "new creation" (6:15–16).

The eschatological age had not arrived completely, however, and in the meantime, some concrete ethical guidance was necessary. Paul finds it in something called "the law of Christ." He does not explain precisely what this is; but he provides a hint about its origins in two places. First, he says that bearing one another's burdens meets this law's requirements (6:2). This is simply an earthy way of expressing Jesus' own summary of the Mosaic law's second table in terms of love for neighbor (Matt. 22:39; Mark 12:31; Luke 10:27; cf. John 13:34; 15:12, 17; 1 John 4:11).[24] Second, Paul grounds his command that the Galatians "enslave" themselves to one another "through love" (5:13) in the dictum, "For the whole law is fulfilled in one word, 'You shall love your neighbor as yourself'" (5:14). Although Paul does not mention Jesus' example and teaching explicitly here, they provide the simplest explanation for the connection between serving as another's slave and the summary of the Mosaic law in terms of the love command in Lev. 19:18. Just as Jesus had summarized the ethical portion of the Mosaic law with Lev. 19:18 and had himself said that his followers should imitate his example of serving rather than seeking to be served (Mark 10:41–45; John 13:1–16), so Paul admonishes the Galatians to love one another as Lev. 19:18 demands and to show that love through service to each other.[25] For Paul, therefore, the law of Christ was Jesus' own ethical teaching and example.[26] Although it had absorbed elements of the Mosaic law, this was a different law and formed the new norm for the people of God during the period of the dawning eschaton.[27]

If this is correct, then it may explain how Paul could say on the basis of Peter's behavior at Antioch that the Jerusalem apostle was a "transgressor" (2:18). Peter had kept the dietary rules of the law of Moses; but by withdrawing from fellowship with Gentile believers, he had violated the requirement of "the law of Christ" that believers show love for their neighbors. Two different laws are in view here: the law of Moses, which builds a wall of division between Jew and Gentile, and the law of Christ, which breaks it down. Peter became a transgressor by violating the law of Christ. He should have known that "in Christ Jesus neither circumcision nor uncircumcision amounts to anything, but faith working through love" (5:6).[28]

In summary, Paul argues in Galatians that God's people violated the Mosaic law and received the law's curses upon the disobedient (2:16; 3:10–14). God has restored his people, as the prophets promised he would, by sending his Holy Spirit among them (3:2–5, 14; 4:6; 5:5), and ethical guidance in this new era is dominated by the twin elements of the Spirit's leading and the law of Christ (2:18; 5:14; 5:16–26; 6:2). Why, then, did God give the Mosaic law? Paul claims in Galatians that it was a temporary institution, operative until the coming of Christ and designed to enclose all things under sin (3:19–4:7). In the age of fulfillment, its divinely appointed function is complete, and it passes from the scene. Gentiles join the people of God, therefore, not through accepting the yoke of the law, but in the same way that God reckoned Abraham to be righteous—through faith alone (3:6–9).

THE LAW, THE GOSPEL, AND THE CHURCH AT ROME

Paul wrote Romans to a Christian community he had never visited. Nevertheless, he had many friends there, all people whom he had met elsewhere in the course of his missionary labors and who, through various circumstances, had settled in Rome. His letter seems to have had three primary purposes.

First, he wanted the Roman Christians to pray for the success of an offering that he was taking from his predominantly Gentile churches in the West to Jewish Christians in Jerusalem. The offering would help relieve suffering in the midst of a Judean famine; but, more importantly, it would demonstrate the spiritual unity of Gentiles and Jews who confess Jesus as Lord (15:25–27, 30–31).[29]

Second, he hoped that the Romans would support his proclamation of the gospel in Spain, where he intended to go after his important work in Jerusalem was complete (15:24). The Romans, however, had heard rumors that Paul's emphasis on God's gracious response to human sin encouraged sinful behavior (3:8; 6:1, 15). Paul writes to set the record straight and to clear the way for the Romans' support of his Spanish mission.[30]

Third, Paul had heard from his friends in Rome that disunity was plaguing the community: a law-observant minority and an anti-Semitic majority were at odds (11:17–20, 25; cf. 12:3). As the apostle to the Gentiles, Paul believed that he had some pastoral responsibility to help restore the unity of this predominantly Gentile Christian community (1:11–15; 15:14–16; cf. 14:1–15:13).[31]

Each of these concerns provided a reason for Paul to place before the Romans an outline of the gospel as he might preach it in a Jewish synagogue. By doing this he would address Roman concerns over his view of the law. At the same time, he would provide a theological foundation for his relief work in Jerusalem and for his exhortation to the Roman Christians that they should be unified. Paul's imaginary Jewish audience, whose presence in the argument is represented by a fictive but skeptical debating partner, is deeply concerned about the place of the Mosaic law in Paul's gospel. This concern, it turns out, is also vitally relevant to the situation of the Roman Christians. Not surprisingly, then, the Mosaic law plays a crucial role in each of the five steps by which Paul's argument proceeds.[32]

The Law of Moses Condemns both Jews and Gentiles (Rom. 1:18–3:20)

Paul begins by arguing that no one can claim exemption from God's just sentence of condemnation on the final day (3:9, 19–20). A synagogue congregation would find this easy to believe for Gentiles, and Paul begins where his work is easiest. Paul's audience would have agreed that Gentiles generally were wicked and that their wickedness was without excuse. God had, after all, revealed to them in his creation "his eternal power and divine nature" (1:20), and they could perceive the "just requirement of God" that their wicked practices deserved death (1:32). Their failure to worship God and their unrighteous social relationships, therefore, are alike "inexcusable" (1:20). In the words of the unknown Jewish author of the Wisdom of Solomon (first century B.C.):

> . . . while they live among his works, they keep searching and they trust in what they see, because the things that are seen are beautiful. Yet again not even they are to be excused; for if they had the power to know so much that they could investigate the world, how did they fail to find sooner the Lord of these things? (13:5–9)

Paul must argue against Jewish exemption from the day of judgment more carefully, however. In Paul's time, as in the time of Jeremiah, some Jews apparently believed that their status as God's elect people, a status that their possession of the Mosaic law proved (Exod. 19:5–6), would protect them from condemnation on the final day. The Gentiles would feel the full brunt of God's wrath on that day, some thought; but God would deal more gently with Israel. "While chastening us," said the author of Wisdom, God will "scourge our enemies ten thousand times more" (12:22; cf. 15:2; 16:2). Against this idea, Paul states a premise that every Jew should recognize from the scriptures: "There is no partiality with God" (cf. Deut. 10:17; 2 Chr. 19:7).[33] If this is true, Paul says, then the author of Wisdom was wrong: the Jew can expect no special treatment on the final day (2:3), for "God will render to each person according to his works," punishment to those who do evil, whether Jew or Gentile (2:9), but "glory and honor and peace" to those who do good, whether Jew or Gentile (2:10).

Against the possible protest that the Gentile has not kept the law, but the Jew has, Paul goes on to say that, as it turns out, Gentiles sometimes keep the law and Jews have often broken it. The law's basic requirement is written on Gentile hearts, and the consciences of Gentiles are able to measure their conduct against this innate standard (2:12–16, 28–29). Jews who know their history, however, will agree that their own record of law-keeping has been far from perfect. Despite their possession of the full record of God's will (2:20; cf. 3:2; 9:4), their disobedience to it often led to suffering. This suffering in turn led to the heckles of the surrounding nations—heckles directed not merely against Israel but against Israel's apparently impotent God (2:21–24; cf. Isa. 52:2 and Ezek. 36:20). The critical issue on the day of judgment, then, will not be whether one possesses the law, or has the mark of physical circumcision, but whether one has kept the law. Like the Gentile, the Jew has failed this test (2:25–29).

Thus, Paul uses the law in the first section of the letter to demonstrate that not even the Jew can claim exemption from God's guilty verdict on the unrighteous at the day of judgment. The Gentiles know enough of the law to render them without excuse for their disobedience to it. Jews cannot legitimately claim that possession of the law exempts them from condemnation. Since God is impartial and since they have violated the law, they too will stand before God without excuse on the final day. Possession of the law provides no immunity from judgment, Paul concludes. Instead, the law defines sin (3:20; cf. 7:7).

The Law of Faith Justifies
both Jews and Gentiles (Rom. 3:21–4:25)

The next step in Paul's argument describes God's gracious solution to the universal plight of sin (Rom. 3:21–4:25). Paul first recounts the action God has taken to deliver people from this plight. He then describes two consequences of this action, using the law's own account of Abraham's faith to prove his claims. In this way he demonstrates, in the face of objections that he has abolished the law, that he has instead established it.

God remedied the universal human plight, says Paul, through the redemption effected by Christ Jesus, "whom God presented as an atoning sacrifice in his blood, [appropriated] through faith" (3:25). This phrase is rich with cultic imagery from the Mosaic law. The Septuagint uses the term "presented" (*protithēmi*) to refer to the presentation of offerings in the sanctuary, especially to the bread regularly "displayed" before the Lord there (Exod. 29:23; 40:23; Lev. 24:8; cf. 2 Macc. 1:8, 15).[34] It also uses the term translated above as "atoning sacrifice" (*hilastērion*) to refer to the cover on the ark of the covenant, the place where, on the Day of Atonement, Aaron was to sprinkle the blood of a bull and the blood of a goat to atone (*exilasasthai*) for his own sins and for the sins of all Israel (Lev. 16:2, 13–15).[35] Since Paul also couples the term with a reference to Christ's blood, all within an explanation of God's remedy for human transgression, he is probably saying that Christ's death was the climactic and final Day of Atonement sacrifice. Through his death, God ushered in a new age (3:21) and provided the final atonement for all previous sin (3:25–26).

Paul next describes the two results of this climactic event. First, he says, its entirely gracious character (3:24) excludes boasting. Paul has just said in the first section of his argument that some Jews boasted in possession of the law (2:17, 23), and he knows from his own experience (Phil. 3:4–6) that some Jews believed that their own obedience to the law played a role in securing their salvation. The law with its prescription of certain works, Paul says, did not succeed in excluding either kind of boast. "The law of faith" (3:27), however, eliminates both. What is the law of faith? It is probably God's climactic work of atonement "by faith in [Christ's] blood," which Paul has just described in 3:25.[36] The graciousness of this event, which Paul stressed in 3:24, makes boasting in either the possession of or the doing of the Mosaic law impossible.

This was even true, Paul goes on to say, for Abraham. As pious as he could claim to be in comparison to other people, he could not boast of his accomplishments before God (4:2). He had to enter a right relationship with God in the same way that all the wicked do—by faith in God's ability to accomplish his promises (4:20–21).

The second result of Christ's climactic sacrifice of atonement is that Gentiles as well as Jews can now belong to the people of God (3:29–30). Not only is the inclusion of the Gentiles consistent with the Jewish conviction that God is sovereign over the whole world (3:30; Deut. 6:4), but it represents the fulfillment of God's promise to make Abraham the father of many nations. Since God had justified Abraham on the basis of his faith prior to his circumcision (4:10), and since through faith uncircumcised Gentiles can now be included in God's people (3:30), the common link of faith had indeed made Abraham the "father" of many nations (4:11).

The fulfillment of this promise would have been impossible, Paul says, if only "the people of the law" were Abraham's heirs. He would then be the father only of Israel, a nation that through its transgression of the law had experienced not blessing but wrath (4:13–15).

Abraham, therefore, demonstrates that God justifies both Jews and Gentiles by faith apart from possession or performance of the Mosaic law. God's promise that Abraham would become the father of many nations also finds fulfillment in the faith of uncircumcised Gentiles in Jesus Christ. Since Abraham's story is recounted in the narrative portion of the Mosaic law, Paul is able to deny that he has abolished the Jewish law in his gospel (3:31).[37] He has instead established the law by showing how the gospel fulfills one of the law's central promises.

The Law of Sin and Death Gives Way to the Law of the Spirit of Life (Rom. 5:1–8:39)

Paul next describes the life that people live who have been justified by faith (5:1–8:39). They live at peace with God (5:1, 11), in the assurance of God's future faithfulness (5:2–5; cf. 8:11, 18–25), and in freedom from sin's domination (6:6–7, 11–14, 17–19, 22; 7:4–6; 8:2, 4, 12–15). The term "law" appears frequently in this description, sometimes playing a positive part, but more often assuming a negative role. It is holy, righteous, good, from God, and correctly asks for the believer's obedience (7:12, 22, 25; 8:7); but it is also allied with transgression, sin and death (5:12–14, 21; 6:14–15; 7:1–25; 8:2). The tension between these two uses of the word "law" comes to a climax in 8:2, where Paul says that "the law of the Spirit of life in Christ Jesus has set you free from the law of sin and death."

How can the Mosaic law play all of these roles? Does Paul contradict himself? Does he have in mind, at least in some of his tensive statements, two ways of understanding the Mosaic law? Does he portray the Mosaic law, despite its holiness, justice, and goodness (7:12), as consistently aligned with sin, speaking positively of the law in 8:2 only in a metaphorical sense? Does he assume the existence of two laws? If we follow Paul's argument carefully in this section, keeping in mind what we have already learned about the law from previous sections, the fog of ambiguity begins to clear.

In 5:12–21 Paul describes the basis for his claim in 5:1–11 that the believer will be saved from God's wrath on the final day.[38] Christ's obedience, he says, has reversed Adam's disobedience and its disastrous effects for all humanity. Adam brought sin and death to all people, but Christ has brought the gift of righteousness and life to all. The basic contrast is straightforward enough, but it leaves three questions unanswered: (1) Since Adam lived before the Mosaic law, does Paul's claim that through Adam's sin "death spread to all people because all sinned" contradict his previous claim that "where there is no law there is no transgression" (4:15)? (2) Does the contrast imply that Adam and Christ are in some way equals, one on the negative side, the other on the positive side? (3) Does it imply that the Mosaic law, which is left out of the contrast, has an insignificant role in God's historical purposes?

Paul's answer to the second question need not detain us; but his responses to the first and third questions reveal a critical element in his understanding of the Mosaic law: both responses link the law with sin. Paul's first clarification (5:12–14) demonstrates that although there is no transgression where there is no law (4:15), sin and its penalty of death still exist because of Adam's disobedience. The law makes it possible to "reckon" (*ellogeō*) sin precisely as transgression against one or more of God's commandments; but it only made worse the rebellion against God that was already in the world from the time of Adam's transgression.[39] Paul's third clarification (5:20) takes the connection between the law and sin further. The law, Paul says, played an important but subsidiary role in salvation history: it transformed Adam's transgression of a single commandment into Israel's rebellion against a whole range of God's commandments.[40] As Paul will say later, the sinfulness of sin is revealed in its insidious use of the good commandment to lead people into death through rebellion against God (7:11, 13). Thus, the law made sin increase and set the stage for the even greater increase of God's grace through the sacrificial death of Christ (3:24).

This, Paul recognizes, is too much for his Jewish debating partner. If an increase in sin were God's purpose in giving the law, then should people not sin in compliance with this purpose (6:1)? Moreover, if the law is as closely allied with sin and death as Paul claims, then is the law not itself evil (7:7, 13)?

Paul answers these objections by pointing to the believer's death with Christ, newness of life, and break with sin's domination. He also clarifies the link between the law and sin. The change through which the believer has passed means that he or she stands ready for service to God and to righteousness (6:2–23) and that the grip of sin over the person, made possible through its alliance with the law, is broken. "Sin shall not be your master," Paul says, "for you are not under law but under grace" (6:14; cf. 6:15), and a few paragraphs later, "you have been put to death with respect to the law through the body of Christ" (7:4; cf. 7:1).

The believer's release from the law because of its entanglement with sin does not mean, however, that the law is evil. Instead, "another law" is responsible for the sin-wracked "body of death" that belongs to unbelievers. This other "law" is sin's grip on the person's "flesh," "body," and "faculties," a grip so firm that even the person who agrees that the law is good and mentally delights in it finds it impossible to do (7:14–25). The law, then, is not at fault: in itself it is entirely good (7:12, 14a, 22). Sin uses the law to deceive the self into rebellion against God (7:11), and to prevent the self, when it is disposed to keep God's law, from fulfilling its good intentions (7:23). Only sin's insidious use of the law for these purposes places the law on the side of sin and death.

Now that Paul has answered his Jewish debating partner's objections to his claim that the law increased the trespass, he returns to his primary theme in chapters 5, 6, and 8: the quality of the life lived by those who have been justified. He describes again the believer's future hope, a hope grounded in God's sacrifice of his own son for us (8:18–39; cf. 5:1–11). He also describes the transformation of the believer's life in the present, a transformation that frees the believer to live in submission to God (8:1–13; cf. 5:12–19; 6:2–13, 16–23).

Here too the connection between the law and sin (5:20–21; 6:14–15) reappears, and, thanks to Paul's clarifications in chapter 7, is now safe from misunderstanding. Drawing upon his discussion of the law in the immediately preceding paragraphs, Paul says that we have been set free from "the law of sin and death" (8:2; cf. 7:7, 13). He says that God has accomplished the condemnation of sin in the flesh, something that "the law, because it was weakened by the flesh" could not do (8:3; cf. 7:14). He also claims, again using ideas familiar from the previous discussion, that the fleshly mind cannot "submit to God's law" (8:7; cf. 7:22–23).

But what is the reader to make of Paul's claim that "the law of the Spirit of life in Christ Jesus has set you free from the law of sin and death" (8:2)? And what does Paul mean when he says that those who live by the Spirit fulfill the law's "just requirement" (8:4)? A close look at the function of these statements within their immediate context and at their connection with statements about the law elsewhere in this section brings clarity to this suddenly positive use of the term "law."

First, in 8:2 Paul refers to two different laws. The "law of sin and death" must be the Mosaic law, since Paul's references to the Mosaic law in the preceding paragraphs have, as we have seen, linked it consistently with sin and death. From this law, Paul says, believers have been "set free," an echo of his claim in 7:3 that the believer "is free from the law." Their freedom from the Mosaic law has been secured by "the law of the Spirit of life in Christ Jesus," an echo of Paul's claim in 7:4–6 that the believer's death to the law "through the body of Christ" means that "we serve in the newness of the Spirit, not in the oldness of the letter." This new law, then, is both the believer's unity with Christ's death and the work of the Spirit in the believer's life. It is reminiscent of the "law of faith" in 3:27, which God also instituted through the death of Christ (3:25) and with which he replaced the Mosaic law.

Second, in 8:4 the believer's fulfillment of the law's "just requirement" comes as a result of Jesus' sacrificial death, which "condemned sin in the flesh" (8:3). Since Paul has described at length only a few sentences earlier sin's use of the flesh to frustrate the desire of the inner self to keep the tenth commandment (7:7–12), he must be speaking here of the believer's newfound ability to keep such commandments. The law that is fulfilled in the believer, then, is to some extent expressed in the Mosaic law. The commandment "You shall not covet" (Exod. 20:17; Deut. 5:21) is as authoritative for those who have experienced the newness of the Spirit as it ever was for ancient Israel.

Nevertheless, Paul's use of the term "just requirement" hints that the believer is not bound by everything in the Mosaic law. Paul has already used the phrase "just requirements of the law" to distinguish between the commandments of the law that the Gentile understands and keeps and other commandments, such as circumcision, that only the Jew keeps. The commandments understood among both Jews and

Gentiles are the "just requirements of the law," and they are the commandments that the true, spiritually circumcised Jew keeps (2:26–29). The believer's fulfillment of the law's "just requirement," therefore, is not a fulfillment of the Mosaic law, but of a new law that excludes parts of the Mosaic law and absorbs other elements of the old law into it.

To summarize, in 5:1–8:39 Paul has argued for an ineluctable connection between the law and sin. The introduction of the law into history caused humanity to violate a whole range of specific statements of God's will (5:20). This happened because in the presence of the law, the sin-dominated self, although knowing and approving of the law's goodness (7:13–25; cf. 1:32), was still deceived by sin into rebellion against God (6:14; 7:5, 7–12). The law was sin's tool for increasing human resistance to God's goodness (5:20; 6:14; 7:5, 8, 11). None of this happened outside of God's design, for God gave the law to show the gravity of sin and so to pave the way for his gracious work in Christ (5:20–21; 7:13). That gracious work has brought the era of the Mosaic law and its alliance with sin to a close for believers. Through this "law of the Spirit of life in Christ Jesus" (8:2), believers can now fulfill God's law, a law that is, however, different from the Mosaic law. Paul will help us to define it more carefully in the final two sections of his letter.

The Mosaic Law and Israel's Misstep
(Rom. 9:1–11:36)

In chapters 9–11, Paul answers a potentially fatal objection to his gospel. If, as Paul's gospel claims, uncircumcised Gentiles have been included among God's people simply on the basis of faith, and many circumcised Jews have been excluded from God's people on the basis of their unbelief, then has not God broken his promises to his people? God's word, after all, says that Israel will be God's special people among all the peoples of the earth, his "treasured possession," his "kingdom of priests," and his "holy nation" (Exod. 19:5–6).

Paul had briefly addressed this objection earlier by saying that God had not broken faith with Israel but that Israel had broken faith with God (3:1–4), a claim that corresponds to the conditional nature of God's promise to make Israel a special people among the nations of the earth ("if you obey my voice and keep my covenant . . . ," Exod. 19:5). That response, however, was too brief to do full justice to the complexities of the problem, and so Paul now undertakes a lengthier treatment. In chapters 9–11 Paul focuses on God's sovereign freedom to dispense his mercy as he chooses. No one, presumably because of human sin, can demand God's favor. Instead, they can only receive God's mercy as a gift and as a result of God's sovereign choice (9:6–24; 11:5–6).[41] In the past this has meant the choice of Isaac rather than Ishmael and of Jacob rather than Esau (9:7–13). In the present it means the choice of a larger number of Gentiles than Jews (9:24–26, 30–31; 10:20–21; 11:8–10). In the future it will mean a great influx of Jews who will turn from their disbelief and join the many Gentiles who have received God's mercy (11:11–32).

God's faithfulness to his promises to Israel can be seen in the midst of this in two ways. First, it appears in the remnant of Jews who presently believe the gospel (9:6, 27–29; 11:1–6), and second, it surfaces in the "mystery" that even the hardening of the Jewish majority is only temporary (11:11–32). Paul recognizes that this scenario did not meet with the expectations of most Jews. Those Jews who held out any hope for the Gentiles during the period of Israel's restoration appear to have assumed that Gentile recognition of Israel's God would follow the restoration of Israel as a nation.[42] Paul's Jewish debating partner would naturally want to know why in the apostle's scheme Gentiles have attained a right standing with God first, ahead of Jews. Paul answers this question in 9:30–10:21, and the Mosaic law figures prominently in his answer.

Paul states the problem in 9:30–31. Gentiles, despite their failure to pursue righteousness, unexpectedly attained righteousness, a righteousness, Paul says, that comes by faith (9:30). Israel, on the other hand, despite pursuing a law of righteousness, did not reach the law (9:31). Paul seems to have in mind two races here. The goal of one was "righteousness," and this race the Gentiles won despite their failure even to step up to the starting line. The goal of the other was "a righteous law," and Israel failed to win this race, although they ran like the wind.

"Why?" asks Paul's Jewish debating partner. Because, says Paul, Israel pursued the goal of the law as if it were to be obtained "by works" and "stumbled" over Christ (9:32–33). Paul seems to be saying that most Jews have rejected the gospel (cf. 10:14–21), and that most of those who have rejected it have done so because their concern to find righteousness by keeping the commandments of the law has led them to miss the goal toward which the law was leading all along.[43]

Changing the analogy slightly, Paul says in 10:1–4 that Christ is the "finish line" (*telos,* 10:4) of the course that the law marked out, but that many Jews, because of their zealous quest to establish their own righteousness by keeping the law have failed to perceive this when they heard the gospel (10:1–3). Succinctly put, Gentiles, although without a righteous law to pursue, obtained righteousness by believing the gospel. Jews, despite their possession of a righteous law that pointed them to Christ, continued to focus on the keeping of the law when confronted with the gospel and so failed to believe in Christ.[44]

How does the law lead to the gospel? Paul answers this question in 10:5–13 where he quotes from Leviticus and Deuteronomy. Paul's quotations from these books remind his Jewish reader that historically Israel has not kept the law and that the law itself pointed to a time when God would transform his people so that they would do his will.

First, Paul allows Moses to describe the righteousness that comes by the law in the paraphrased words of Lev. 18:5: "The person who does them [my commandments and decrees] shall live by them." As Leviticus recognizes, however, Israel would fail to perform the commandments and decrees set out in the law, and the law's curses would come upon Israel (Lev. 26:14–39). Lev. 18:5, when read in context, then, was a reminder that the law had not been kept.

Second, Paul personifies "the righteousness that comes from faith" and makes her speak the language of Deut. 8:17; 9:4; 30:12 and 14. The first two passages (8:17 and 9:4) emphasize the inadequacy of Israel's ability and righteousness. They admonish Israel not to think that "the might of [their] own hand" or "[their] righteousness" has enabled them to seize the land. This thought stands in direct continuity with Paul's claim that by rejecting the gospel, Israel has abandoned God's righteousness in an effort to establish its own (10:3).

The second pair of quotations (30:12 and 14), however, is more puzzling. Deut. 30:11–14 asserts the accessibility of the Mosaic law in a way that makes Israel's failure to choose obedience and life (30:15–20) impossible to excuse:

> Surely, this commandment that I am commanding you today is not too hard for you, nor is it too far away. It is not in heaven, that you should say, "Who will go up to heaven for us, and get it for us so that we may hear it and observe it?" Neither is it beyond the sea, that you should say, "Who will cross to the other side of the sea for us, and get it for us so that we may hear it and observe it?" No, the word is very near to you; it is in your mouth and in your heart for you to observe.

How can Paul use this passage to describe the gospel's answer to the human inability to keep the law and live? The context of Deut. 30:11–14 may provide the crucial clue. As we have already seen, Deut. 30:1–10 looks beyond Israel's disobedience and experience of the law's curse to the time when God would circumcise the hearts of his people (30:6), they would turn to him, and he would restore them (cf. Deut. 4:25–31). On the basis of Deut. 30:1–14, then, Paul is saying that God's will had been accessible to his people in the Mosaic law, but they had failed to obey it, whereas in "the word of faith" God's will is not only accessible but fulfillable. It is fulfilled when people confess Christ as Lord with their mouths and believe with their hearts that God raised him from the dead (Rom. 10:9–10).

The law of Moses, then, stands both in continuity and in discontinuity with "the word of faith." The law is continuous with the gospel because it led the way to Christ, but it is discontinuous with the gospel because it spells the end of the Mosaic covenant. Israel's failure lay in following the law up to Christ but then stumbling over him rather than believing that he was the law's fulfillment. How could Israel be expected to recognize that Christ was "the end of the law"? The law itself, Paul argues, points beyond Israel's failed attempt to keep its commandments to the eschatological period of circumcised hearts.[45] Israel should have recognized the coming of Christ as the inauguration of that period. Instead, they continued the pointless pursuit to establish their own righteousness by keeping the stipulations of the Mosaic law.

Love for Neighbor Fulfills the Mosaic Law (Rom. 12:1–16:27)

Unlike the present Israelite majority, however, the Roman Christians to whom Paul was writing had believed the gospel. In the letter's final section (12:1–16:27) Paul explains how God's extension of mercy to the believers in Rome should shape the way they live. Here, as elsewhere, the Mosaic law plays a central role.

Paul begins the section with a description of the foundation for Christian ethics. The foundation has two pillars: the presentation of the body as a living sacrifice to God and the transformation of the self by the renewal of the mind. Both pillars have implications for Paul's

understanding of the law. The first implies that the sacrificial prescriptions of the Mosaic law are now to be replaced with lives transformed by God's mercy. The idea of making a costly gift to God in
gratitude for his mercy survives the transition to the new age, but this
statement implies that in light of Jesus' ultimate sacrifice (3:25), literal
obedience to the sacrificial regulations is no longer necessary.[46] The
second pillar implies that the detailed prescriptions of the Mosaic law
have been replaced for believers in part by the inner renewal predicted
by the prophets (Jer. 31:33; Ezek. 11:19; 36:26–27) and so desperately
needed in the era before Christ (7:14–25, esp. vv. 22–23). Believers have
begun the transition from "this age" to the age in which their renewed
minds can perceive "the good and acceptable and perfect will of God"
(12:2).

This approach finds concrete expression in Paul's admonitions to
the law-observant minority and the nonobservant majority in the
Roman churches "to welcome one another" (15:7). At least some
within the Roman church continued to restrict their diet and to judge
one day, presumably the sabbath, as different from others in conformity with the Mosaic law.[47] Others within the majority, however, ate
whatever they liked and treated every day the same. Advocates of conformity to the Mosaic commands were judging those who did not follow their example, and those who refused to conform were despising
those who did. In his response to this problem Paul is unambiguous
about his own convictions on the dietary issue. He is confident "in the
Lord that nothing in itself is unclean" (14:14) and labels those who
think otherwise "the weak in faith" (14:1; cf. 15:1). Thus, he agrees
with the majority that the Mosaic commands concerning diet are no
longer binding. He does not state what he thinks about sabbath observance, but since he describes the contention over sabbath observance
in the same breath with his description of the trouble over dietary matters, he probably intended the Romans to see his own views on the two
issues as analogous. If so, Paul would have agreed with those who
treated every day alike.[48]

Two practical elements temper this conviction, however. First, Paul
believes that those who are weak in faith will sin if they act, against
their own inner convictions, as if they are free from the Mosaic law
(14:5b, 14b, 23). The majority, therefore, should not coerce people of
weak faith to adopt their position (14:13–23). Presumably God, who is
at work within the weak, will continue to renew their minds and bring
them closer to the truth.

The role of the majority, who have the technically correct position, should be to "walk in love" toward the weak (14:15). Here Paul alludes to his claim in 13:8–10 that those who love others fulfill the Decalogue. The claim almost certainly originates in the teaching of Jesus. Like Jesus, Paul summarizes the Mosaic law's social regulations using Lev. 19:18 ("You shall love your neighbor as yourself"), and, like Jesus, Paul claims that the law is fulfilled in not doing wrong to one's neighbor.[49]

Jesus' teaching here is crafted out of the Mosaic law, but for Paul it is something different (cf. 8:4). The Mosaic law requires the observance of dietary customs and special days, and Paul is convinced in the Lord Jesus that such observances are no longer necessary. The Roman Christians are obligated, however, to live by Jesus' own reshaping of the Mosaic law. Since that reshaping emphasizes love of neighbor, the non-observant majority in Rome should not despise their weaker fellow believers, but, following God's example, should welcome them into their fellowship (15:7).

In this concluding passage, then, Paul's convictions about the role of the Mosaic law during the transition to the new age become clear. The Mosaic law is no longer binding on believers. Believers instead must conform to the teaching of Jesus, teaching that absorbs within it elements of the Mosaic law, such as the Decalogue (except for the sabbath commandment, at least as commonly understood) and Lev. 19:18. Perhaps this corresponds to "the pattern of teaching" to which Paul claimed in 6:17 the Roman Christians had become obedient "from the heart."

In addition, the mind of each believer is the object of God's transforming power, and some believers have been more fully transformed than others. As a result, in some matters of minor importance, a concern for the mutual edification of believers should lead those whose faith is strong to be tolerant of behavior that is technically inconsistent with the believer's freedom from the Mosaic law.

If we now look back over the winding trail of Paul's argument in Romans, the basic elements of his approach to the Mosaic law in the letter come clearly into view. Paul believed that the Mosaic law, although itself good, was closely allied with sin. It both revealed sin (3:20; 7:7) and was used by sin to increase rebellion against God (5:20; 6:14; 7:5, 8, 11). Christ's death and God's Spirit, however, have released the believer from the grip of this deadly alliance between the law and sin (7:4–6; 8:2) and have brought the era of the Mosaic law to its divinely appointed close (9:30–10:13). The refusal to recognize this implies, whether explicitly (3:27–30) or implicitly (9:30–10:4), that human effort plays a role in salvation. This mistaken notion, moreover, is consistent with neither the law (4:1–8) nor the gospel (3:24, 27–30).

All of this means that the believer no longer looks directly to the Mosaic law for ethical guidance, but instead relies on God's renewal of the mind and on the teachings of Jesus for direction (12:1–2; 13:8–10; 14:1–15:13; Jer. 31:33–34). Since the teachings of Jesus include elements of the Mosaic law, some continuity between the two exists (13:8–10; cf. 15:4). Nevertheless, believers have been released from the law (7:4–6), its entanglement with sin (6:14–15; 7:5, 7–25; 8:2), its now obsolete ethnic boundaries (2:28–29; 3:28–30; 4:16–17; 10:5–13), and its penultimate provisions for atonement (3:25–26; 12:1). It is therefore impossible to say that the Mosaic law, as it was commonly understood in Paul's time, supplies the substance of his moral vision.[50]

PAUL AND THE MOSAIC LAW: SOME CONCLUSIONS

With Paul's statements about the Mosaic law in Galatians and Romans before us, we are now in a position to comment on some of the classic questions that have been raised over the centuries about his view. To what extent does Paul's gospel stand in continuity with the Mosaic law? What is the theological significance of Paul's contrast between faith in Christ and the works of the law? Does this contrast imply that the Judaism of Paul's time was a legalistic religion? Are Paul's statements about the law consistent with one another?

Continuity and Discontinuity

If the understanding of Paul's statements about and allusions to the Mosaic law proposed here is correct, then a reasonably clear picture emerges of the relationship between the law and the gospel. We can summarize this relationship in three points.

1. In both Romans and Galatians Paul argues that the era of the Mosaic law has passed away. Paul says this explicitly in passages where he speaks of the believer having been "released" (*katargeō*) from the Mosaic law (Rom. 7:2, 6; cf. Gal. 2:19) and of the

law's temporary function of identifying, punishing, and increasing sin. This function, Paul says, has now ceased with the coming of Christ and the Spirit (Gal. 3:19–25; 4:1–5; 5:18; Rom. 3:20; 5:20; 6:14–15; 7:1–25; 8:2). Paul also implies the cessation of the Mosaic era when he claims that central elements of the Mosaic law such as circumcision (Gal. 5:2, 6; 6:15), dietary regulations (Gal. 2:11–14; Rom. 15:14), the observance of special days (Gal. 5:10; Rom. 14:5–6), and the temple cult (Rom. 3:25–26; 8:3; 12:1), are no longer necessary.

2. In Galatians Paul says explicitly, and in Romans he implies, that the new era has brought with it a new law, "the law of Christ" (Gal. 6:2). In Galatians, Paul links this law to the teaching of Jesus by saying that it is fulfilled when believers "bear one another's burdens," a statement that echoes Jesus' own summaries of the law's second table in terms of "the golden rule" and Lev. 19:18 (Matt. 7:12; 19:19; 22:39; Mark 12:31; Luke 10:27; cf. Luke 6:31). Paul's independent use of Lev. 19:18 to summarize the law's requirements (Gal. 5:14; Rom. 13:8–10), and his claim that an unloving insistence on the Mosaic law's dietary regulations is a transgression (Gal. 2:18), increase the likelihood that he considered Jesus' teaching on love for neighbor to be part of this new "law of Christ." The new law, then, incorporates parts of the Mosaic law within it, but apparently only insofar as the teaching of Jesus reaffirms their validity.[51]

3. The demise of the Mosaic law and the introduction of the law of Christ does not mean, however, that the Mosaic law ceased to function as authoritative scripture for Paul. Specific passages within the Mosaic law, such as the Abraham narrative (Gal. 3:6–18, 29; 4:21–5:1) and the Decalogue (Rom. 13:9) continue to offer guidance for the Christian community—indeed, like all the scriptures, they were written precisely for the Christian community (Rom. 15:4)—but they are interpreted through the eschatological lens of the gospel.[52]

If we step outside Paul's letters to the Galatians and the Romans briefly, we find a hint in the Corinthian correspondence about the origin of this complex set of convictions. In both Corinthian letters Paul borrows the language of Jer. 31:31 to speak of the gospel as a "new covenant" (1 Cor. 11:25; 2 Cor. 3:6), and in 2 Corinthians he recalls passages from both Jeremiah (31:33) and Ezekiel (11:19; 36:26) to say that the gospel was "written not on tablets of stone but on the tablets of fleshy hearts" (2 Cor. 3:3). In 2 Cor. 1:22 Paul can use the language of Ezekiel's prophecy that God would put his Spirit within his people (Ezek. 11:19; 36:26) to describe the presence of the Spirit among the Corinthians. These prophetic glimpses of the time of Israel's restoration, therefore, probably provide the source for Paul's claims in Galatians and Romans that believers have been released from the Mosaic law, are obligated to walk in the Spirit, and fulfill the law of Christ.

Works and Righteousness

Several passages in Galatians and Romans claim that a right standing before God ("justification") cannot be realized through "works of the law" but only through faith. Protestant Christians have traditionally interpreted these statements to mean that a right standing with God cannot be secured through doing the good works that the law requires. Instead, justification comes solely through faith in the effectiveness of Christ's death to atone for transgression of the law.

Against this classic interpretation, some recent scholars have advocated the notion that when Paul contrasts works of the law with faith he is primarily interested in denying a nationalistic understanding of the law among Jews.[53] The problem Paul addresses in Galatians and Romans, it is said, is the claim among some Jews and Jewish Christians that the Mosaic law delineates the boundaries of the people of God. The phrase "works of the law" then refers to doing the law as a means of demonstrating membership in God's people. Since circumcision, dietary observances, and sabbath keeping were the most visible social markers of the Jewish people, these works were especially important, but viewing any or all of the law as the symbol of membership in a social group is Paul's primary concern.

The advantage of this new outlook on Paul's approach to the law is that it makes Paul fully intelligible within the social and cultural matrix of his time. Scholars have pointed out for decades that Jews of Paul's time did not typically believe that perfect obedience to the law was necessary for a right standing with God on the final day. Means of atonement were available for transgression, and every Israelite could appeal, even in the face of heinous sin, to God's abundant mercy.[54] Thus Paul himself could claim that he was "blameless with respect to the righteousness in the law" (Phil. 3:6). In other words, he had kept the law as well as he could and, when he sinned, had followed the law's provisions for forgiveness. The attitude toward the law that the new approach advocates, on the other hand, is present in a wide range of Jewish literature from Paul's time.[55] Many Jews of Paul's day rallied around the law as a national symbol, insisting especially on the identity markers of circumcision, dietary observance, and sabbath keeping. If the new understanding of the contrast between works of the law and faith in Paul's letters is correct, then Paul becomes fully intelligible against the backdrop of his own Jewish context.[56]

The new approach, however, is probably off the mark. Both the broader context of the phrase "works of the law" in the passages where it occurs and Paul's perspective on human works in his letters generally demonstrate the problems with this recent hypothesis. First, although Paul speaks of "works of the law" in Gal. 2:16 within the context of a dispute over observance of the food laws, his claim that "by works of the law shall no flesh be justified" cannot be limited to concerns over the social function of the law. This phrase, as we have seen, is a conscious echo of Ps. 143:2, and that passage is a general statement that in God's presence no one can claim to be righteous. Paul uses virtually the same phrase, echoing the same Psalm, in Rom. 3:20, and there the phrase summarizes Paul's general claim in 3:9–19 that everyone, even the Jew, is "under sin" (3:9).

Most important of all, in Rom. 3:27–4:8, Paul claims that boasting is excluded by faith rather than by works (3:27) and that a person is "justified by faith apart from works of the law" (3:28). Certainly, one conclusion Paul draws from this is that justification by faith excludes the social function of the law: "Or is God the God of the Jews only? Is he not also God of the Gentiles? Yes, of the Gentiles also!" (3:29). But as the discussion of Abraham's faith in the subsequent paragraph (4:1–8) shows, the faith–works contrast prohibits boasting in human effort generally, not simply in the use of the law to draw social boundaries. Here works earn payment (4:4); those who do not work are ungodly (4:5); and the wicked need the forgiveness of the God who justifies apart from works (4:6–8). In these assertions, the social function of the law is not at issue. Paul is claiming that no one can achieve a right standing with God by doing what is good. The boast that is excluded (4:2), then, is not a boast in possession of the Mosaic law but in doing the good things that the law requires.[57]

In their understanding of the works–faith contrast, then, the Protestant Reformers were correct. Has Paul then misrepresented Judaism as a religion in which God's favor is secured by human effort?

Jewish Legalism

Before considering this question, we must first identify the opponents against whom Paul was arguing when he contrasted works with faith. In Galatians, where this contrast first occurs historically, Paul is arguing not against Judaism generally but against Jewish Christians who have added to faith in Christ the requirement that the law must be kept.[58] For Paul, adding this requirement implies that human effort, in the form of keeping the Mosaic law, justifies. Paul is convinced that this implication is thoroughly un-Jewish, and therefore urges the Galatians to return to the gracious religion of his—and his opponents'—ancestors: "We who are by nature Jews and not Gentile 'sinners' know," he says, "that a person is not justified by works of the law" (2:15–16). Far from misrepresenting Judaism, Paul calls the Galatians back to a truly Jewish understanding of the human need for God's eschatological mercy.

In Romans Paul attacks Jewish boasting in keeping the law (3:27–4:8), but this is not an argument against Judaism generally.[59] It targets only those Jews who believed that their own works cooperated with God's grace to guarantee their right standing before God. Ample evidence is available for such notions within Judaism of the Second Temple period. The pre-Christian Paul himself had confidence that not only his Jewish identity (Phil. 3:4–5a) but also his own accomplishments (Phil. 3:5b–6; cf. Gal. 1:14) would gain acquittal before God on the final day (Phil. 3:9).[60] Luke says that Jesus told the parable of the Pharisee and the publican to "certain people who had confidence in themselves that they were righteous, and despised the rest" (Luke 18:9). In the parable itself, the aim of both the Pharisee and the publican was apparently to leave their time of prayer "justified" (18:14). Only the publican, however, who realized his sinful condition and cast himself wholly on God's mercy, succeeded.[61] The existence within Judaism of people such as the pre-Christian Paul and the Pharisee in the parable should occasion no surprise: the belief that one's own status and accomplishments will secure God's favor was probably as prevalent among first-century Jews as it was and remains in many other religious groups.

Paul, moreover, did not limit his criticism of this attitude to Jews who hoped to gain righteousness before God through compliance with the Mosaic law. To the Gentile Corinthian Christians, some of whom were placing an improper confidence in the social group to which they belonged (1 Cor. 1:12; 8:1–2; 11:18–19), Paul issues a reminder that "God chose the low and the despised things of the world—the things that are not—in order that he might nullify the things that are, so that no flesh might boast in his presence" (1 Cor. 1:29). To the Gentile majority among the Roman Christians, he issues a warning that they dare not "boast over" Jews who have not become believers. "Do not think haughty thoughts, but fear," Paul says, "for if God did not spare the natural branches, neither will he spare you" (11:20–21).

Did Paul not go further with Judaism, however? In Rom. 9:30–10:13 does he not accuse all Israel of the notion that righteousness comes through doing good works? Paul does say in 9:31–32 that Israel failed to attain the law's goal because they pursued the law "as if it were by works" and sought to establish "their own righteousness" (10:3), but we must be careful to read these claims with two qualifications in mind. First, Paul is not making a statement about all Jews for centuries past, nor is he describing "the Jewish doctrine of salvation." Instead, as 10:14–21 reveals, he is commenting on the approach to the Jewish law among Jews who have recently rejected the gospel. Second, Paul's claim that these Jews have rejected Christ in favor of a redoubled effort to keep the law does not mean that they imagined themselves to be sinless or that they failed to recognize a need for God's mercy. An important part of law-keeping was offering the sacrifices prescribed to atone for sin, and Paul, like all Jews, would have assumed this. The error of these Jews lay in imagining that their "own righteousness" could play any part in mending the broken Mosaic covenant (cf. Phil. 3:4–6, 9).

Paul, then, did not characterize Judaism as a legalistic religion. He recognized that the confidence of some Jews in their ability to contribute something to their standing before God on the final day had led them to reject the gospel. But he did not attribute this conviction to all Jews or to the Jewish religion generally. Moreover, he would have assumed that even these Jews recognized their need, at least to some extent, for God's mercy.

Paul's Consistency

If the understanding of Paul's approach to the law proposed here is correct, then Paul is consistent both with himself and with the Judaism of his time. His understanding of the relationship between the Mosaic law and his gospel is certainly complex, and his logic is a biblical logic; but if we enter this symbolic world, his view of the law makes sense. Like many Jews of his time, Paul believed that the Jewish people lived with the reality of the law's curse: they were subject to foreign domination because they had broken the covenant. Like many Jewish Christians of his time, Paul believed that the period in which God would reverse the law's curse and restore the fortunes of his people had dawned with the coming of Jesus.[62]

For Paul, unlike many others, the death of Jesus and the unexpectedly immediate inclusion of the Gentiles entailed the end of the Mosaic law rather than its vigorous reinforcement. But even here, Paul's thinking is not unprecedented. Other believers had probably also drawn the conclusion that the death of Jesus atoned for sin in some climactic way and therefore obviated the need for the temple cult.[63] The biblical book of Jonah paints a remarkable picture of God's surprising inclusion of Gentiles within his merciful purposes apart from any conformity to the Jewish law (cf. Isa. 42:6–7; 49:6). Paul, then, was not the enigma that later interpreters have sometimes thought him to be.

But even if we can explain Paul's statements about the law on the basis of these convictions, do Paul's comments really arise from any coherent view? Are they not hastily assembled arguments intended to answer the crisis of the moment rather than considered reasons why Christians should remain loyal to the Pauline gospel?[64]

If we move outside Galatians and Romans to, for example, 1 Corinthians, we find that this is not the correct approach to Paul's admittedly complex statements about the law. In 1 Corinthians the law is not Paul's central concern, and the letter was probably written prior to Paul's encounter with the judaizing "agitators" of Galatians. Yet Paul appears to assume the understanding of the law that he spells out more fully in Galatians and Romans. He assumes that the Corinthians, although predominantly Gentile, are part of the chosen people of God (1:2, 24, 27–28; 10:1) and are obligated to a concrete set of ethical standards that Paul calls variously "the commandments of God," "the law of God," and "the law of Christ" (7:19a; 9:21). Nevertheless, he also assumes that circumcision is irrelevant to membership in the people of God and that the Mosaic dietary code is no longer binding (7:19b; 10:27).

What has happened to the Mosaic law? Paul unintentionally provides an answer in a parenthetical remark that occurs within an argument on the resurrection: "the sting of death is sin," he says, "and the power of sin is the law" (1 Cor. 15:56). If we have read Rom. 7:1–25 we know what this means. The law defines sin, provides sinful people with an opportunity to rebel against God, and pronounces the curse of death on those who disobey. It does not, however, provide the remedy to this situation, and so believers are released from it. Paul had worked all this out, then, well before the composition of Galatians and Romans and apparently had made it so clear to the Corinthians when he was among them that he could assume they would understand his offhand and highly condensed reference to it here.[65]

All of this is evidence that Paul's thinking about the Mosaic law was mature by the time he wrote 1 Corinthians. Certainly he hammered out his comments in Galatians and Romans on the anvil of controversy. But the situations that called forth those letters provided occasions for his views to be expressed, not the matrix in which they were first formed.

The church's painstaking attempt from ancient times to understand Paul's view of the law and its implications, therefore, has not been misdirected. Despite its complexity and the incompleteness with which his occasional letters articulate it, Paul's understanding of the Mosaic law is worthy of the deepest theological reflection.

NOTES

1. See Rom. 3:8; 6:1, 15; Acts 21:20–21; cf. James 2:14–26 and the discussion in Peter Stuhlmacher, "Paul's Understanding of the Law in the Letter to the Romans," *SEÅ* 50 (1985): 87–104.

2. See, e.g., Tertullian, *Against Marcion* 1.20; and the Nag Hammadi text *The Testimony of Truth* 73.20–30.

3. See the Council of Trent, *Decree on Justification,* 6.10–11; and John Calvin, "Antidote to the Council of Trent" in *Tracts,* 3 vols. (Edinburgh: Calvin Translation Society, 1861), 3:110–11.

4. See John Calvin, *Institutes of the Christian Religion* 2.7.12–17 (ca. 1559); and, in contrast, Dietrich Philips, "The Church of God" (ca. 1560) in *Spiritual and Anabaptist Writers,* ed. George Huntston Williams and Angel M. Mergal, LCC 25 (Philadelphia: Westminster, 1957), 235–37.

5. Surveys of the recent debate over Paul's view of the law can be found in Stephen Westerholm, *Israel's Law and the Church's Faith: Paul and His Recent Interpreters* (Grand Rapids, Mich.: Eerdmans, 1988), 1–101; Thomas R. Schreiner, *The Law and Its Fulfillment: A Pauline Theology of Law* (Grand Rapids, Mich.: Baker, 1993), 13–31; Frank Thielman, *Paul and the Law: A Con-*

textual Approach (Downers Grove, Ill.: InterVarsity, 1994), 14–47; and Colin G. Kruse, *Paul, the Law, and Justification* (Peabody, Mass.: Hendrickson, 1996), 27–53.

6. Cf. Martin Noth, "'For All Who Rely on Works of the Law are under a Curse,'" in *The Laws of the Pentateuch and Other Studies* (Edinburgh: Oliver & Boyd, 1966), 108–17.

7. In the Septuagint, the Greek Bible that Paul often used, these passages take on a clearly prophetic tone.

8. On Ezek. 20:25, see Leslie C. Allen, *Ezekiel 20–48*, WBC 29 (Dallas, Tex.: Word Books, 1990), 11–12.

9. See Frank Thielman, *From Plight to Solution: A Jewish Framework for Understanding Paul's View of the Law in Galatians and Romans*, NovTSup 61 (Leiden: Brill, 1989), 36–45; and idem, *Paul and the Law*, 48–68.

10. On the importance of character to the ancient art of persuasion, see George A. Kennedy, *New Testament Interpretation through Rhetorical Criticism* (Chapel Hill, N.C.: University of North Carolina Press, 1984), 15.

11. On the specific dietary problem in view here, see James D. G. Dunn, *The Epistle to the Galatians*, BNTC 9 (Peabody, Mass.: Hendrickson, 1993), 117–22.

12. See Hans Dieter Betz, *Galatians*, Hermeneia (Philadelphia: Fortress, 1979), 113–14; Richard N. Longenecker, *Galatians*, WBC 41 (Dallas, Tex.: Word Books, 1990), 80–81; Frank J. Matera, *Galatians*, SP 9 (Collegeville, Minn.: Liturgical Press, 1992), 98; Jan Lambrecht, "Paul's Reasoning in Galatians 2:11–21," in *Paul and the Mosaic Law*, ed. James D. G. Dunn, WUNT 89 (Tübingen: J. C. B. Mohr [Paul Siebeck], 1996), 53–74, here at 66; and Ben Witherington, *Grace in Galatia: A Commentary on Paul's Epistle to the Galatians* (Grand Rapids, Mich.: Eerdmans, 1998), 170.

13. Cf. James D. G. Dunn, *The Theology of Paul the Apostle* (Grand Rapids, Mich.: Eerdmans, 1998), 134–35.

14. The rhetorical question, "Is Christ, therefore, a servant of sin?" may recall Jesus' own willingness to eat with those whom the Pharisees and scribes considered "sinners" (as in, e.g., Mark 2:15; Luke 15:1). See Heinrich Schlier, *Der Brief an die Galater*, MeyerK 7, 11th ed. (Göttingen: Vandenhoeck & Ruprecht, 1951), 59; Dunn, *Galatians*, 141–42. Is it possible that this question, in addition, reminds the Galatians that Christ himself dispensed with the food laws (Mark 7:15; Matt. 15:17–18)?

15. Cf. Jan Lambrecht, "Transgressor by Nullifying God's Grace: A Study of Gal 2,18–21," *Bib* 72 (1991): 217–36; idem, "Paul's Reasoning in Galatians 2:11–21," 64–66.

16. In the Dead Sea document 4QMMT, this is the solution proposed as a remedy for the plight of living during the time of the law's curse. See James D. G. Dunn "4QMMT and Galatians," *NTS* 43 (1997): 147–53, here at 148.

17. See Thielman, *From Plight to Solution*, 68–69; idem, *Paul and the Law*,

49–55, 126–28; N. T. Wright, *The Climax of the Covenant: Christ and the Law in Pauline Theology* (Edinburgh: T & T Clark, 1991), 137–56; and James M. Scott, "'For as Many as are of Works of the Law are under a Curse' (Galatians 3.10)," in *Paul and the Scriptures of Israel*, ed. Craig A. Evans and James A. Sanders, SSEJC 1 (Sheffield: Sheffield Academic Press, 1993), 187–221.

18. Witherington, *Grace in Galatia*, 243.

19. Betz, *Galatians*, 168; Dunn, *Galatians*, 191; Witherington, *Grace in Galatia*, 258–59.

20. Cf. Betz, *Galatians*, 171–73; and Longenecker, *Galatians*, 143.

21. Witherington, *Grace in Galatia*, 261–62.

22. See J. Louis Martyn, "The Covenants of Hagar and Sarah," in *Faith and History: Essays in Honor of Paul W. Meyer*, ed. John T. Carroll, Charles H. Cosgrove, and E. Elizabeth Johnson (Atlanta: Scholars Press, 1990), 160–92.

23. John M. G. Barclay, *Obeying the Truth: Paul's Ethics in Galatians* (Edinburgh: T & T Clark, 1988), 68–72.

24. Cf. Dunn, *Galatians*, 322–23; and David Wenham, *Paul: Follower of Jesus or Founder of Christianity?* (Grand Rapids, Mich.: Eerdmans, 1995), 256–61.

25. Cf. Wenham, *Paul*, 255–56.

26. On the balance between the Spirit's guidance and concrete ethical admonition in Paul, see the sage comments of Dunn, *Galatians*, 321–24. On the example of Jesus as the law of Christ, see Richard B. Hays, "Christology and Ethics in Galatians: The Law of Christ," *CBQ* 49 (1987): 268–90. Cf. Bruce W. Longenecker, "Defining the Faithful Character of the Covenant Community: Galatians 2.15–21 and Beyond," in *Paul and the Mosaic Law*, ed. James D. G. Dunn, WUNT 89 (Tübingen: J. C. B. Mohr [Paul Siebeck], 1996), 75–97, here at 92–94; and Witherington, *Grace in Galatia*, 192 and 423–24.

27. Paul may have formulated the phrase "the law of Christ" to demonstrate that this new law replaced "the Law of Moses." "The law of Moses" was a standard way of referring to the Jewish law both in scripture and in non-canonical literature from Paul's era. See, e.g., Josh. 23:6; 2 Kgs. 23:25; Dan. 9:11; Tob. 7:13; Bar. 2:2; Sus. 62; and 1 Esdr. 9:39.

28. See Thielman, *Paul and the Law*, 141–43; and Witherington, *Grace in Galatia*, 424–25. Cf. Barclay, *Obeying the Truth*, 223.

29. See A. J. M. Wedderburn, *The Reasons for Romans* (Minneapolis, Minn.: Fortress, 1991), 37–41, 70–75.

30. See Stuhlmacher, "Paul's Understanding of the Law in the Letter to the Romans," 87–104.

31. Cf. Wright, *Climax of the Covenant*, 247–48; Wedderburn, *Reasons for Romans*, 88–91.

32. Cf. Dunn, *Theology of Paul the Apostle*, 131.

33. For an extensive list of references to this notion in ancient Jewish literature, see Joseph A. Fitzmyer, *Romans: A New Translation and Commen-*

tary, AB 33 (New York: Doubleday, 1993), 303. For the currency of this notion in Paul's time, see especially Wis. 6:7; Sir. 35:15–16; *Jub.* 5:15–16; and *Pss. of Sol.* 2:18.

34. Peter Stuhlmacher, "Recent Exegesis on Rom 3:24–26," in *Reconciliation, Law, and Righteousness: Essays in Biblical Theology* (Philadelphia: Fortress, 1986), 94–109, here at 102; Arland J. Hultgren, *Paul's Gospel and Mission: The Outlook from His Letter to the Romans* (Philadelphia: Fortress, 1985), 56 and 76–77 n. 79. The term may also recall the public display of blood at the covenant ratification ceremony in Exod. 24:5–8. See James D. G. Dunn, *Romans 1–8*, WBC 38A (Dallas, Tex.: Word Books, 1988), 170. Lexically, the verb can also mean "foreordained," but ample reasons for the meaning "presented" in this passage are supplied by Christian Maurer, "προτίθημι, κτλ.," *TDNT* 8:165–67.

35. Adolf Schlatter, *Romans: The Righteousness of God* (Peabody, Mass.: Hendrickson, 1995; orig. ed., 1935), 98–99; Stuhlmacher, "Recent Exegesis," 96–103; Hultgren, *Paul's Gospel and Mission*, 58–60. For a historical survey of the vigorous debate over the meaning of *hilastērion* in 3:25, see Hultgren, ibid., 47–55.

36. Cf. Douglas Moo, *The Epistle to the Romans*, NICNT (Grand Rapids, Mich.: Eerdmans, 1996), 249–50. Because sacrificial blood was used in the ratification of the Mosaic covenant (Exod. 24:1–11), Paul may have viewed Christ's sacrificial blood not only as a Day of Atonement sacrifice but as the ratification of the new covenant as well.

37. This part of the law, says Paul, was written not only on account of Abraham, "but also on our account" (4:23–24), and so the law preaches the gospel. Cf. 10:6–8 and the comments of Richard Hays, "Three Dramatic Roles: The Law in Romans 3–4," in *Paul and the Mosaic Law*, ed. James D. G. Dunn, WUNT 89 (Tübingen: J. C. B. Mohr [Paul Siebeck], 1996), 151–64, here at 154–55 and 158–64.

38. Moo, *Romans*, 316–18.

39. The Greek term *ellogeō* was used in the commercial world to mean "charge to one's account." Paul uses it this way in Philemon 18, its only other use in the New Testament. See Carl Heinz Preisker, "ἐλλογέω," *TDNT* 2:516–517.

40. When Paul says "where sin increased, grace became more abundant," his "where" probably refers to Israel. See C. E. B. Cranfield, *The Epistle to the Romans*, 2 vols., ICC (Edinburgh: T & T Clark, 1975, 1979), 1:293; Wright, *Climax of the Covenant*, 39.

41. See Frank Thielman, "Unexpected Mercy: Echoes of a Biblical Motif in Romans 9–11," *SJT* 47 (1994): 169–81; and Stephen Westerholm, *Preface to the Study of Paul* (Grand Rapids, Mich.: Eerdmans, 1997), 106.

42. They may have understood Isa. 2:2–3; 56:6–7; and 60:1–7 this way. The liveliness of this expectation during Paul's era is evident from, for example,

Pss. Sol. 17:29–31 and possibly James's quotation of and commentary on Amos 9:11–12 in Acts 15:14–21. See James D. G. Dunn, *Romans 9–16*, WBC 38B (Dallas, Tex.: Word Books, 1988), 572; Moo, *Romans*, 684 n. 2; and Witherington, *Grace in Galatia*, 237–38.

43. See Moo, *Romans*, 626–27.

44. By continuing the race through their own "works" and righteousness, they have also forgotten that God chooses those to whom he shows mercy on the basis of his sovereignly dispensed grace, not on the basis of works (9:11, 16; 11:5–6).

45. Cf. Douglas J. Moo, "The Law of Christ as the Fulfillment of the Law of Moses: A Modified Lutheran View," in *Five Views on Law and Gospel*, ed. Greg L. Bahnsen, Walter C. Kaiser, Jr., Douglas J. Moo, Wayne G. Strickland, and Willem A. Van Gemeren (Grand Rapids, Mich.: Zondervan, 1996), 319–76, here at 324–27.

46. Cf. Moo, *Romans*, 750.

47. See John M. G. Barclay, "'Do we undermine the Law?': A Study of Romans 14.1–15.6," in *Paul and the Mosaic Law*, ed. James D. G. Dunn, WUNT 89 (Tübingen: J. C. B. Mohr [Paul Siebeck], 1996), 287–308, here at 288–93.

48. On this, see Herold Weiss, "Paul and the Judging of Days," *ZNW* 86 (1995): 137–53.

49. See Dunn, *Romans 9–16*, 779; Wenham, *Paul*, 255–56; and Stuhlmacher, "Paul's Understanding of the Law," 100–101.

50. *Contra* Karin Finsterbusch, *Die Thora als Lebensweisung für Heidenchristen: Studien zur Bedeutung der Thora für die paulinische Ethik*, SUNT 20 (Göttingen: Vandenhoeck & Ruprecht, 1996).

51. Cf. Moo, "Law of Christ," 367–70; Dunn, *Galatians*, 322–24; and idem, "'Law of Faith,'" 75–80.

52. Cf. Paul's admonitory use of the narrative portions of the law in 1 Cor. 10:1–13 and Phil. 2:14–16 and his universalizing of Exod. 20:12/Deut. 5:16 in Eph. 6:2–3. On Paul's eschatological hermeneutics, see Richard B. Hays, *Echoes of Scripture in the Letters of Paul* (New Haven, Conn.: Yale University Press, 1989), 168–73.

53. See especially James D. G. Dunn, *Jesus, Paul and the Law: Studies in Mark and Galatians* (Louisville, Ky.: Westminster/John Knox, 1990), 215–41; idem, "Yet Once More—'the Works of the Law': A Response," *JSNT* 46 (1992): 99–117; idem, *Romans 1–8*, 153–55; idem, *Galatians*, 135–38; idem, *Theology of Paul the Apostle*, 354–66.

54. See, e.g., George Foot Moore, *Judaism in the First Centuries of the Christian Era: The Age of the Tannaim*, 3 vols. (Cambridge, Mass.: Harvard University Press, 1927–30), 2:93–95; and E. P. Sanders, *Paul and Palestinian Judaism: A Comparison of Patterns of Religion* (Philadelphia: Fortress, 1977), 1–428.

55. On the literary evidence, see Dunn, *Romans 1–8*, lxix–lxxi.

56. This is the point of Dunn's 1983 article, "The New Perspective on Paul," reprinted in *Jesus, Paul and the Law*, 183–206.

57. Cf. Westerholm, *Israel's Law and the Church's Faith*, 117–19; idem, "Paul and the Law in Romans 9–11," in *Paul and the Mosaic Law*, ed. James D. G. Dunn, WUNT 89 (Tübingen: J. C. B. Mohr [Paul Siebeck], 1996), 215–337, here at 229–31; Schreiner, *Law and Its Fulfillment*, 41–71; Moo, *Romans*, 211–17; Witherington, *Grace in Galatia*, 175–78; and I. Howard Marshall, "Salvation, Grace and Works in the Later Writings in the Pauline Corpus," *NTS* 42 (1996): 339–58.

58. Cf. Kruse, *Paul, the Law, and Justification*, 69, 111–12.

59. James D. G. Dunn correctly comments that Paul regards his statement in Rom 4:4–5 as a Jewish principle ("In Search of Common Ground," in *Paul and the Mosaic Law*, ed. James D. G. Dunn, WUNT 89 [Tübingen: J. C. B. Mohr (Paul Siebeck), 1996] 309–34, here at 331–32).

60. Cf. Kruse, *Paul, the Law, and Justification*, 287.

61. Mark A. Seifrid shows that the community that stands behind the *Psalms of Solomon* also attributed saving significance to the works of "the pious" (*Justification by Faith: The Origin and Development of a Central Pauline Theme*, NovTSup 68 [Leiden: E. J. Brill, 1992] 109–33). Cf. the comments of Trypho in Justin's *Dialogue with Trypho the Jew* 8.4; 47.1; and 67.6 and the observations of Graham Stanton, "The Law of Moses and the Law of Christ: Galatians 3:1–6:2," in *Paul and the Mosaic Law*, ed. James D. G. Dunn, WUNT 89 (Tübingen: J. C. B. Mohr [Paul Siebeck], 1996), 100–116, here at 105–6. Justin had read Paul's letter to the Romans (see 23.3 and 27.4), however, and this may have influenced his presentation of Trypho's viewpoint.

62. See, e.g., the hope expressed in Luke 1:68–79; 2:29–32; 24:21; Acts 1:6.

63. On the traditional character of Rom. 3:21–26, see Stuhlmacher, "Recent Exegesis," 94–109.

64. Heikki Räisänen, *Paul and the Law*, WUNT 29 (Tübingen: J. C. B. Mohr [Paul Siebeck], 1983), 256–63; and E. P. Sanders, *Paul, the Law, and the Jewish People* (Philadelphia: Fortress, 1983), 4, 150. Cf. J. Christiaan Beker, *Paul the Apostle: The Triumph of God in Life and Thought* (Philadelphia: Fortress, 1980), 53; and Hans Hübner, *Law in Paul's Thought* (Edinburgh: T & T Clark, 1984).

65. See Frank Thielman, "The Coherence of Paul's View of the Law: The Evidence of First Corinthians," *NTS* 38 (1992): 235–53, here at 248–52.

3

Treasures New and Old: The Mosaic Law in Matthew's Gospel

MANY INTERPRETERS OF MATTHEW'S GOSPEL believe that its author and the community for which he wrote were devoted adherents of the Mosaic law. The provocative stand that Jesus takes in the Gospel on matters such as sabbath keeping and dietary observance, it is often thought, reveal differences over how to apply the law between Matthew's Jewish-Christian community and the dominant Jewish milieu in which its members lived. Matthew and his community elevated the command to love and show mercy over cultic concerns, and they were committed to a mission to the Gentiles; but they never abandoned the Mosaic law. Although they differed from most of their Jewish neighbors in the emphasis they gave to these matters, the Mosaic law was common ground.[1]

A quick reading of Matthew with an eye on his statements about the law shows the plausibility of this understanding of the Gospel. After his baptism but before his preaching of the kingdom begins, Jesus faces the Tempter in the wilderness for a period of testing. The first temptation reveals Jesus' attitude toward Deuteronomy, the centerpiece of the Mosaic law. The Tempter urges Jesus to break his fast of forty days and nights to satisfy his hunger by turning the stones around him into bread. Jesus' response comes virtually word for word from the Greek rendering of Deut. 8:3, a passage that tells how God allowed Israel to go hungry in the wilderness and then fed them with manna to teach them that "one shall not live by bread alone, but by every word that comes from the mouth of God" (cf. Matt. 4:4). In the rest of the temptation narrative, Jesus demonstrates the truth of this sentiment by responding to Satan's enticements only with the words of Deuteronomy. Clearly, the Mosaic law is God's word to Jesus, and as essential to life as bread.

Once Jesus' teaching ministry is in full swing, this initial impression only becomes stronger. In the Sermon on the Mount, Jesus puts to rest any notion that he is interested in destroying the law or the prophets (5:17). He has instead come to fulfill them. Focusing his attention specifically on the law, he says that heaven and earth must first pass away before its smallest requirement is nullified (5:18). He goes on to resist the notion that any commandment ought to be interpreted to make its observance easier (5:19) and insists that those who enter God's kingdom have a greater level of righteousness than that of the scribes and Pharisees (5:20). Whereas the scribes and Pharisees often neglect the weightier matters of the law in their obsession with minor concerns, Jesus' followers should attend to the law's fundamental demands without neglecting minor requirements (23:23; cf. 23:3). Indeed, they should strive for perfection (5:48; 19:21).

Thus, it comes as no surprise that Jesus often appeals to the law in his ministry. He criticizes the Pharisees for using their tradition to avoid obedience to the law's commandment to honor one's parents (15:3–9). He meets the Sadducee's insinuation that Moses did not teach the resurrection from the dead with a quotation from the law that, he says, is the very speech of God to the Sadducees on the subject (22:31; cf. Exod. 3:6). He answers the rich young man's question about how to enter life with the Mosaic law's instructions for those who want to live: "keep the commandments" (19:17). Can anyone reasonably doubt that "Matthew's interpretation of biblical law is neither an abrogation nor a surpassing of that law, but a correct understanding and fulfillment of it"?[2]

A close look at the passages in Matthew where the Mosaic law is under discussion, however, shows that Matthew's view of the law is more complex than these initial impressions reveal. There is much continuity between Jesus' teaching in the Gospel and the Mosaic law, but discontinuity is also present. Careful attention to this tension between continuity and discontinuity reveals the special way in which Jesus "fulfills" the law. He does so not by requiring submission to its every detail but by reducing the law to its fundamental principles and reissuing the result as his teaching.

This understanding of the Mosaic law emerges from considering the following points:

1. The programmatic statement about the law's fulfillment in 5:17–20 should be interpreted in light of the antitheses in 5:21–47 and the concluding statement in 5:48. The "antitheses" stand in contrast to parts of the law, but show that Jesus' teaching is continuous with the law's most fundamental principles. This approach to the law appears again in Jesus' demand of perfection from the rich young man (19:16–22) and in Jesus' summaries of the law (7:12; 22:34–40; 23:5–7; and 23:23).

2. In the course of Jesus' ministry, these broadly stated convictions reappear in his approach to four specific sections of the Mosaic law: the purification ritual for lepers (8:1–4), the prohibition of work on the sabbath day (12:1–14), dietary restrictions (15:1–20), and the observance of Passover (26:17–29).

3. The way in which Matthew describes both Jesus' teaching and his role as teacher shows that Matthew considered Jesus to be Moses' greater replacement, and believed that his teaching replaced the Mosaic law.

JESUS' GENERAL STATEMENTS ABOUT THE LAW

In a number of passages, Jesus speaks in a general way about the Mosaic law. In 5:17–48 he discusses his approach to the law at length, providing first a basic statement of it and then six illustrations of how his basic convictions apply to specific legal issues. Other shorter but equally broad statements about the Mosaic law found elsewhere in the Gospel (7:12; 19:16–22; 22:34–40; 23:5–7, 23) cohere with the approach that Jesus describes in 5:17–48.

The Fulfillment of the Law
(5:17–48)

In 5:17–48, Matthew provides a full statement of his convictions concerning the Mosaic law. The position of the passage at the beginning of the Gospel and near the beginning of the largest block of ethical teaching within the Gospel demonstrates its programmatic character.

Matthew intends for the reader to interpret Jesus' controversies with the scribes and Pharisees over the law in the rest of the Gospel, and to interpret Jesus' ethical teaching elsewhere in the Gospel, in light of his comments here on the Mosaic law. He hoped that the passage would provide his readers with a hermeneutical key for understanding the complex relationship that he and his community had with the Mosaic law. Judging from the way the passage begins ("Do not think that I have come to abolish the law or the prophets . . ."), he also hopes to dispel antagonistic misinterpretations of his community's approach to the scriptures of Israel.

The passage is part of Jesus' Sermon on the Mount, a section of the Gospel addressed to his disciples (5:1) and concerned primarily with how they should live in order to be "salt" and "light" in the world (5:13–16). The passage begins with a general statement about Jesus' relationship to the law (5:17–19) and continues with six illustrations of that relationship (5:21–47). At the end of the illustrations stands a statement that summarizes the basic point of the passage (5:48).

The passage begins with a sentence that looks like an unambiguous affirmation of the continuing validity of the Mosaic law for Jesus' disciples. Jesus denies that he has come to abolish the law or the prophets, claiming instead that he intends to "fulfill" them. Focusing directly on the law, he then says that until heaven and earth pass away and everything has been accomplished, not the smallest part of the law will disappear (5:17–18; cf. Luke 16:17).[3] Whoever abolishes a single commandment will be least in the kingdom of heaven, he says, and whoever practices and teaches the law will be considered great (5:19).

The next statement summarizes this introductory paragraph by saying that Jesus' disciples, if they are to enter the kingdom of heaven, must possess a level of righteousness that outstrips the righteousness of the scribes and the Pharisees (5:20). Since the previous verses speak of upholding every particular of the Mosaic law, the term "righteousness" probably means conformity with the law. Furthermore, since the Pharisees were widely regarded as the most meticulous interpreters of the law in Matthew's time (Acts 26:5; Josephus, *Life* 191), Jesus seems to be saying that his followers must overtake even the law's most zealous disciples in the accuracy with which they keep the law.

Because this opening statement has focused on keeping the Mosaic law in the smallest particulars—every stroke of the pen, every commandment, and more strictly than the most painstaking observers of the law among the Jews of Matthew's time—we might expect Matthew's understanding of the law to be concerned with how to live in conformity with even the smallest details of the Mosaic code. When Jesus illustrates the meaning of 5:20 in the following verses, however, the reader discovers that Matthew has in mind a kind of conformity to the requirements of the Mosaic law different from what we might first expect.

In 5:21–47, Jesus explains the meaning of his admonition to keep the law at a level that even the scribes and Pharisees have not reached. He lists six illustrative commands, drawn directly from, or implied by, the Mosaic code and then comments on how his disciples should conform to these commands. The most obvious, and in light of the introduction, the most confusing aspect of this section of commands and commentary is its antithetical character. Jesus speaks of what "was said to the people who lived long ago" (5:21, 33), alluding to what God said to the Israelite generation of the exodus.[4] He then contrasts the word of God during the time of the exodus with his own teaching using the phrase, "But I say to you . . . ." The contrast is not between the interpretation of the law among Jesus' contemporaries and Jesus' own understanding, but between the law and its implications as they appear in sacred scripture and Jesus' own instruction. The question that cries out for an answer in light of this is how Jesus can teach the fulfillment of every detail of the law and then immediately contrast his own instruction with the law's commands. The answer lies in the meaning of the term "fulfill" and in the nature of the contrasts.

Matthew uses the term "fulfill" (*plēroō*) in his Gospel most often to refer to the realization of biblical prophecies about Jesus.[5] Since Jesus mentions the prophets alongside the law in 5:17, and since in 11:13 Matthew can refer explicitly to the law as something that prophesies, Matthew probably intended the word "fulfill" in 5:17 to carry this prophetic nuance.[6] The primary difficulty with this view is that the law consists of commands, and it is difficult to know how commands can "prophesy" or point forward to some eschatological fulfillment. The puzzle begins to be solved, however, when we look at the nature of the contrasts that Jesus draws between the law and his own teaching in 5:18–48.

Here we find that in each case Jesus replaces a Mosaic command with instruction that expresses the ethical goal toward which the Mosaic law points. In cases where the Mosaic law in question is a pragmatic attempt to legislate a less than ideal situation, Jesus nullifies the command altogether by demanding a change in the situation itself so radical that, if it takes place, the legislation becomes unnecessary.[7] The antitheses, then, illustrate how Jesus' ethical teaching identifies the prophetic element in the Mosaic law and fulfills the law's "prophecy" by bringing it to completion.

This understanding of the antitheses appears to be confirmed when we consider Matthew's use of the term "it was said" in each antithesis. Matthew uses precisely the same term, in the same tense and voice, in the introduction to his fulfillment quotations. These quotations claim that "the thing spoken" (*to rhēthen*) by a certain prophet "was fulfilled" in some aspect of Jesus' life (3:3; 1:22; 2:15, 17, 23; 4:14; 8:17; 12:17; 13:35; 21:4; 22:31; 24:15; 27:9). By analogy, in the antitheses of the Sermon on the Mount, the ethical teachings of Jesus "fulfill" what "was said" (*errethē*) in the Mosaic law by bringing it to its divinely intended goal.

In the first antithesis (5:21–26) Jesus quotes word for word from the Decalogue ("You shall not kill," Exod. 20:13; Deut. 5:17), and then follows the quotation with a summary of the Mosaic teaching about what should happen judicially if one person kills another. The murderer, according to the Mosaic law, should be punished with death, a penalty that is normally applied after a court has reached judgment on a particular case (Num. 35:30; cf. Exod. 21:12; Lev. 24:17; Num. 35:16–21, 29–31). In place of this law, Jesus says that those who are angry with another or who use fighting words have done something worthy of a court appearance (5:22–23a) and that whoever calls a brother or sister a fool is guilty enough to merit hell's fire (5:23b). He then comments on the urgency of the offender's need to seek reconciliation from the person offended (5:24–26).

Jesus addresses the emotional and relational problems that lead to murder and claims that these prior conditions have no place among the people of God. In addition, his mention of hell's fire as a penalty for hurling an angry epithet at a fellow member of the community implies that the ultimate penalty for violation of his teaching is not the judicial action provided for in the Mosaic law but the eschatological action of God himself. If the disciple lives by Jesus' instructions and in light of the eschatological judgment, judicial action against murder, and by implication, the Mosaic law's prohibition of murder become unnecessary.

There is much discontinuity here. Jesus contrasts his teaching with that of the Mosaic law and obviates the Mosaic law's prohibition by addressing the fundamental cause of the action that the law was designed to curtail. But we can also see how Jesus' teaching stands in continuity with the law. By forbidding the kind of anger against a fellow member of the community that degenerates into name calling, and by commanding reconciliation, Jesus has, by implication, forbidden murder. Jesus' teaching, therefore, fulfills the law's prohibition of murder by forbidding the attitude from which murder springs.

The second antithesis (5:27–30) follows the same pattern. Jesus quotes verbatim the Decalogue's prohibition of adultery (Exod. 20:14; Deut. 5:18; cf. Lev. 18:20) and then contrasts with it his own teaching that the man who looks at a woman in order to "lust" (*epithymēsai*) has already committed adultery with her in his heart. The law provided a means for determining whether a woman suspected of adultery had actually committed the offense (Num. 5:11–31) and mandated the death penalty for both men and women who violated the statute (Lev. 20:10; Deut. 22:22–24; cf. Sus. 22, 41; John 8:5). In contrast, Jesus provides the eschatological penalty of being cast into hell (5:29, 30).

As with the first antithesis, there is both discontinuity and continuity here. The discontinuity lies in a prohibition that is more strict and a penalty that is more severe than the comparable provisions in the Mosaic law. The continuity appears in the way that Jesus' prohibition and penalty strike at the root of the problem that the Mosaic law attempts to address. Jesus implies that a man's lustful heart betrays the godless orientation of his life. Even before the man with a lustful heart commits adultery and breaks God's command, then, his fate on the eschatological day of God's judgment is sealed by his wayward heart.

Continuity also appears in the way the Hebrew scriptures and Jewish tradition anticipated this understanding of adultery prior to Jesus. The Decalogue itself tells the Israelite not to "lust" for his neighbor's wife (Exod. 20:17 LXX; Deut. 5:21 LXX; cf. Gen. 39:6b–15; Prov. 5:1–23; 6:20–35; 7:6–27) and Jewish tradition advised avoiding not merely adultery itself but situations and thoughts that might lead to it (e.g., Sir. 9:9; *Test. Jos.* 9:2). Jesus' teaching transcends the Mosaic law in a direction already anticipated by hints in the law itself and traditional interpretations of the law. He obviates the need for a prohibition against adultery by pushing the prohibition toward the more fundamental question of the inner deliberation of one's heart.

The next antithesis (5:31–32) does not quote the law itself, but draws an inference about what the law allows from a statute that regulates a different matter. Deut. 24:1–4 forbids remarriage to a previously divorced wife if, in the meantime, she has been married and has lost her second husband either through divorce or death. In the course of regulating this specific situation, the passage describes the legal basis for divorce and the means by which it could be accomplished: a man who discovers some "indecency" in his wife may write her a certificate of divorce and evict her from his house (24:1, 3).

"Indecency" could be interpreted to mean adultery, as in the metaphorical reference in Jeremiah to God's divorce of his people for their "adulteries" with other nations and their gods (Jer. 3:1, 8; cf. Isa. 50:1). It was often interpreted broadly, however, to mean anything that the husband found displeasing (Matt. 19:3), and divorce by means of certificate for reasons other than adultery was not uncommon.[8] Indeed, a vigorous debate was under way in first-century Palestine about which of these interpretations of "indecency" was correct (Matt. 19:3, 7). Here, however, Jesus bypasses the debate. He seems to assume that Moses permitted divorce not only for adultery but for other reasons as well, and contrasts his own, more restrictive view with Moses' understanding.

The discontinuity between Jesus' teaching on this point and the Mosaic law is clear: Jesus forbids what the Mosaic law, on Jesus' own interpretation, permits.[9] An element of continuity is more difficult to find, perhaps because the antithesis is so brief and because Matthew knows that a more detailed discussion of Deut. 24:1–4 will surface later in his Gospel.

If we turn to that passage (Matt. 19:3–12), we discover that the element of discontinuity between Jesus' position on divorce and the Mosaic legislation remains firm. Jesus assumes that Deut. 24:1 and 3 permit divorce for reasons other than adultery as a concession to the hard-heartedness of the Israelites, but Jesus is unwilling to make any such concession. Appealing to the account of the origin of marriage in Gen. 1:27 and 2:23–24, Jesus argues that these passages are more fundamental to the issue of divorce than Moses' concession in Deut. 24:1–4. The Genesis account, says Jesus, shows that marriage is from God. Since human beings may not separate what God has joined, he concludes, divorce is permissible only on the basis of sexual infidelity.[10]

Amid this discontinuity, however, an element of continuity also emerges. Jesus' comment that Moses permitted divorce because of Israel's "hard-heartedness" (19:8) reveals that Jesus believed the Mosaic legislation to be an attempt to regulate a sinful situation.[11] Jesus, then, contrasts his own teaching with the Mosaic legislation, but in the process implies that his teaching is in accord with the ideals of that legislation itself. At least in this more elaborate discussion of divorce and remarriage, then, we again find the pattern that appeared in the first and second antitheses: Jesus contrasts his own teaching with the teaching of Moses but implies that his own teaching addresses the ultimate concern of the law itself.

The next antithesis (5:33–37) alludes to several passages in the Hebrew scriptures, most of them in the five books of Moses, that urge people to keep their oaths. As with the teaching on divorce, no biblical text commands oath taking, but the practice is everywhere assumed and carefully regulated.[12] Thus, when Israelites swear, they should not use the names of pagan deities, but only God's name (Deut. 6:13; 10:20), and oaths in God's name are not to be taken lightly (Exod. 20:7; Deut. 5:11; cf. Lev. 19:12). Those who vow to the Lord either to do something or to abstain from something must keep their word (Num. 30:2; Deut. 23:21, 23; Pss. 15:4; 51:14; Eccl. 5:4; cf. Exod. 20:16; Deut. 5:20). At times, these admonitions not to make vows rashly and to keep any vow that has been made become reminders that vows are not necessary (Deut. 23:22) and that not vowing at all is better than failure to keep one's word (Eccl. 5:5).

In contrast to the implication in these texts that vows are permissible, Jesus forbids them. He could hardly be clearer: "But I say to you, do not swear at all" (5:34). Anything other than an emphatic yes or no, he says, is evil (5:37). As in the case of divorce, however, Jesus' position pushes the tendency of the law itself toward its ultimate significance. The law regulates a custom that was ubiquitous in the ancient Near Eastern world. It makes this custom compatible with monotheism and coopts it for service to the God of Abraham, Isaac, and Jacob. But swearing is not commanded, rash oaths are forbidden, and occasionally discussion of oaths becomes so fraught with caution that the reader receives the impression that it is better not to use them at all. Jesus' teaching obviates all this regulation by forbidding the practice entirely. What the law recognizes as unnecessary and prone to abuse, Jesus prohibits.

Jesus next turns to the Mosaic code's law of retaliation, citing the two elements of the law that are common to all three of its occurrences in Hebrew scripture (Exod. 21:23–24; Lev. 24:19–20; Deut. 19:21): "eye for eye, tooth for tooth." This principle appears also in the Laws of Hammurapi and was apparently a common ancient Near Eastern means of limiting punishment to a penalty no more severe than the inflicted injury.[13] Thus, under this law an entire family could not be destroyed simply because a wayward son had fought with a member of some other clan. In a society whose basic unit was the family and the larger tribe, the law of retaliation, imposed by an overarching government, could stop the cycle of retributive violence and prevent the society from spiraling downward into vengeful self-destruction.[14] The law also assured that members of various social classes would be treated equally: the upper classes could no longer escape punishment for inflicting physical injury on someone else simply through payment of a fine.[15] Rather than a relic of primitive retribution, then, the law was actually a merciful advancement over mob violence and oppressive elitism.[16]

Jesus directly opposes the principle, however, with his own law of nonretaliation.[17] Whether the issue is physical violence, a lawsuit, conscription into the service of an occupying military force, a request for clothing, or an appeal to borrow money, the disciple of Jesus must not retaliate or turn away from an evildoer. Indeed, in the event of physical violence, lawsuits, and conscription into service, Jesus' disciple is to comply with the evil person's request even beyond that person's expectations or the law's provision (5:39b–41; cf. Exod. 22:25–26; Deut. 24:12–13).[18]

The difference between Jesus and the Mosaic law on this point is clear: the Mosaic law permits retaliation; Jesus forbids it. Nevertheless an element of continuity lies beneath the surface of both the law of retaliation and Jesus' principle of nonretaliation: both principles limit physical violence. The law of retaliation does this by implicitly forbidding the injured party to retaliate beyond the scope of its own injury, and Jesus' teaching accomplishes the same purpose by explicitly forbidding any retaliation. The Mosaic law took over a common legal formula because it represented a merciful advance over more ruthless and socially destructive forms of justice. In a way that is consistent with this tendency toward mercy, the law itself admonishes Israelites not to take vengeance into their own hands but to leave it to the Lord (Lev. 19:18; Deut. 32:35; cf. Prov. 20:22; 24:29).[19] Jesus now pushes this tendency to its ultimate extreme: rather than stopping the cycle of violence after one round of injury and retribution, Jesus stops it immediately. His disciples must live as if violence were not an option.[20]

In the final antithesis (5:43–47), Jesus contrasts his teaching with the legal maxim "You shall love your neighbor and hate your enemy"

(5:43). The command to love one's neighbor comes from Lev. 19:17–18, which in its complete form says this:

> You shall not hate in your heart anyone of your kin; you shall reprove your neighbor, or you will incur guilt yourself. You shall not take vengeance or bear a grudge against any of your people, but you shall love your neighbor as yourself: I am the LORD.

A few paragraphs later, this command is extended to cover the alien who resides in the land of Israel also, "for," the Lord says, "you were aliens in the land of Egypt" (Lev. 19:33–34; cf. Deut. 10:19). Thus, the command covers both kinspeople and strangers who live within Israel's territory.

Israel's national enemies, however, received harsher treatment. Although the Mosaic law contains no command to hate one's enemies, Deuteronomy says that the Israelites should "utterly destroy" the peoples who occupy the land of promise. Israel is to "make no covenant with them and show them no mercy" (Deut. 7:2; cf. 20:16; Exod. 34:11–12; Pss. 26:5; 137:7–9; 139:19–22). Because the Ammonites and Moabites opposed God's people during the time of the exodus, and because they hired Balaam to curse the Israelites (Deut. 23:3–5; cf. 30:7), Israel should "never promote their welfare or their prosperity" (23:6).

At the heart of these commands lies the desire to protect God's often wayward people from the idolatry characteristic of their national enemies and to preserve Israel as "a people holy to the LORD" (Deut. 7:4–6; Exod. 34:13–17). From the perspective of the law itself such commands were necessary because of Israel's tendency to stray from worship of the Lord into idolatry, or, as Matthew might put it, because of the "hardness" of their "hearts" (19:8).

In contrast, Jesus urges his disciples to love not only their neighbors but their enemies also. They are to pray for their persecutors (5:44; cf. 5:11–12) and greet not only their kin but others also (5:47). The basis for this unusual attitude among Jesus' disciples is their relationship to their heavenly Father. They are his children, and as children they should imitate his gracious actions toward both the good and evil, the just and the unjust (5:45). Thus, Jesus tells his disciples to love not merely their neighbors and aliens who pose no threat to them, but to love those who actively seek their harm. The seeds of this development can be seen in God's own unmerited love for Israel, expressed in the law itself (Deut. 7:7–8) and in other passages that advise treating individual enemies mercifully (Exod. 23:4–5; cf. 1 Sam. 24:17–19; Prov. 24:17–18 and 25:21–22).[21] Again, Jesus follows the path of the law itself past love for the neighbor and resident alien to the ultimate goal of love for one's enemy.

In each of the antitheses, then, Jesus pushes a tendency already present in the Mosaic law toward its ultimate conclusion. Actions that the Mosaic law forbids, such as murder and adultery, Jesus expands to cover fundamental attitudes and actions such as anger, fighting words, a refusal to seek reconciliation, and the lustful look. Actions that the Mosaic law seems to permit as concessions to less than perfect social conditions, such as divorce, swearing, the principle of retaliation, and hatred of the enemy, Jesus simply forbids, demanding that his disciples live in a way that concedes nothing to evil.

This is the way in which Jesus' teaching fulfills every aspect of the law. Every part of the law pointed collectively toward the fundamental principles that comprise Jesus' teaching. The law itself implied these principles and occasionally expressed them explicitly, but its concerns with regulating the behavior of an entire nation to preserve it from social disintegration and unholy alliances with surrounding groups prevented it from making these principles its primary concern.

Jesus has no interest in the legal refinements necessary for making a society work politically, however. The fundamental principles lying beneath the Mosaic law become for Jesus the law itself, and the sanctions for violating those principles are not legal penalties subject to court review but eschatological penalties administered on the final day by an all-seeing God.

This is why the passage ends with the admonition to Jesus' followers that they "shall be perfect as [their] heavenly Father is perfect" (5:48). The term "perfect" translates the Greek adjective *teleios*, which means "having attained the end or purpose, complete." Jesus' followers are to conform their behavior not merely to the requirements of the Mosaic code but to a set of deeper principles that bring the Mosaic commandments to their ultimate goal. This is the sense in which their righteousness is to exceed the righteousness of the scribes and Pharisees (5:20). Because the scribes and Pharisees refuse to acknowledge Jesus' approach to the Mosaic law, they are mired in conformity to a penultimate ethic. Jesus has moved beyond them to an eschatological ethic that expresses the law's ultimate concerns. His disciples, he says, must do the same. Their prayer must be that God's will be done on earth as it is in heaven (6:10).[22]

The Law and Perfection (19:16–22)

This approach to the law appears again in Matthew's record of Jesus' encounter with the rich young man (19:16–22). The man asks Jesus what good thing he must do to have eternal life. Jesus responds in the language of the law itself (Deut. 4:2–4; 6:18, 24; 28:1–14; cf. Sir. 15:15–17) that in order to have life one must keep the commandments. When the man asks further which of these he should keep, Jesus lists five commandments from the second table of the Decalogue. He then adds to these commandments one that both summarizes them and implies the tenth commandment: "You shall love your neighbor as yourself" (Lev. 19:18). The man responds that he has kept all these things. "What," he asks, "do I still lack?" Jesus answers that if he wants to be "perfect" he must sell all that he has and follow him, and the result will be treasure in heaven. The man then leaves sadly, however, "for he had many possessions."

Matthew's interest in telling this story was from the first Jesus' claim that if the rich young man would be "perfect" he must sell his possessions, give to the poor, and follow Jesus. This is clear from the focus in the young man's first question on the one "good thing" that he must do to have eternal life (19:16). As it develops, the story reveals that this one thing is not the commandments, which the man claims to have kept, but the one thing that he lacks: love for the poor (19:20). This one thing will make the man "perfect" (*teleios*) and thus lead to eternal life.

As in 5:21–48, perfection entails pushing beyond the Mosaic law's formal requirements for love of neighbor to something far more demanding. The Decalogue pointed in this direction with its list of each person's concrete responsibilities toward his or her neighbor, and elsewhere the law commanded an open heart and an open hand to the poor person's need, "whatever it may be" (Deut. 15:7–8). But in Matthew's narrative Jesus perceives that this man has managed to keep, or at least to avoid breaking, these formal requirements without showing love to the poor. Jesus, then, raises the man's vision beyond the Mosaic law to something that will expose the division of loyalty in his heart: he must sell everything he has, give to the poor, and follow Jesus. If this man follows Jesus, he must walk with him so far down the pathway marked out by the Mosaic law that he arrives at the law's ultimate goal. He must not merely keep the law's second table and its command to love one's neighbor, nor must he simply "lend" to the needy poor from his wealth (Deut. 15:8); but he must sell his own possessions and "give" the proceeds to the poor (19:21).

Once again, both continuity with the Mosaic law and discontinuity emerge from this passage. The Mosaic law demanded love for neighbor and care for the poor, just as Jesus demands them here. But the definition of love for neighbor preserved in the second table of the Decalogue, at least in this man's case, did not go far enough. Despite this man's commitment to the law's formal statement of his responsibility to his neighbor, his concern for his neighbor stopped short of an unfettered love for the poor. Thus, he was able to deceive himself into thinking that he had fulfilled God's requirement when instead he had neglected the law's fundamental principle of self-giving love for all. Jesus identifies this problem and calls the man to comply not with the law's letter but with this fundamental principle.

The Law Summarized
(7:12; 22:34–40; 23:5–7, 23)

Jesus' summaries of the law and comments on the central aspects of the law in Matthew's Gospel are consistent with this approach. In six brief passages, Jesus reveals what he believes to be the fundamental concern of the law—the ultimate goal toward which other aspects of the law point.

In two passages Jesus offers summaries of the law. In 7:12 he says that the message of "the law and the prophets" can be summarized in the dictum, "Everything that you want people to do for you, precisely these things you should also do for them." The meaning of this phrase is virtually identical to a commandment of the law itself, "You shall love your neighbor as yourself" (Lev. 19:18), and Jesus chooses this commandment to summarize the law's ethical requirements when a hostile Pharisee asks him to state the law's greatest commandment (22:34–40).[23] These summaries, like the stress on perfection in 5:48 and 19:20, cut through the Mosaic law's concern to regulate the life of a large society. They claim that in matters of ethics the primary interest of Jesus' disciple should be the basic principle on which the Mosaic law is constructed: love for the other must sacrifice nothing to love for oneself.

This concern also lies beneath two otherwise puzzling references to the Mosaic law in chapter 23. In 23:2–7 Jesus says that the scribes and Pharisees sit on Moses' seat and that in light of this Jesus' disciples should "do and keep whatever they say" to them (23:3). Jesus' disciples should not, however, do as the scribes and Pharisees do because they weigh people down with burdens that are heavy but do nothing to lighten them (23:4) and because their conformity with the law is motivated by the desire for praise from people (23:5–7). Later in the same chapter, Jesus criticizes the scribes and Pharisees for attending to such minute concerns of the law as tithing herbs but neglecting the law's more important concern with judgment, mercy, and faith. Rather than this approach, says Jesus, the scribes and Pharisees ought to attend to the small matters without neglecting the more important ones (23:23).

These passages appear startling when we remember Jesus' antithetical approach to the Mosaic law's regulation of divorce, swearing, and retaliation. They are even more surprising in light of Jesus' disagreements both in this chapter (23:16–24) and elsewhere in the Gospel (12:1–14; 15:1–20) with scribal and Pharisaic interpretations of the law. Does Jesus now, in the Gospel's eleventh hour, contradict the radical stance he has taken on the Mosaic law in the preceding chapters?

This impression originates in a misunderstanding of these passages. Jesus does not commend to his disciples the approach that the scribes and Pharisees take to the law when he tells them to do whatever they say. Instead, he simply commends the law itself to the disciples and implies that if the disciples are to have access to the law, they can only get it through the scribes and Pharisees who sit on Moses' seat. In a culture where literacy was relatively uncommon and copies of the Mosaic law were not widely available, the disciples would have to hear the law in the synagogue, where the scribes and Pharisees were responsible for revealing its contents.[24] Jesus tells them to do this, but he tells them precisely not to keep the law in the way the scribes and Pharisees keep it. The primary concern of his disciples should be with the law's weightier matters of judgment, mercy, and faith (23:23; cf. 23:4), and they should observe no part of the law in order to gain praise from people (23:5–7). The validity of the law is affirmed, but in a way that distinguishes first between the law and corrupt interpretations of it and second within the law itself between less important and more important matters.

If this approach is correct, then Jesus' statement in 23:23 that the scribes and Pharisees should do the lighter matters of the law without neglecting the weightier matters is not a claim that the lighter matters remain valid for his disciples. The command is directed first to the scribes and Pharisees as a way of exposing their own unwillingness to distinguish between less important and more important commandments in the law. For Jesus' disciples and Matthew's readers the message is simply that the weightier matters are the critical ones (cf. 9:13 and 12:7).[25]

JESUS' APPROACH TO SPECIFIC LAWS

When we move from Jesus' statements about the law generally to his teaching on specific laws, we discover the same principle as it is worked out in the concrete situations of Jesus' ministry. Here too Jesus' position on the law bears the marks of radical discontinuity at one level, but on a more fundamental plane, especially when the passages are taken together, a profound continuity emerges.[26]

The Purification of Lepers (8:1–4)

After teaching his disciples on the mount, Matthew says that Jesus went down from the mountain accompanied by throngs of people. Among them was a leper who prostrated himself before Jesus and asked him for cleansing (8:2). Jesus touched the man, saying "I will. Be cleansed" (8:3). He then told him to go show himself to the priest and to offer the "gift" that Moses commanded should be presented in such cases. The man was to do this, says Jesus, "in order to bear witness to them" (8:4).

According to a common reading of this passage, Jesus affirms the authority of the Mosaic law by telling the man whom he has healed to obey the law's prescriptions for cleansing from leprosy (Lev. 14:2–32). Some who adopt this reading believe that Jesus' final statement directs the man to follow the Mosaic prescriptions as a testimony to the priests that, contrary to the claims of the scribes and Pharisees, Jesus keeps the law of Moses.[27]

Close attention to the passage, however, shows that this is not the best way to understand it. The legal procedures that Jesus tells the man to observe were not intended for certifying that a recovered leper had been cleansed but were for the actual cleansing of the leper. The law commanded that when the leper appeared before the priest certain sacrifices should be offered "for the one who is to be cleansed" (Lev. 14:4, 7, 8, 14, 17, 18, 19, 25, 28, 29). Only after these procedures had been followed was the leper pronounced clean (14:7, 8, 9, 20, 23, 31). The priest himself is the previously healed leper's "purifier" (14:11). The healed leper was not ritually pure from the law's perspective, therefore, until the priest cleansed him by means of the prescribed ritual. In contrast to this, Jesus in Matt. 8:1–4 plays the part not only of healer but of priest, curing the man's leprosy and cleansing his impurity at the same time with a single touch.[28]

Why, then, did Jesus send the man to the priest? The answer lies in the phrase "as a testimony to them" at the end of the account (8:4). Since "them" is plural, it cannot refer to the "priest." Instead, it probably refers to every one who might see the leper at the temple. The man would serve as a testimony to all who saw him of Jesus' power to heal and of his sovereign authority over the Mosaic law. Jesus has bypassed the details of the law's requirements for cleansing, but has done so in a way that achieves the ultimate goal of the law in this instance—the cleansing of the leper. Jesus has, therefore, provided a practical and public demonstration of the approach to the law that he has just articulated in 5:17–48.[29]

Rest on the Sabbath (12:1–14)

In 12:1–14, Jesus redefines the law's requirement that God's people refrain from "any work" on the sabbath. Just prior to this passage, Jesus has invited the weary and heavily burdened to take his easy yoke upon them (11:28–30). The heavy burdens to which Jesus refers are the legal interpretations and ancillary requirements that the scribes and Pharisees have tied up into heavy bundles and placed upon their followers' shoulders (23:4a). In contrast to the scribes and Pharisees, who have been unwilling even to move a finger in order to lighten this load (23:4b), Jesus invites people to take up his easy yoke and light burden (11:30). He will, he says, give them "rest" (11:28–29). To illustrate the difference between the "rest" provided by the Pharisees and the "rest" provided by Jesus, Matthew links Jesus' statement to two debates between Jesus and the Pharisees over the law's requirement that God's people "rest" on the sabbath.[30]

In the first of these passages (12:1–8), the Pharisees criticize Jesus for allowing his disciples to pick and eat grain from the fields on the sabbath, a violation of the commandment to rest from "any work" on that day (Exod. 16:22–30; 20:10; 35:3; Num. 15:32–36; Deut. 5:14; Jer. 17:19–27; Neh. 10:31; 13:15–22; Isa. 58:13). Jesus responds by reminding the Pharisees that according to the scriptures David broke a commandment in order to satisfy his own hunger and the hunger of those with him (1 Sam. 21:1–6); that even the priests in the temple, whose sacral duties require them to work on the sabbath (Lev. 24:5–9; Num. 28:9–10), profane the day; and that the scriptures elevate mercy over sacrifice (Hos. 6:6; cf. 1 Sam. 15:22; Pss. 40:6; 51:16–17; Prov. 15:8; Amos 5:21–24; Mic. 6:6–8). Thus, Jesus concludes, the disciples are as innocent of violating the sabbath as the temple priests, and the Son of Man is Lord of the sabbath.

In order to understand the significance of this passage for Matthew's approach to the law we must appreciate the two separate lines of reasoning Jesus takes in defense of the disciples. First, and most obviously, Jesus claims that the disciples are innocent on the basis of scripture itself. When David and those with him satisfied their hunger with the temple's sacred showbread, he points out, they technically broke the law's command that only priests should eat this bread. In some instances, therefore, the scriptures permit the technical violation of a legal command in order to satisfy human need. In addition, the law makes no provision for the priests to rest from their duties in the temple on the sabbath. Under certain sacred conditions, therefore, work on the sabbath is permissible. Finally, scripture elevates showing mercy over the rote observance of ritual technique, and therefore where sabbath observance conflicts with showing mercy to others, sabbath observance must give way.

According to this first line of defense, then, scripture allows for certain types of work on the sabbath. Specifically, it permits the satisfaction of human hunger as a merciful act even if the way in which this act of mercy is performed violates the sabbath. The disciples are innocent, therefore, because their sabbath work falls into the category of permissible sabbath "violations." Had Jesus left matters here, his conflict with the Pharisees would have found a comfortable place within the world of ancient Jewish disputes over how to observe the sabbath.

Entwined with this first line of defense, however, is a second and more radical argument: Jesus, as Lord of the sabbath, has authority to define how the sabbath should be observed. Thus, Jesus' first two examples depend for their validity not only upon the notion that they provide a precedent for doing work on the sabbath but upon the authority of the central figure or institution in the example. In the first example, it is not any Israelite, but the great David, who satisfies his hunger in a way that violates the Mosaic law. In the second example, it is not service in any Israelite institution but in the temple itself that technically violates the sabbath. David and the temple possess a divine authority that gives them an element of freedom from the law not available to others. For these two examples to serve as true precedents for the activity of Jesus' disciples, Jesus must be at least as great as David and the temple.

This claim would be radical enough; but Jesus takes it even further. "I tell you," he says, "that one greater than the temple is here" (12:6), and then, in a proclamation that brings the passage to a climactic close, "For the Son of Man is Lord of the sabbath" (12:8).[31] The disciples are innocent, therefore, not merely because their breech of the sabbath commandment has biblical precedent, but because Jesus has absolute authority over how the sabbath ought to be observed.

How should it be observed? The passage also addresses this question. Jesus claims that the Pharisees' mistaken accusation against the disciples arose from their inability to understand the biblical principle that mercy was more important than sacrifice. Thus, the sabbath ought to be observed not by a definition of rest that excludes mercy but by defining rest in terms of showing mercy to others.

As if to underline this point, Matthew recounts a second dispute between Jesus and the Pharisees over the sabbath. Here Jesus enters a synagogue controlled by the Pharisees (12:9, 14; cf. 12:2) where a man with a paralyzed and atrophied hand is in attendance. The Pharisees ask Jesus what they hope will be a damning question, "Is it permitted to heal on the sabbath?" (12:10). Jesus responds by reminding them of their own allowances for showing mercy to a distressed animal on the sabbath (12:11), and concludes that since a man is more valuable than an animal, doing good on the sabbath, and therefore healing on the sabbath, is permissible (12:12). Jesus then heals the man (12:13), and the Pharisees depart to plot his death (12:14).

This passage takes the issue of Jesus' authority over the sabbath to a new level.[32] Now the question is not merely whether one can permit the occasional preparation of food on the sabbath as an act of mercy, but whether one can heal someone on the sabbath who was chronically ill and might just as easily have been healed the previous day. Jesus' position on this question is that the sabbath is a day for "doing good" and that healing, even if the healing does not respond to some emergency, is therefore permissible on the sabbath. This claim opens the sabbath to all kinds of merciful activity. Indeed, for Jesus, whose healing activity was an essential part of his day-to-day vocation, it made the sabbath day like any other day.[33]

As he had done in the first encounter with the Pharisees over the sabbath, Jesus' points out that the Pharisees' refusal to acknowledge his authority over the sabbath leads them to have greater concern for a sheep in distress than for a chronically ill man. If they had recognized Jesus' authority to redefine the law in terms of its own most fundamental principles, he argues, they would not seek to defend such a ridiculous position. The Pharisees can only respond to this by plotting Jesus' death—the penalty that the law mandates for those who flagrantly violate the sabbath (Exod. 31:14; 35:2; Num. 15:32-36; cf. *Jub.* 2:25–27).

With these two accounts, Matthew has illustrated the meaning of Jesus' claim in 11:28–30 that he can give rest to those who labor under the heavy burden of traditional elaborations of the Mosaic law. As the Lord of the sabbath he has the authority to merge the commandment to rest on the sabbath with the prophetic elevation of mercy over sacrifice.[34] By allowing his disciples to prepare food on the sabbath and by healing a chronically ill man on this day, he shows that the sabbath, like every other day, is a time for doing good and showing mercy.[35]

Dietary Restrictions (15:1–20)

In Matt. 15:1–20 the debate revolves around "the traditions of the elders" rather than the Mosaic law, but as the discussion develops, Jesus implies that the law's dietary restrictions are no longer binding. The trouble begins when the Pharisees and scribes criticize Jesus' disciples for failing to wash their hands before eating. In response, Jesus claims that the scribes and Pharisees have elevated their traditions above the commandment of God. He substantiates this charge with the further claim that they avoid obeying God's instructions to honor father and mother by means of a special understanding of the biblical command to keep one's vow (Num. 30:2). Their tradition claims that if a son vows to give all personal profit from his own wealth to the temple, that vow could not be broken even to care for his father and mother. Peripheral cultic matters have provided an opportunity for escaping the law's fundamental concern with showing respect toward and mercy to one's parents. Jesus then summons "the crowd" and explains further that one is defiled not by what enters the mouth but by what comes out of it. Informed by his disciples that this statement has offended the Pharisees, Jesus explains it. What goes into the mouth, he says, merely passes through the body; but what comes out of the mouth originates with the heart, and the heart produces the evil designs that result in murder, adultery, immorality, theft, false witness, and blasphemy. These evils, not failure to wash one's hands, says Jesus, are true defilement.

If Matthew has used Mark's Gospel as his primary source for this narrative, then he has made three changes that are significant for understanding his approach to the law. First, he omits Mark's explicit comment that by this teaching Jesus had pronounced all foods clean (Mark 7:19). Second, he emphasizes that the primary question at issue was hand washing by adding to the end of the narrative Jesus' words, "but eating with unwashed hands does not defile a person" (Matt. 15:20b). Third, he trims Mark's list of twelve sins that originate with the heart (Mark 7:21–22) to seven. The first of these seven sins ("evil designs") is apparently the source for the other six, all of which are violations of the Decalogue (Matt. 15:19).

These changes have led many interpreters to conclude that Matthew edited Mark's account to make its approach to the law less radical.[36] Thus, in Matthew Jesus does not disavow the food laws but limits the significance of his comments to eating with unwashed hands, a custom whose origins do not lie in the Mosaic code. In Matthew, it is sometimes said, Jesus is the loyalist to the Mosaic law and the scribes and Pharisees are the law's transgressors. However, this approach does not adequately account for the radical implications of Jesus' teaching on "what enters the mouth." Since this phrase can only refer to food, and since Jesus says as explicitly in Matthew as in Mark that "what enters the mouth does not defile the person" (Matt. 15:11; cf. Mark 7:16), Jesus unambiguously rejects the continuing validity of dietary restrictions.[37]

At the same time, he affirms the continuing validity of much of the Decalogue both in his illustration of how scribal and Pharisaic tradition nullifies the Decalogue's fifth commandment and in his list of sins that flow from the heart's evil thoughts: murder violates the sixth commandment; adultery, interpreted by Jesus to include sexual immorality, violates the seventh commandment; theft the eighth; false witness the ninth; and blasphemy the first, second, and third. The tenth commandment, which forbids the sinful attitude of coveting, is covered by the first sin in Jesus' list, "evil thoughts." Thus, the only commandment of the Decalogue not reaffirmed in Matt. 15:1–20 is the fourth, "Remember the sabbath day and keep it holy" (Exod. 20:8–11; cf. Deut. 5:12–15), and this is consistent with our discovery above that Jesus redefined the biblical understanding of rest on the sabbath.

In Matt. 15:1–20, then, Jesus rejects the food laws along with the traditions of the scribes and Pharisees about hand washing before eating. At the same time he reaffirms nine of the Decalogue's ten commandments, omitting only the commandment to rest on the sabbath, a commandment that he has already implied was no longer in force in the traditional sense.

Observance of Passover (26:17–29)

This method of affirming but changing the Mosaic law reappears in Jesus' celebration of Passover in Matthew's Gospel (26:17–19). The law required every Jew who was ritually clean and not outside the land of Israel to celebrate Passover during the seven days from the fourteenth to the twenty-first of Nisan (Num. 9:13). In Matthew, as in the other Gospels, Jesus and his disciples gathered on the night of Jesus' arrest for a Passover meal (26:17–19). They ate the meal at night on the first day of the feast of Unleavened Bread as the law instructed. They also ate it, in conformity with the law's instructions, in Jerusalem (26:18) rather than outside the city in Bethany, where they were staying (21:17; cf. Deut. 16:7).[38] Bread (26:26), wine (26:27), and a dish containing either salty water or a fruity paste (26:23) were all part of the meal for Jesus and his disciples, just as they were for other first-century Jews.[39] The meal also included an interpretive element in agreement with the law's requirement that the meaning of the meal be explained (Exod. 12:26–27).

The interpretation that Jesus gave to the meal, however, was different from the one that the Mosaic law dictated. Rather than reminding his disciples of God's mercy to his people at the time of their exodus from Egypt (Exod. 12:11, 27), Matthew tells us that Jesus used the bread and the wine to describe his coming death—his broken body and shed blood. His shed blood, he explains, inaugurates "the covenant" and effects forgiveness of sins "for many" (26:28). The language seems to be drawn from Jer. 31:31–34, where the prophet speaks of a "new covenant" unlike the one that God's people violated. This new covenant, says the prophet, will transform the hearts of God's people so that they will all know God and understand instinctively what he wants them to do. At the time when this covenant is established, Jeremiah says, God will "forgive their iniquity, and remember their sin no more" (31:34).

Here too Jesus observes but transforms an important requirement of the Mosaic law. A ritual designed to recall God's greatest act of redemption for his people is reinterpreted as a reference to another great act of redemption predicted by the prophets and fulfilled in Jesus' death. Jesus does not abolish the Mosaic law at this point but alters it so radically that it becomes something different.

JESUS' TEACHING
AS A NEW LAW IN MATTHEW

How are we to explain this complex mingling of continuity and discontinuity, of bold assertion of authority over the law and yet concern to show consistency with the law at a fundamental level? The answer to this question begins to emerge when we investigate Matthew's hints throughout his narrative that Jesus has brought a new law, not inconsistent with but nevertheless different from the Mosaic law.

In four places in his Gospel, Matthew shows that he believes Jesus' own teaching is a replacement of the Mosaic law. Jesus' own words, including his affirmation of the Mosaic law's ultimate goal and many of its specific requirements, constitute not a new interpretation of the Mosaic law but a supersession of it.

The Sermon on the Mount

When Jesus teaches his disciples from "the mountain" (5:1), the setting of his teaching parallels Moses' mediation of the law, received on Mount Sinai, to the people below.[40] But Jesus' words are more than simply an interpretation of the Mosaic law or an addition to it. As the antithetical character of 5:21–47 shows, they are intended to function as a substitute for the law. Moreover, the sermon ends with a definitive statement about the authority of Jesus' words (7:24–27). Disciples of Jesus should build the conduct of their lives on the foundation of Jesus' words, for not to do so will spell disaster. Success or failure depends no longer on whether one keeps the Mosaic law, but on whether or not one hears Jesus' words and does them (7:24).

The Permanence of Jesus' Teaching

Near the end of the eschatological discourse in Matthew, Jesus, who has just spoken of end of the age, makes the solemn pronouncement that although heaven and earth will pass away, his words will not pass away (24:35). He is probably referring chiefly to his prophetic utterances on the end of the age, but two considerations lend the statement a more general significance as well. First, the sentence is unconnected by any conjunction with Jesus' preceding statement about the present generation not passing away until the occurrence of all the events he has just described. The primary link between the statement and its context instead seems to be the catchword "pass away" (*parerchomai*), which is used once in v. 34 and twice in v. 35. This makes v. 35 stand out from its context and urges the reader to apply it to Jesus' teaching throughout the Gospel rather than to his eschatological comments in this section alone.

Second, this sentence inevitably reminds the alert reader of a similar solemn pronouncement near the beginning of the Gospel, "Truly I say to you, until heaven and earth pass away, neither one iota nor one stroke of the pen will pass away from the law, until all is accomplished" (5:18). Here too the word "pass away" (*parerchomai*) appears twice and the second time is negated in a particularly emphatic way (*ou mē* + the aorist subjunctive), just as it is in 24:35. The subtle message behind this verbal and grammatical correspondence is that just as 5:18 referred to the Mosaic law in general, so 24:35 refers to Jesus' words in general.

If this is a correct understanding of 24:35, then a contrast emerges between the Mosaic law and Jesus' words. Eventually, 5:18 implies, the Mosaic law will pass away; but according to 24:35, Jesus' teaching in the Gospel will not pass away, even when the end of the age has arrived.[41] Jesus words, then, are not an interpretation of the Mosaic law but a permanent and eschatologically oriented replacement for it.

Teaching the Commandments of Jesus

At the end of the Gospel Jesus instructs his disciples from a mountain (28:16) just as he had at the beginning (5:1), and again Jesus' commands are an important element in the instruction:

> All authority has been given to me in heaven and upon earth. Go, there-fore, and teach all the gentiles, baptizing them in the name of the Father and of the Son and of the Holy Spirit, instructing them to keep (*tēreō*) everything I have commanded you (*entellō*). And, behold, I am with you all the time, indeed until the end of the age. (28:18–20)

Matthew's use of the word "commanded" here recalls his use of the closely related term "commandment" (*entolē*) in the rest of the Gospel, a word that always refers to the Mosaic law (5:19; 15:3; 19:17; 22:36, 38, 40) and is once coupled with the verb "keep" (*tēreō*), as "commanded" is here, to refer to keeping the Decalogue (19:17). In addition, Jesus mentions having received all authority in heaven and on earth, a statement that recalls the response of the crowds to Jesus' commandments in the Sermon on the Mount (7:29).

These characteristics send a clear message: Jesus replaces Moses, and his teaching replaces the Mosaic commandments. Just as Moses spoke from a mountain, so Jesus speaks from a mountain here. Just as Moses gave commandments with the intention that his hearers should keep them, so Jesus intends that his commandments should be kept. Just as Moses spoke with authority, so Jesus speaks with an unsurpassed authority. Jesus and his teaching, in short, have superseded Moses and the law.

NEW AND OLD TOGETHER IN MATTHEW

Jesus' approach to the law in Matthew's Gospel, then, is characterized by both continuity and discontinuity. Matthew shows that by focusing on the law's fundamental concerns, Jesus replaced the Mosaic law itself with the ethical ideal toward which it pointed. He redefined the commandment to rest on the sabbath, placing it squarely beneath the requirement to show mercy.[42] He elevated the rest of the Decalogue above the law's dietary restrictions and implied that those restrictions were no longer valid. He summarized the law and the prophets in terms of the basic principles on which they depend—love for God and neighbor. Matthew demonstrates by his emphasis on the authority of Jesus' words and his comparison of Jesus' words with Moses' commands, that Jesus' teaching, although consistent with the tendency of the Mosaic law, is something new and a replacement for it. The law and the prophets, says Jesus, prophesied until John (11:13), but Jesus' teaching represents their fulfillment and therefore their divinely appointed end.[43]

This intermingling of new and old is not merely an implication of Jesus' teaching in Matthew's Gospel or an unintentional by-product of the tension between Matthew's Jewish origins and his new Christian commitments. It is instead Matthew's purposeful theological commitment. This is especially clear in a brief parable preserved only in Matthew that describes the activity of the Christian scribe, the kind of person that Matthew probably considered himself to be. The parable occurs at the end of Matthew's collection of Jesus' parables in chapter 13. Several of these parables have stressed the way in which Jesus' proclamation of the kingdom of God has overwhelmed the old, but has done so in a way that is consistent with the old (13:31–33, 44–46). "Have you understood all these things?" Jesus asks the disciples (13:51). After the disciples have responded with a perhaps too optimistic "Yes," Jesus describes the kind of interpreters of his proclamation that he wants them to be:

> Every scribe who has been discipled in the kingdom of heaven is like the master of a house who brings out of his treasure chest things both new and old. (13:52)

This is precisely the way that Matthew has approached the Mosaic law in his Gospel. Jesus raises the fundamental principles of the Mosaic law to the highest level of importance and brings its ultimate tendencies to full expression. In the process he has created something new.

NOTES

1. Representative of this approach are Gerhard Barth, "Matthew's Understanding of the Law," in Günther Bornkamm, Gerhard Barth, and Heinz Joachim Held, *Tradition and Interpretation in Matthew* (Philadelphia: Westminster, 1963), 58–164, especially 62–75; Rudolf Smend and Ulrich Luz, *Gesetz*, Biblische Konfrontationen (Stuttgart: Kohlhammer, 1981), 79–86; Roger Mohrlang, *Matthew and Paul: A Comparison of Ethical Perspectives,*

SNTSMS 48 (Cambridge: Cambridge University Press, 1984), 7–26; Ingo Broer, "Anmerkungen zum Gesetzesverständnis des Matthäus," in *Das Gesetz im Neuen Testament*, ed. Karl Kertelge, QD 108 (Freiburg: Herder, 1986), 128–45; J. Andrew Overman, *Matthew's Gospel and Formative Judaism: The Social World of the Matthean Community* (Minneapolis: Fortress, 1990), 23–30, 70, 86–90; Anthony J. Saldarini, *Matthew's Christian-Jewish Community* (Chicago: University of Chicago Press, 1994), 124–64; and Ulrich Luz, *The Theology of the Gospel of Matthew* (Cambridge: Cambridge University Press, 1995), 20–21, 53, 57, 147.

2. Saldarini, *Matthew's Christian-Jewish Community*, 162.

3. The phrases "until heaven and earth should pass away" and "until all is accomplished" probably both refer to the end of time. The second phrase adds to the first an emphasis on the end of God's saving purposes (cf. 24:34). See Douglas J. Moo, "Jesus and the Authority of the Mosaic Law," *JSNT* 20 (1984): 3–49, here at 27.

4. The phrase "it was said" translates the Greek term *errethē*, which is in the aorist tense and passive voice. Matthew's frequent use of this verb in this tense and voice refers in every instance outside 5:18–48 to the words of God. Moreover, because what "was said" in three of the antitheses is a *verbatim* quotation of the Mosaic law, it is likely that the phrase "to the generations of old" refers to the generation who received the law at Mount Sinai. See John P. Meier, *Law and History in Matthew's Gospel*, AnBib 71 (Rome: Biblical Institute Press, 1976), 132; Robert A. Guelich, *The Sermon on the Mount: A Foundation for Understanding* (Waco, Tex.: Word Books, 1982), 179–82; and W. D. Davies and Dale C. Allison, *A Critical and Exegetical Commentary on The Gospel According to Saint Matthew*, 3 vols., ICC (Edinburgh: T & T Clark, 1988–97), 1:506–7, 510–11.

5. Out of sixteen uses of this word in Matthew, only three (3:15; 13:48; 23:32) do not refer to prophetic fulfillment.

6. R. J. Banks, *Jesus and the Law in the Synoptic Tradition*, SNTSMS 48 (Cambridge: Cambridge University Press, 1975), 210, 217–18; Meier, *Law and History in Matthew's Gospel*, 165; Guelich, *Sermon on the Mount*, 138–42; Moo, "Jesus and the Authority of the Mosaic Law," 24–25; D. A. Carson, "Matthew," in *The Expositor's Bible Commentary*, 12 vols. (Grand Rapids, Mich.: Zondervan, 1976–92), 8:143–44; Yong-Eui Yang, *Jesus and the Sabbath in Matthew's Gospel*, JSNTSup 139 (Sheffield: Sheffield Academic Press, 1997), 108–11. *Contra* Meinrad Limbeck, *Das Gesetz im Alten und Neuen Testament* (Darmstadt: Wissenschaftliche Buchgesellschaft, 1997), 130–31, who thinks that the term "fulfill" in Matthew means "confirm" (cf. 1 Kgdms. 1:14 LXX).

7. Cf. Guelich, *Sermon on the Mount*, 262–63; and Yang, *Jesus and the Sabbath in Matthew's Gospel*, 120–29.

8. For the texts of two Jewish bills of divorce, one from husband to wife and the other from wife to husband (cf. Mark 10:12) and dating from the first and

second centuries A.D. respectively, see Tal Ilan, "Notes and Observations on a Newly Published Divorce Bill from the Judean Desert," *HTR* 89 (1996): 195–202. Jesus' disciples were amazed at his conservative position when divorce comes up again in Matt. 19:3–9. "If this is the situation of a man with his wife," they respond, "it is not advantageous to marry!" (Matt. 19:10).

9. The Qumran community apparently held a position on divorce that was as strict as that of Jesus, but, unlike Jesus, attempted to show that their position was the position of the Mosaic law. See 11QTemple[a] 57:15–19 and CD 4.19–5.6 and the discussion of these texts in Joseph A. Fitzmyer, "Divorce among First Century Palestinian Jews," in *H. L. Ginsberg Volume*, ErIsr 14 (Jerusalem: Israel Exploration Society, 1978), 103–10.

10. The meaning of "sexual infidelity" (*porneia*) is hotly disputed. Hans Dieter Betz is correct in observing that since Matthew uses a different word for adultery in the same verse, this term must have a broad meaning and probably refers to "unspecified acts of sexual immorality" (*The Sermon on the Mount* [Hermeneia; Minneapolis: Fortress, 1995], 250).

11. Betz argues that the purpose of the legislation in Deuteronomy (22:13–19, 28–29; 24:1–4) was to curtail rather than to legitimate and expand divorce (*Sermon on the Mount*, 246, 249).

12. Meier believes that the Old Testament commands the taking of oaths in Exod. 22:6–7, 10; Num. 5:19–22; Deut. 6:13; and 10:20 (*Law and History in Matthew's Gospel*, 152). But Moo correctly observes that the Deuteronomy passages only regulate a custom already in place and that the other passages describe judicial situations different from the everyday practice of oath taking at issue in Matt. 5:33–37 ("Jesus and the Authority of the Mosaic Law," 44 n. 148).

13. See, e.g., the Laws of Hammurapi §§196, 197, and 200. Ancient interpreters of the biblical text were aware of this explanation for the law of retaliation. See Josephus, *Jewish Antiquities* 4.280; Tertullian, *Against Marcion* 4.16; and John Chrysostom, *Homilies on Matthew* 18.1.

14. Shalom M. Paul, *Studies in the Book of the Covenant in the Light of Cuneiform and Biblical Law*, VTSup 18 (Leiden: E. J. Brill, 1970), 73–77.

15. Ibid., 76–77.

16. J. J. Finkelstein, "Ammiṣaduqa's Edict and the Babylonian 'Law Codes,'" *JCS* 15 (1961): 98–104, here at 98.

17. The Greek word *anthistēmi* should be translated "retaliate," in accord with the illustrative examples in 5:39b–42 rather than "resist" as in many translations. The retaliation in view is the return of evil for evil. See Betz, *Sermon on the Mount*, 280–81.

18. Guelich, *Sermon on the Mount*, 222.

19. See Davies-Allison, *Matthew*, 1:541.

20. Cf. John Chrysostom, *Homilies on Matthew* 18.1, who says, "But if any one accuses the ancient law, because it commands such retaliation, he seems to me very unskilled in the wisdom that becomes a legislator, and ignorant of

the virtue of opportunities, and the gain of condescension. For if he considered who were the hearers of these sayings, and how they were disposed, and when they received this code of laws, he will thoroughly admit the wisdom of the lawgiver, and see that it is one and the same who made both those laws and these, and who wrote each of them exceedingly profitably, and in its due season" (NPNF 10:123–24). See also Augustine, *Sermon on the Mount* 56.

21. See Donald A. Hagner, *Matthew 1–13*, WBC 33A (Dallas: Word Books, 1993), 134; and Betz, *Sermon on the Mount*, 310.

22. This line of the Lord's Prayer is unique to Matthew's Gospel, since the most probable text of Luke's version (11:2–4) omits it.

23. Hagner, *Matthew 1–13*, 176–77.

24. Mark Allan Powell, "Do and Keep What Moses Says (Matt 23:2–7)," *JBL* 114 (1995): 419–35. This understanding of the passage is preferable to the claim that the statement is more general than Matthew really intends or that Jesus is using irony. For the first position, see H. N. Ridderbos, *Matthew* (Grand Rapids, Mich.: Zondervan, 1987), 422–23; and Donald A. Hagner, *Matthew 14–28*, WBC 33B (Dallas: Word Books, 1995), 659; and for the second, see Joachim Jeremias, *New Testament Theology* (London: SCM, 1971), 210: and Carson, "Matthew," 473. On literacy levels in the ancient Roman world, see William V. Harris, *Ancient Literacy* (Cambridge, Mass.: Harvard University Press, 1989), 259–82.

25. See Carson, "Matthew," 481.

26. I do not treat Jesus' statement, "Let the dead bury their dead" (8:22; cf. Luke 9:60) in this section. although these words are sometimes understood as Jesus' most radical statement on the Mosaic law (Martin Hengel, *The Charismatic Leader and His Followers* [New York: Crossroad, 1981; orig. German ed., 1968], 1–15; and E. P. Sanders, *Jesus and Judaism* [Philadelphia: Fortress, 1985], 252–55). As Marcus Bockmuehl has shown, the legal status of the statement is ambiguous ("'Let the Dead Bury Their Dead' (Matt. 8:22/Luke 9:60): Jesus and the Halakah," *JTS* 49 [1998]: 553–81).

27. E.g., Alan Hugh McNeile, *The Gospel According to St. Matthew* (Grand Rapids, Mich.: Baker, 1980; orig. ed., 1915), 103; Francis Wright Beare, *The Gospel according to Matthew*, HNTC (New York: Harper & Row, 1981), 205; Ulrich Luz, *Das Evangelium nach Matthäus*, 3 vols., EKK 1 (Zurich: Benziger; Neukirchen: Neukirchener Verlag, 1985–), 2:10; Joachim Gnilka, *Das Matthäusevangelium*, 2 vols. (Freiburg: Herder, 1988), 1:297.

28. This account appears in all three Synoptic Gospels, but Matthew places special emphasis on Jesus' ability to make people ritually pure apart from the Mosaic law. Matthew emphasizes the leper's testimony to the priests by referring to it in the last line of his version of the story (contrast Mark 1:45 and Luke 5:15). In addition, Matthew omits the phrase "concerning your cleansing" in Jesus' command to the man to follow the law's procedure for sacrifice (Mark 1:44; Luke 5:14) and therefore clarifies for his reader that the man was already clean prior to offering the sacrifice that the law considered necessary

for cleansing. For a similar perspective on the passage, see Robert H. Gundry, *Matthew: A Commentary on His Handbook for a Mixed Church under Persecution*, 2nd ed. (Grand Rapids, Mich.: Eerdmans, 1994), 140.

29. Gundry, *Matthew*, 140.

30. Cf. D. A. Carson, "Jesus and the Sabbath in the Four Gospels," in *From Sabbath to Lord's Day: A Biblical, Historical and Theological Investigation*, ed. D. A. Carson (Grand Rapids, Mich.: Zondervan, 1982), 57–97, here at 75; and Yang, *Jesus and the Sabbath in Matthew's Gospel*, 157.

31. Unlike Mark, Matthew does not include the statement that the sabbath was made for man, not man for the sabbath. Like Luke, Matthew simply says that Jesus is Lord of the sabbath. If Matthew was editing Mark at this point, then he probably intended to focus the reader's attention on the authority of Jesus over the sabbath.

32. Cf. Hagner, *Matthew 1–13*, 332.

33. Commentaries on Matthew's Gospel often attempt to illumine this passage by prolific quotation from later rabbinic debates over whether someone should be healed on the sabbath. Strictly speaking, these debates are irrelevant to the issue here since they speak only to the occasional healing of some infirmity on the sabbath, not to the regular work of healers.

34. The merciful character of the original sabbath command is evident in Exod. 23:12 and Deut. 5:14, where the purpose of the sabbath is described as giving rest and refreshment to ox and ass, bondmaid's son and alien. Matthew probably does not bring this merciful purpose of the commandment to the surface because he wants to keep the emphasis of the passage on the authority of Jesus to deal sovereignly with the sabbath. See Daniel J. Harrington, "Sabbath Tensions: Matt 12:1–4 and other New Testament Texts," in *The Sabbath in Jewish and Christian Traditions*, ed. Tamara C. Eskenazi, Daniel J. Harrington, and William H. Shea (New York: Crossroad, 1991), 45–56, here at 51; and Davies-Allison, *Matthew*, 2:218 n. 59.

35. In 24:20 Jesus tells his disciples to pray that their flight from the time of suffering before the end of the age would not happen on a sabbath. Since Mark at this point only refers to prayer that the time of suffering may not happen in winter (Mark 13:18), many interpreters take Matthew's additional reference to the sabbath as evidence that his community observed the sabbath. But the addition probably only refers to the inconveniences, if not outright persecution, that one who fled on the sabbath would encounter within a predominantly Jewish culture. See Carson, "Matthew," 501; and Graham N. Stanton, *A Gospel for a New People* (Edinburgh: T & T Clark, 1992), 192–206.

36. See, e.g., Daniel J. Harrington, *The Gospel of Matthew*, SP 1 (Collegeville, Minn.: Liturgical Press, 1991), 231; Hagner, *Matthew 14–28*, 429; and Saldarini, *Matthew's Christian-Jewish Community*, 134–41. For a different perspective, closer to the one adopted here, see Carson, "Matthew," 347–53.

37. The statement of Eduard Schweizer (*The Good News according to Matthew* [Atlanta: John Knox, 1975], 326) that Matthew "could not have writ-

ten verse 11 if the community had not considered the Old Testament dietary laws to be binding" is puzzling. Verse 11 seems to show just the opposite.

38. Joachim Jeremias, *The Eucharistic Words of Jesus* (London: SCM, 1966), 42–43.

39. On the identification of the dish mentioned in 26:23, see Gnilka, *Matthäusevangelium,* 2:396.

40. See especially Dale C. Allison, Jr., *The New Moses: A Matthean Typology* (Minneapolis: Fortress, 1993), 172–80.

41. See Adolf Schlatter, *Der Evangelist Matthäus: Seine Sprache, sein Ziel, seine Selbständigkeit: Ein Kommentar zum ersten Evangelium* (Stuttgart: Calwer Verlag, 1929), 713; and Gnilka, *Matthäusevangelium,* 2:336.

42. Cf. 23:23, where Jesus relativizes the commandment to tithe by subordinating it to the weightier matters of judgment, mercy, and faithfulness.

43. Cf. Davies-Allison, *Matthew,* 1:484–87.

4

Grace in Place of Grace:
Jesus Christ and the Mosaic Law
in John's Gospel

J OHN CONDUCTS AN INTENSE DEBATE with "the Jews" in his Gospel.[1]
Already in the second chapter, Jesus appears in the temple, whip in
hand, driving out of his Father's house those within it who profit
from the exchange of money and the sale of sacrificial animals. "The
Jews," in response, demand that he produce a sign to demonstrate his
right to act with such prophetic zeal. Jesus answers with a statement
that on the literal level sounds ridiculous, but at a deeper, symbolic
level is profoundly true: "Destroy this temple, and in three days I shall
resurrect it." This begins a series of confrontations in which "the
Jews" or "the Pharisees" so thoroughly misunderstand the deeper significance of Jesus' deeds and words that they eventually claim he has
a demon and seek to kill him. Jesus can only conclude from this firm
rejection that they are children of the devil.

The Mosaic law plays a key role in this controversy. The Jews proclaim their allegiance to the Mosaic law and believe that this loyalty
is fundamentally incompatible with belief in Jesus. In their view, Jesus
breaks the law (5:18), and leads others to do the same (5:10–12; 7:47; cf.
7:12). His offenses against the law are so severe that the law demands
his death (8:59; 10:31–33; 19:7; cf. 5:18), and loyalty to Moses requires
the excommunication from the synagogue of all who confess that he is
the Christ (9:22, 34; cf. 12:42; 16:2). Even entertaining the notion that
Jesus is the Christ (7:40–44) reveals ignorance of the law and that one
lies under a curse (7:49). "We are disciples of Moses," the Pharisees
assert, "We know that God has spoken to Moses but we do not know
where this man is from" (9:28–29).

John, however, is unwilling to concede the point. Far from leading people astray on the law, Jesus and his teaching are in step with Moses' ultimate purposes. Jesus offers a defense for his supposed legal infractions (5:17; 7:21–24; 10:34–36) and claims that Moses wrote about him in the law (1:45; 5:46). Those who believe what Moses wrote, Jesus asserts, will believe in him (5:46), and Moses becomes the accuser of those who do not believe (5:45). Even the Jews' hatred of him fulfills the "law," broadly interpreted in this instance to cover the other scriptures also (15:25).

Some of this tug-of-war over the law takes place on Jewish turf, as if John understood the conceptual world of Judaism and wanted to speak its language. In response to the claim that he broke the law by healing a lame man on the sabbath, Jesus claims that just as the command to circumcise is more important than the command to rest on the sabbath, so the healing of one's entire body is more important than strict observance of the sabbath (7:22–23). This is a classic argument from legal precedent and would have seemed reasonable to some Jews.[2]

Similarly, when Jesus defends his claim to be the Son of God by saying that the law itself calls people gods (10:34–36; cf. Ps. 82:6), his extension of the term "law" to cover all of scripture and the interpretive method he uses to defend himself on the basis of "the law" were familiar features of first-century Jewish exegesis.[3] The same can be said for Jesus' claim that the world's rejection of him fulfilled the statement in the "law" that reads, "They hated me without a cause" (15:25; Ps. 35:19; 69:5).[4] John's "Jews" certainly rejected the conclusions that he drew from these interpretations of the law, but they would have found the exegetical method adopted here familiar.

On the other hand, this common ground with Judaism lies next to features of John's approach to the law that come from a different conceptual world. When Jesus speaks of the Mosaic law, he typically distances himself from it: speaking to the Jews he refers to the law as "your law" (8:17; 10:34), and to his disciples he calls it "their law" (15:25). Such statements do not mean "the law as Jews misinterpret it," for Jesus says explicitly that Moses gave the law to "you," meaning the Jews (7:19; cf. 7:22), not to "us," and it is precisely "their" law that Jesus fulfills (15:25). Just how far this places Jesus from his Jewish opponents becomes clear when we find the Roman governor Pilate also referring to the Mosaic law in dialogue with the Jews as "your law" (18:29).

Where Jesus does adopt Jewish interpretive presuppositions in his debate with the Jews over his deeds and claims, moreover, he never fully answers their concerns in terms of the law. That circumcision on the eighth day is more important than avoiding work on the sabbath is true enough (7:23), for an infant's eighth day never comes again. But Jesus could have waited another day to heal a man who had been crippled for thirty-eight years, and he certainly did not need to tell him to carry his mat. The same problem arises during Jesus' debate with the Jews over whether by claiming unity with the Father (10:30) he has blasphemed God (10:31, 33). Despite Jesus' Jewish method of argumentation from "the law," the passage that he cites does not answer in an obvious way the Jews' concern over Jesus' claim of unity with the Father, for although that passage uses the term "gods" of human judges, it does not attribute divinity to them.[5] At the same time that Jesus adopts Jewish methods of interpreting the law, therefore, he demonstrates that his relationship to the law is unique. It does not apply to him in the way that it has applied to other Jews for centuries past.

John, then, affirms the law as a witness to Jesus and reveals an accurate knowledge of the way first-century Jews understood the law. At the same time, his Gospel holds the law at a distance.[6] What understanding of the Mosaic law lies beneath these two tendencies? When John says in the prologue to the Gospel that "the law came through Moses; grace and truth through Jesus Christ" (1:17), does he mean that the law was devoid of grace and truth but that these are found in Jesus?[7] Or, pointing back to his mention of "grace in place of grace" (1:16), does he affirm the graciousness of the law and only claim that its graciousness was exceeded in Jesus Christ?[8]

Like other elements of the prologue, the meaning of this statement only becomes clear after pondering the rest of the Gospel. We shall attempt to grasp John's understanding of the law in the rest of the Gospel by taking the following steps:

1. We shall look at the two great legal controversies that face Jesus. One of these focuses on Jesus' attitude toward the sabbath and the other on his claim to be equal with God. Jesus' opponents believe that in both instances he has violated the Mosaic law. To this Jesus responds that his opponents have failed to understand the law's deeper meaning.

2. We shall examine the ways in which Jesus' person and teaching replace the law. He replaces the law's purification rituals, its temple, its festivals, and its ethical teaching with his person and with his own "new commandment." This replacement theme is

not a criticism of the law but an expression of John's belief that the law pointed to Jesus.

3. We shall apply these two aspects of John's approach to the law to his statement in 1:16–17. Here John claims not that Jesus stands against the law or that the law was devoid of grace and truth but that the grace of the law pales in comparison to the grace brought by Jesus.

SABBATH WORK, EQUALITY WITH GOD, AND THE MOSAIC LAW

Beginning in chapter 5, controversy breaks out between Jesus and the Jews (or Pharisees) over Jesus' activity on the sabbath and his claims for himself.[9] By the end of chapter 10, the issues in the dispute between Jesus and his Jewish opponents are clearly defined, and the legal basis for the opposition to Jesus has hardened into the form it will take when the Jews accuse Jesus before Pilate.[10] "We have a law," the Jews tell Pilate in 19:7, "and according to that law he ought to die, because he made himself out to be the Son of God." This charge is based on Jesus' dispute with the Jews about his person and work in 5:1–47; 7:1–52; and 8:12–10:39. In these passages, the Jews and the Pharisees assert, first, that Jesus violates the sabbath and, second, that he blasphemes God.

The First Charge: Sabbath Work (5:1–18; 7:21–24; 9:1–41)

The trouble begins with the healing of the lame man at the pool of Bethzatha in Jerusalem (5:1–9). The man had been ill for thirty-eight years and had hoped to elicit a magical cure from the pool by dipping himself into the water before anyone else after the water had been disturbed (5:5–7). Bypassing all this, Jesus simply told the man to get up, pick up his mat, and walk (5:8). The man was instantly healed (5:9a). The last line in this part of the narrative, however, sounds a forbidding note: "And that day was the sabbath" (5:9b).

In the second part of the account, "the Jews" register no objection to the miracle itself, but have three problems with the way in which Jesus effected the healing. First, he told the man whom he had healed to carry his mat on the sabbath. The importance of this concern is evident from John's almost ponderous repetition of Jesus' instructions:

> Jesus said to him, "Rise, *pick up your mat and walk."* And instantly the man became healthy and *picked up his mat and walked.* And that day was the sabbath. The Jews therefore were saying to the man who had been healed, "It is the sabbath, and it is not permitted to you to *pick up your mat."* But the man answered them, "The man who made me healthy—that man said to me, *'Pick up your mat and walk.'"* They asked him, "Who is the man who said to you, *'Pick up and walk'?"* (5:8–12)[11]

Already in the Mosaic law itself the fourth commandment's instruction not to do "any work" on the sabbath day (Exod. 20:8–11; Deut. 5:12–15) was interpreted strictly (Num. 15:32), and this strict interpretation is reaffirmed in the prophets (Jer. 17:19–27) and the writings (Neh. 13:15–22) where the carrying of burdens on the sabbath day was expressly forbidden.[12] The Jews were concerned that this law was being violated, and so they questioned the formerly lame man about his activity.

Second, the Jews quickly learned that the man was not violating the sabbath on his own initiative but because the one who had healed him told him to carry his mat (5:11–12). Their concern, therefore, shifted to Jesus (5:15). He had healed a chronically ill person on the sabbath—to their mind another violation of the commandment to avoid "any work" on the sabbath (5:16).

Third, the subsequent narrative reveals the concern of some of "the crowd" and of "the Pharisees" that Jesus was leading people astray (7:12, 47). The seed of that concern may lie in Jesus' instructions to the lame man to carry his mat on the sabbath. Jesus had not only violated the sabbath himself (5:18), but he had led someone else to violate it also.

The sabbath controversy arises again in chapter 9, where Jesus opens the eyes of a man who had been born blind (9:1–2, 19, 32). Here too Jesus not only heals on the sabbath but makes clay from his spittle to anoint the man's eyes and tells the man to go and wash in the pool of Siloam, additional activity that John again emphasizes by repetition (9:6–7, 11, 14, 15; cf. 9:26). For the second time, Jesus has not only healed someone who was chronically ill on the sabbath but has also led someone else to perform unnecessary activity on this day.

Thus, Jesus has much to answer for in the eyes of his Jewish opponents. The Pharisees insist that he cannot be from God and is a sinner because "he does not keep the sabbath" (9:16; cf. 5:18). To their dismay, however, his defense only produces what, from their perspective, is a more serious breech of the law. Jesus claims that he is justified in working on the sabbath because of his unity with God. "My Father is working until now, and I am still working," he says (5:17). In the discourses that follow this provocative statement, Jesus frequently repeats in various ways its essence. He does what his Father does (5:19–21); he accomplishes the work his Father assigns to him (5:22, 27, 30; 9:3–4, 33; 10:25, 32, 37–38; cf. 14:10–12; 15:24; 17:4); and he does nothing from himself, but only speaks what the Father has taught him (8:28). The implications are clear. Jesus is not subject to the command to avoid work on the sabbath because he is equal to God. Since God is exempt from sabbath rest (5:18; cf. 10:30), Jesus is also.[13]

The formerly blind man, now Jesus' "disciple" (9:28) offers a similar defense. Whereas the Pharisees who interrogate him are convinced that someone who does not keep the sabbath is a sinner and not from God, the blind man is equally convinced that Jesus' sabbath activity does not disqualify him from being a "prophet" (9:17) and "from God" (9:33). Indeed it does not disqualify him from being the Son of Man himself (9:35).

The Second Charge: Blasphemy
(8:12–59; 10:22–39)

In 8:12–59 and 10:22–39, Jesus' violation of the sabbath fades from view, and his close relationship with the Father becomes the primary issue. "The Jews" articulate clearly the central concern of 8:12–59 in 8:25 when they ask Jesus, "Who are you?" and in 8:53, "Who do you make yourself out to be?" This section of the Gospel places the differences between Jesus and his opponents on this issue in bold relief. Jesus claims to be the light of the world (8:12), the revealer of truth (8:32, 45–46), the one who can set others free from sin (8:24, 34–36), and the one who can prevent them from experiencing death (8:51). Most important of all, Jesus claims to have a breathtakingly close relationship with God. Jesus claims that God, his Father, bears witness to the truth of his claims (8:18), that to know him is to know the Father (8:19; cf. 8:55), that his origins and destiny lie with the Father (8:21, 23–24), that the Father sent him (8:26, 29), that he speaks as the Father taught him (8:28, 38, 40; cf. 8:55), that he only does what is pleasing to the Father (8:29), that he came from the Father (8:42), and that the

Father glorifies him (8:54). Finally, in a climactic way, Jesus says that he existed before Abraham as the "I am"—the God of Israel himself (8:58).

This crescendo of claims, climaxing in the ultimate self-assertion is matched on the Jewish side by ever increasing dismay and rejection. At first the Jews do not understand Jesus. "Where is your Father?" they ask (8:19), and, "Who are you?" (8:25). They are befuddled by Jesus' statement that they will be unable to follow him to his destination. Is he speaking of suicide? (8:22). As the claims persist, the Jews become more hostile. Surely Jesus has deviated from normal Jewish belief—he is a Samaritan—or is demon-possessed (8:48, 52). Finally, as Jesus' assertions about his identity reach their startling climax, the Jewish response is fittingly dramatic. When they realize that Jesus is claiming eternal unity with God himself, the Jews pick up stones to stone him (8:59).

The discussion in chapter 10 is shorter, but advances the same claims with the same results. The issue again is who Jesus claims to be. "How long are you going to annoy us?" the Jews ask. "If you are the Christ, tell us plainly" (10:24). The question is appropriate, since Jesus, calling on imagery from Ezekiel 34, has just cast the Jews in the role of those who would harm God's flock and himself in the role of God who would shepherd his people through a Davidic king. Since some first-century Jews expected the Messiah to fill the role of David as described in the prophets (Jer. 23:5–6; Ezek. 34:23–24; 37:23–25; Luke 1:69–70; Acts 13:23; Rom. 1:2–3), the question of the Johannine Jews is fully intelligible. You have been speaking in irritatingly allusive biblical metaphors, they seem to be asking, now tell us plainly what you mean: Are you the Christ?

Jesus quickly leaves the category of Messiah behind, however, as he claims that the Jews do not belong to his sheepfold and that no one is able to snatch those who do belong to his fold from his hand. That is to say, he goes on, no one is able to snatch them out of "the Father's hand" (10:28–29). In light of the previous discussion, the implications of this statement are clear; but as if to avoid any misunderstanding Jesus says, "I and the Father—we are one" (10:30).

Once again, the Jews pick up stones to stone Jesus (10:31), and this time, John reveals their reasoning with as much clarity as Jesus has used in revealing his identity. It is now Jesus' turn to ask the questions. "I have shown you many good works from the Father," he says. "For which of these do you stone me?" (10:32). The Jews retort that they are not troubled by any good work Jesus might do, but because he—a mere man—makes himself out to be God. He is, they claim, a blasphemer (10:33). Jesus, therefore, is a lawbreaker because he has violated the law's prohibition against blasphemy. In accord with the law's penalty for that violation, he must die by stoning (Num. 15:32–36; Lev. 24:16; cf. John 19:7).

The Jews oppose Jesus, then, because he violates the law by breaking the sabbath and blaspheming God, and he not only does these things himself but leads others to do them also. Jesus' disciples, who believe his claims for himself, must be excluded from the synagogue in accord with the law's instructions to "purge the evil from Israel" (9:22).[14] Jesus himself must die. John summarizes this in 5:18:

> This is why, therefore, the Jews were seeking to kill him: he not only broke the sabbath, but was also calling God his own Father, making himself equal to God.

Jesus' Defense

Despite these charges, Jesus consistently refuses to be labeled a violator of the law. His accusers, he insists, are the violators of the law, since they read the law as if nothing has changed and fail to perceive that the law is actually about him.[15] This perspective emerges from five passages.

The Jews Reject Moses and Violate Their Central Creed (5:31–47)

In 5:31–47 Jesus speaks of God's testimony concerning the truth of his claims. As helpful as the testimony of John was in bearing witness to the truth concerning Jesus and in pointing the way to salvation through him (5:33–34), the testimony of the Father is greater. Jesus benefits from this greater testimony in the form of the works that the Father has given him to do (5:36–37a). The Jews have just rejected the testimony of those works, however. Because Jesus healed the lame man and therefore worked on the sabbath (5:1–9), and because Jesus' explanation of this action implied equality with God (5:17), the Jews began persecuting Jesus and seeking his death (5:16, 18).

In 5:37b–47 Jesus claims that this refusal to recognize him arises from the Jews' hard-hearted misreading of the Mosaic law.[16] He begins by contrasting them with Moses and the ancient Israelites, who, according to the Hebrew scriptures, heard God's voice and saw his form.[17] God has given to the Jews access to his voice and form again in Jesus, for Jesus speaks the words of God (3:34; 17:8), and those who have seen Jesus have seen God (1:18; 14:9). Unlike Moses and the ancient generation of Israelites, however, Jesus' Jewish opponents have rejected this most recent revelation of God's voice and form, and therefore the word of God does not remain within them (5:37–38).[18]

John takes this thought further in his next statement. The Jews search the scriptures, he says, because they think that they will find life in this way, but the scriptures point to Jesus as the source of life, and the Jews have rejected him (5:39–40). Here John alludes to the claim within the scriptures themselves, particularly within the law, that only those who affirm and obey God's instruction will find life.[19] He says that the Jews, because of their desire to have the eternal life promised in the scriptures, search them diligently. But then he points out that the result of this diligent search is rejection of Jesus—the one who gives the life promised in the scriptures to those who come to him (5:39–40). Their rejection of him on the basis of the law (5:18; 7:52; 8:13; 9:16; 19:7), he implies, is ironically rejection of the very blessing that the law promises to those who keep it.

John next claims that the Jews' rejection of Jesus implies that they have violated the law's central confessional statement. In Deut. 6:4–5 Moses restates the essence of the Decalogue's first commandment:

> Hear, O Israel: The LORD our God is one LORD; and you shall love the LORD your God with all your heart, and with all your soul, and with all your might. (RSV)

The two aspects of this confession, that only the Lord is Israel's God and that Israel should love him with their whole being, reappear in John 5:42 and 44. Here Jesus claims that the Jews' refusal to glorify God through acknowledging Jesus means that they do not love God (5:42). Moreover, their willingness to receive from each other the glory that belongs to God alone is not consistent with the scriptures' insistence that God is the only God, and that he alone deserves praise (5:44).[20] Rejection of Jesus, once again, means violation of the Mosaic law.

Finally, John states explicitly what he has said allusively up to this point in the passage: Moses wrote about Jesus, and at the root of the Jews' refusal to believe Jesus lies a rejection of Moses himself (5:46–47). Just as the Jews search the scriptures to find eternal life in them (5:39), so they set their hope on Moses (5:45; cf. 9:28). But in both cases, they have become so fixed on scripture and Moses, that they have failed to perceive the role of the law as a witness to someone beyond itself. Moses therefore no longer intercedes for them as he did in the days of the exodus (Exod. 32:30–34; 33:12–16). Instead, he becomes their accuser (5:45).[21]

The Jews Violate the Sixth Commandment and Misunderstand the Sabbath (7:19–24)

In 7:19–24 Jesus charges the Jews with breaking the Mosaic law by their attempt to kill him for healing the lame man on the sabbath (5:16, 18; 7:1). Their efforts violate the law at two levels. On one level, by trying to kill an innocent person, they are breaking the sixth commandment of the Decalogue, "You shall not murder" (Exod. 20:13; Deut. 5:17). At a deeper level, their rejection of Jesus' sabbath healing shows that they do not understand the law's own witness to the secondary importance of the sabbath. Jesus argues that the commandment to avoid any work on the sabbath is linked with the Mosaic commandment to circumcise male offspring. It is widely recognized, he says, that the commandment to circumcise male children on their eighth day of life takes precedence over the commandment to avoid work on the sabbath. Circumcision involves work, but if the male child's eighth day falls on the sabbath, this important work nevertheless goes forward (7:22). To this extent, Jesus' unbelieving Jewish audience would have agreed with his reasoning.

Additional elements of Jesus' argument, however, would have brought sharp disagreement. First, Jesus concludes from the practice of circumcising on the sabbath that Moses gave the circumcision commandment to God's people precisely so that it might show the existence of circumstances that call for the violation of the sabbath (7:22). Jesus claims, therefore, that God intended for the circumcision commandment to reduce the importance of the sabbath commandment. Second, Jesus closes his argument by claiming that his sabbath healing activity, like circumcision, takes precedence over the sabbath commandment. If circumcision is permissible on the sabbath and involves bringing only one part of the body into conformity with God's will, he reasons, then how much more appropriate that the sabbath commandment should not prevent the restoration to health of "a whole man" (7:23).

Jesus' opponents could easily retort that if a male child's eighth day fell on the sabbath, circumcision could not be performed either early or late without violating the commandment: circumcision on the seventh or the ninth day would not do, for the law stipulates that circumcision must occur on the eighth day. The lame man, on the other hand, had been sick for thirty-eight years. Surely he could have been healed the previous day or could have waited another day for healing. Moreover, even if Jesus' argument on this point were conceded, he had violated the sabbath in another way when he told the man to carry his mat.

For John, however, these objections were invalid. Healing the lame man was not an effort to keep one statute of Moses by breaking another, but an effort to accomplish the life-giving work assigned to Jesus by the Father (5:21, 24–29, 39–40).[22] If this involved breaking the sabbath commandment, then that commandment would have to be swept away before the all-consuming current of God's greater work in Jesus. Ignoring the sabbath commandment in order to perform circumcision simply illustrated this principle on a smaller scale. Jesus' opponents are mired in the fretful pursuit of conformity to the details of the Mosaic law, but Jesus exposes the law's deep theological structure, fulfills it, and is therefore beyond submission to its details.

The Pharisees Ignore the Law's Weightier Matters (7:45–49)

In 7:45–49, John gives an example of the Jews' faithfulness to the details of the law at the expense of understanding its deeper fulfillment in Jesus. Here, the assistants to the chief priests and Pharisees return to their superiors after failing to complete their mission of arresting Jesus (7:45; cf. 7:32). The assistants, it turns out, had followed the crowd and fallen under the influence of Jesus' remarkable words. As a result, they could not bring themselves to lay hands on him (7:46). This brings a sharp rebuke from the Pharisees, who are amazed at their assistants' gullible preference for the judgment of "the crowd" over their own immense learning (7:47–48). "This crowd," they claim, does not know the law and is accursed (7:49).

Immediately, however, an interchange with one of their own group belies their claim to understand the law. Nicodemus points out that the law of the Jews ("our law") does not condemn a person without first hearing from him and knowing what he is doing (7:51). No text in the Mosaic law explicitly says this, although several assume it (Exod.

23:1; Deut. 1:16–17; 17:2–5; 19:15–19), and it is an elementary principle of justice that people should not be convicted, especially of a capital crime, on the basis of evidence obtained through hearsay.[23] The effect of this reminder is to show that despite the disgust of Jesus' accusers at the legal ignorance of the mob, they themselves have failed to understand the law.

Once again, however, this failure goes deeper than an unwillingness to hear the evidence for and against Jesus objectively. At its root lies the unbelief of Jesus' opponents. They have not merely failed to hear him and know what he does in a legal sense; they have failed to hear in his words the word of God (8:43, 47; cf. 10:26–27) and to see in what he does the will of God (4:34; 6:38; 8:29; 14:31).[24] Their technical violation of the law in their eagerness to condemn Jesus without a trial is merely a symptom of their hard-hearted unwillingness to believe his words and works.

Because of their disbelief, their only response to Nicodemus's challenge is to inform their colleague that Jesus does not meet the criteria for the Messiah that they have constructed on the basis of their reading of the law. "The prophet" like Moses (Deut 18:15), they insist, could not come from Galilee (cf. 1:46) because the scriptures say nothing about the origins of the prophet in that region.[25] Once again, their concern with Jesus' nonconformity to legal details prevents them from seeing in Jesus the ultimate life toward which the scriptures point (5:39–40).

Jesus Stands above the Law of Testimony (8:12–20)

In 8:12–20 Jesus claims to be the light of the world and answers the objection of the Pharisees to this claim by appealing to the Jewish law of testimony. The Pharisees phrase their objection in two straightforward statements: "You testify about yourself. Your testimony is not true" (8:13). This objection echoes the Mosaic law's requirement that only evidence corroborated by two witnesses can be used to convict someone accused of a crime (Deut. 17:6; 19:15).[26] It also recalls Jesus' statement in 5:31, "If I testify about myself, my testimony is not true." The Pharisees seem to be saying that by testifying to himself that he is the light of the world, Jesus is violating a law that even he has previously recognized to be valid.

Jesus responds to this charge in two ways. First, he shows that the

Pharisees have misunderstood his earlier statement. "Even if I testify about myself," he says, "my testimony is true because I know where I have come from and where I am going" (8:14). His testimony about himself is true, therefore, because his unique relationship with the Father reveals its truth. When Jesus said in 5:31 that his testimony would not be true if he testified about himself, the term "testimony" referred precisely to this unity with the Father, as the ensuing discussion shows (5:19, 21, 26, 30; cf. 8:16). In 5:31, then, Jesus has not uttered a legal principle at all but only described the Father's testimony to the unity of Father and Son. That the Pharisees recall this statement as a legal principle and use it against him in 8:13 shows that they have misunderstood it. Thus, they can make judgments only on the level of the flesh (8:15). They are mired in legal details and are unable to see beyond them to the meaning of Jesus' words.[27]

Second, Jesus argues that for him, formal conformity with the law's requirement for at least two corroborating witnesses is unnecessary (8:16) and, if it is to be sought at all (8:17), must come in this form: "I am he who bears witness to myself, and the Father who sent me bears witness to me" (8:18). Jesus, in other words, must be allowed to serve as one of his two corroborating witnesses. Since the law demands two witnesses besides oneself, Jesus once again claims that his relationship with the Father places him beyond the reach of the kind of legal details with which the Pharisees are concerned.

The Pharisees can only respond by asking where Jesus' Father is (8:19), presumably so that at least he might be summoned to corroborate Jesus' witness. Still thinking on the level of the flesh, their concern with conformity to the details of the Mosaic law has obscured for them the identity of Jesus' Father and the truth of Jesus' claims.

Jesus' Claim of Unity with God Is Lawful (10:31–39)

In 10:31–39 Jesus, who has just said, "I and the Father—we are one,"defends himself against the charge of blasphemy (10:33) by appeal to "the law." The text to which he appeals, Ps. 82:1, is not within the Mosaic law proper, but Jesus follows the custom of extending to other parts of scripture the same authority that Jews accorded the Pentateuch.[28] In this Psalm, the judges of God's people are called "gods" (vv. 1, 6) and "sons of the Most High" (v. 6), despite their wickedness (vv. 2–5) and mortality (v. 7), because the word of God came to them in their role as judges (John 10:35; cf. Deut. 1:17).[29] How much more, Jesus argues, can the one whom the Father consecrated and sent into the world, rightfully claim the title "Son of God" (10:36).[30]

Interpreters often observe that Jesus' defense seems to miss the point of his opponents' concern. The Jews have not charged Jesus with claiming the title "son of God" in the innocuous sense in which the Psalm uses it of human judges, but with making himself God. A wide range of explanations has been advanced for this discrepancy. Some have said that Jesus is parodying his opponents' misuse of scripture.[31] Some have claimed that Jesus is following the terminological focus of rabbinic exegesis without realizing the fallacious reasoning involved in it.[32] Some have claimed that the argument is an *ad hominem* attempt under the pressure imposed by a lynch mob to stave off premature execution.[33] Some have tried to place less than obvious meanings upon phrases within Jesus' words to provide a logic for them that otherwise is missing.[34]

It seems best, however, simply to view Jesus' argument here, as so often in the Gospel, as operating on a different level of discourse from that of his opponents.[35] His opponents cannot see beyond the scandal of the words he uses to the truth that lies behind them. Jesus' claim to be one with the Father is not blasphemous if it is true, but this is a possibility that Jesus' opponents, blinded and hardened as they are, refuse to entertain. In 10:34–36, then, Jesus offers an explanation for a passage from their "law" that only those who believe in him can appreciate.[36] To those who believe, Jesus' exegesis demonstrates the preeminent propriety of his claim to be one with God: if people are sometimes labeled sons of the Most High, surely the one whom the Father consecrated and sent to reveal his word can lay claim to that title. To Jesus' opponents, who read the law in another way, however, this defense misses the point of their concern, and so their only response is, once again, to seek Jesus' arrest (10:39).

Jesus' Legal Status in John's Gospel: A Summary

Jesus' controversy with "the Jews" and "the Pharisees" over the law in chapters 5–10 reveals a clear if complex approach to the Mosaic law. Jesus stands above the law as its termination and fulfillment. He not only works on the sabbath in imitation of his Father but directs others to do the same. He therefore "broke" the sabbath commandment (5:18) and demonstrated that it was no longer applicable either to him or to his disciples. On the other hand, Jesus affirms that "the scripture cannot be broken" (10:35) and that to believe Moses was to believe him (5:46).

These two apparently contradictory attitudes toward the Mosaic law are bound together by the notion that Moses wrote about Jesus (5:46), that Abraham rejoiced to see his day (8:56), and that Isaiah saw Jesus' glory and spoke about him (12:41). The law, like all of scripture, points forward to Jesus (5:39), who dispenses with Israel's law in the name of Israel's God. To become Jesus' disciple, despite the reality that to do so was to cease being a disciple of Moses (9:28), was to keep the law in the most profound sense. In the same way, to reject Jesus because he and his disciples do not conform to the detailed commandments within the Mosaic law is to dishonor Moses and to fail to keep the law that he gave. Thus, the Jews who want to kill Jesus because he did not keep the sabbath become lawbreakers themselves in the only sense that really matters (7:19–24).

JESUS' REPLACEMENT OF THE MOSAIC LAW

This understanding of the Mosaic law also emerges from John's Gospel in more subtle ways. John shows at many points how Jesus fulfills, and therefore replaces, key elements of the Mosaic law. The first of Jesus' signs shows how Jesus replaces Jewish purification rituals. It is immediately followed by an incident that foreshadows Jesus' replacement of the temple, a theme present elsewhere in the Gospel as well. Later the narrative shows how Jesus replaces three great pilgrimage festivals prescribed in the Mosaic law: Passover, the feast of Unleavened Bread, and the feast of Booths. Finally, in the farewell discourses Jesus replaces the Mosaic law with a new commandment of his own.

Purification Water Becomes
Eschatological Wine (2:1–11)

As is well known, John has organized the first part of his Gospel around a group of Jesus' mighty works. For John, these events point beyond themselves to the identity of Jesus, and therefore John calls them "signs." They should have provoked belief in Jesus' claims about himself from all who saw them during Jesus' ministry, and should lead to belief among all who read John's record of them in later days. "These [signs] have been recorded," John tells his readers near the end of his Gospel, "that you might believe that Jesus is the Christ, the Son of God, and that by believing you should have life in his name" (20:31).

In the first of these signs Jesus, who is attending a wedding in Cana of Galilee with his mother and disciples, transforms the water in six stone jars into wine to make up for an embarrassing lack of supplies (2:1–11). Prior to the sign, the disciples' understanding of Jesus had been framed in purely Jewish terms. Jesus is a rabbi (1:38), the Messiah (1:41), the one foretold by Moses and the prophets (1:45), the Son of God (1:49), and the king of Israel (1:49). In the first sign, however, John shows that Jesus not only fulfills but transcends the boundaries of traditional Jewish religion. John carefully points out that the water Jesus changed into wine was held in "six stone jars" used for "the purification rites of the Jews" (2:6). The jars were stone so that they would not have to be broken if they contracted impurity from a dead swarming thing (Lev. 11:33) or from the touch of a man with a discharge (Lev. 15:12).[37] They contained water for the purification of objects and people that had been defiled in various ways (see, e.g., Leviticus 11–15).[38] Perhaps these jars were present so that the guests at the wedding feast could wash their hands before eating, a ritual not prescribed by the Mosaic law but encouraged by the Pharisees (Mark 7:1–5; cf. Matt. 15:2; Luke 11:38).[39] In this instance, John comments, each pot held "two or three measures," or between eighteen and twenty-seven gallons.[40] When filled "to the top" at Jesus' instructions they would have supplied at least one hundred and eight gallons of water.

Jesus turns this enormous quantity of water into wine. Abundant wine is a frequent image in the biblical prophets and in the apocalyptic literature from the Second Temple period for the prosperity that will come to Israel during the time of its eschatological restoration.[41] According to the early church father Irenaeus (ca. 130–ca. 200), some who knew the disciple John claimed he spoke of Jesus' teaching that

> The days will come, in which vines shall grow, each having ten thousand branches, and in each branch ten thousand twigs, and in each true twig ten thousand shoots, and in each one of the shoots ten thousand clusters, and on every one of the clusters ten thousand grapes, and every grape when pressed will give five and twenty metretes of wine. (*Against All Heresies* 5.33.3)[42]

This is very close to *2 Apoc. Bar.* 29:5, which was written about the same time that Irenaeus recorded these words and, whether Irenaeus knew it or not, is probably their ultimate source. It is unlikely, then, that Jesus actually said this; but the association of this picture of the eschatological age with the traditional author of the Fourth Gospel suggests that the Gospel's author and his circle would have been familiar with the image. If so, they would also have recognized in the superabundant supply of wine at the wedding in Cana a sign that the eschaton had come.

The implications of this first sign for John's understanding of the law now become clear. Jesus fulfills the eschatological expectations of Israel as they appear in the law and the prophets, but in fulfilling them he replaces them with his own revelation of the Father. His revelation is as superior to the Mosaic law as a lavish supply of wine is to stone jars emptied of their purifying water. Indeed, so lavish is this new wine that at the symbolic level it meets traditional expectations for the eschatological restoration of Israel.

Jesus Becomes the Temple's Eschatological Replacement (1:14; 2:13–22; 4:19–24; 11:48)

John makes much the same point in the next section (2:13–22), which recounts Jesus' cleansing of the temple in Jerusalem. The focus of this passage lies neither on the cleansing itself, the details of which occupy only about a third of it, nor on Jesus' motives for the cleansing, which are described only with his ambiguous rebuke, "Do not make my Father's house a market-house" (2:16). The emphasis lies instead on the interpretive dialogue between Jesus and "the Jews," which is bordered at its beginning and end by the interpretive memory of the disciples (2:17–22).

The theme of this interpretive section is the death and resurrection of Jesus and how these events together signify Jesus' assumption of the temple's role. John says at the beginning of this part of the passage that when Jesus drove the merchants, sheep, and oxen out of the temple with a whip he had fashioned himself, the disciples recalled the passage of scripture that says, "Zeal for your house will consume me" (2:17; Ps. 69:9). This is an exact quotation of the Septuagint (Ps. 68:10), except that John has replaced the Septuagint's past tense verb "consumed" (*katephagen*) with a future, "will consume" (*kataphagetai*).[43]

This change foreshadows the nervous comment of the chief priests and Pharisees much later in the narrative that if Jesus is allowed to continue revealing his identity through his signs, "the Romans will come and take away both our place [the temple] and our nation" (11:48). Not only was Jesus consumed with zeal for his Father's house, but he, like the author of Psalm 69, would be led to suffering by his zeal for God's cause (v. 7). That suffering, moreover, would come through those who were zealous for God's house. The misguided zeal of the chief priests and scribes for the temple would eventually "consume" Jesus on the cross.

In the interchange between the Jews and Jesus that follows 2:17, Jesus describes his own death and resurrection as the establishment of a new temple. The Jews ask Jesus to work some sign that will demonstrate his right to act with the prophetic zeal he has just displayed. Jesus enigmatically responds, "Destroy this temple, and in three days I shall resurrect it" (2:19). This statement inevitably recalls for the Christian reader Jesus' own destruction on the cross and resurrection from the tomb; but John wants no one to miss the allusion—". . . That one," he says, "was speaking about the temple of his body" (2:21). The crucified and resurrected Jesus, therefore, replaces the physical temple.

This notion also stands behind other, less explicit statements in the Gospel. When John says, "The Word became flesh and lived among us" (1:14), the term translated "lived" is *eskēnōsen*. It appears only here in the Gospel and recalls the language that the Bible in both its Hebrew and Greek forms uses for the tabernacle (*miškān, skēnē*), the portable prototype of the temple and the ancient "dwelling place" of God.[44] Thus, John has carefully chosen a term to describe the Word's incarnation that recalls the ancient biblical image of God dwelling among his people in a tabernacle during the period of the wilderness wandering.[45]

Similarly, in 4:20–24 the Samaritan woman, perceiving that Jesus is a prophet, brings up the principal difference between the Jews and the Samaritans on the issue of worship. The Samaritans, she says, worship on Mount Gerizim, but the Jews claim that "Jerusalem is the place (*ho topos*) where it is necessary to worship" (4:20). Mention of "the place" recalls the language that Deuteronomy uses for the temple (12:5, 11, 21; 14:23–25; 16:2, 6, 11, 16), language with which John is clearly familiar (11:48).[46] At issue here then is not merely the contrast between Mount Gerizim and Jerusalem, but the temples at each location and the legitimacy of each.

Jesus responds to the question with a subtle reference to the future belief of the Samaritan woman and her people. "An hour is coming," he says, "when you [pl.] will worship the Father neither on this mountain nor in Jerusalem" (4:21). The coming hour probably refers, as it does so often in John, to the time of Jesus' death, resurrection, and departure to the Father (7:30; 8:20; 12:23, 27; 13:1; 16:21, 25, 32; 17:1). At that time, the many Samaritans who believed in Jesus through the woman's testimony (4:39), through the testimony of Jesus himself (4:42), and through the testimony of Jesus' disciples (4:35–38; cf. Acts 8:4–25), would discover that worship in their own temple was misguided. This newfound belief would not, however, lead them to worship in the Jerusalem temple. Despite the origin of salvation with the Jews and the orthodoxy of Jewish worship in comparison with the practices of the Samaritans (4:22), in the future true worshipers from both peoples—indeed from the whole world (4:42)—would worship God in Spirit and in truth. Worship in the Spirit will take place after the glorification (7:39) of Jesus and the sending of the Spirit of truth (14:17; 16:13), who will bear witness to Jesus (15:26), although insofar as people respond to Jesus in faith in the present, that future time "is now" (4:23).[47]

Worship in Spirit and in truth, therefore, is no longer localized in the Jerusalem temple, but in Jesus, who takes the temple's place. He is the fulfillment of the prophetic longing for the days when God would miraculously reestablish his temple and would once again dwell among his people (Ezek. 37:27–28; 43:2–7).[48]

Jesus Fulfills and Replaces the Feasts of Passover, Unleavened Bread, and Booths (6:1–71; 7:37–39; 8:12)

John also shows how Jesus fulfills and replaces three festivals closely associated with the temple in the first century: Passover, Unleavened Bread, and Booths.

Jesus Is the Real Food and Drink of Passover and Unleavened Bread (6:1–71)

The Mosaic law mandates that God's people should celebrate Passover the day before the seven-day feast of Unleavened Bread (Lev. 23:5–6; Num. 28:16–17). Both festivals commemorated God's rescue of his people from slavery in Egypt (Exod. 12:14, 17, 24–27; 13:8; Deut. 16:3, 6). During twilight on the fourteenth day of the first month, Israelite families were to slaughter a year-old male lamb, being careful to break none of its bones (Exod. 12:6, 46; Num. 9:5, 12). They were to place some of its blood on the two door posts and the lintels of their houses, then roast the meat and eat it with unleavened bread and bitter herbs (Exod. 12:5–8). They were to burn completely any unfinished portion so that nothing would be left over (Exod. 12:10; Deut. 16:4) and were to eat this meal with belt fastened, feet shod, and staff in hand to commemorate the haste in which their ancestors had consumed the first Passover on the night of their redemption from Egypt (Exod. 12:11). The story of this original Passover was to be told to the children in the family each year when Passover was observed (Exod. 12:25–27; 13:8; cf. 13:11–15). According to Numbers and Deuteronomy, Passover should be observed only in Jerusalem (Deut. 16:5–6; cf. Num. 9:10–12).

For seven days after this sacrifice, God's people were to observe the feast of Unleavened Bread by purging their homes of all leaven (Exod. 12:19–20; Deut. 16:4). Consumption of unleavened bread during this period would remind Israel of the conditions under which God had brought them out of slavery in Egypt (Deut. 16:3). In biblical times, both festivals were observed in Jerusalem and therefore involved pilgrimage for all who lived outside the city (2 Kgs. 23:23; 2 Chr. 30; 35:1–19).

During the first century, Jews observed these annual celebrations much in the way that the Mosaic law stipulates.[49] People flocked to Jerusalem before the festivals began (Luke 2:41–42; Josephus, *Jewish War* 6.427), scrupulously maintaining their purity so that they might participate (*Jub.* 49:9; Philo, *Special Laws* 2.148; John 18:28; Josephus, *Jewish War* 6.425). Passover sacrifices were brought to the temple and slaughtered from the fifth to the ninth hour on the fourteenth of Nisan (Josephus, *Antiquities* 3.248; *Jewish War,* 6.423; cf. *Jub.* 49:10–12), roughly complying with the biblical requirement for the slaughter of sacrifices at twilight on the fourteenth day of the first month.[50] The biblical emphasis on the feast as a reminder of God's gracious work of redemption in the exodus was well understood in the Second Temple period. Thus, the author of *Jubilees* (second century B.C.), the Jewish epic poet Ezekiel (second century B.C.), and the author of the Wisdom of Solomon (first century A.D.) all tell the story of the exodus in a way that links it to the observance of Passover during their own day.[51]

Passover was probably also a time for looking toward God's future redemptive work among his people. The biblical descriptions of the feast emphasize its character as national symbol: aliens who want to observe it must first be circumcised (Exod. 12:48; cf. Josh. 5:8–10), and any Israelite who fails to observe it for reasons other than impurity or distance from Jerusalem was to be cut off from Israel (Num. 9:13; cf. Exod. 12:47 and *Jub.* 49:9). During the first century, participation in the feast was strictly limited to Jews (Josephus, *Jewish War* 6.427). The prophets spoke of Israel's future national restoration as a new exodus, similar to or greater than the first (Isa. 11:15–16; Jer. 16:14–15; 23:7–8; 31:32; Hos. 2:15), and during the Second Temple period, the eschatological age was sometimes described as a time when manna would again fall from heaven (*2 Apoc. Bar.* 29:8; *Sib. Or.* 7.148–49). Since the Bible links the celebration of Passover to God's provision of manna (Josh. 5:11–12), it is easy to see how the feast could become a time of fervent eschatological hope. Perhaps this explains why in Josephus's writings the feasts of Passover and Unleavened Bread were so frequently times of political unrest (*War* 2.10–13, 224–27; cf. *Antiquities* 20.105–12).[52]

John's Gospel presents Jesus as the fulfillment of these feasts, the national memories of the ancient exodus that they evoked, and the eschatological promise that they held. The theme appears in several places in the Gospel (1:29, 36; 3:14; 19:36), but is especially prominent in chapter 6.

Around the time of the Passover (6:4), John tells us that Jesus fed a "great crowd" (6:2) with a miraculous supply of bread and then crossed the Sea of Galilee on foot. The crowd was impressed by both signs, and was especially fascinated with Jesus' miraculous gift of bread. "This is truly the prophet who is coming into the world," they began to say (6:14), probably referring to the future prophet like Moses, described in Deuteronomy and expected among many Jews from at least the time of the Maccabees (Deut. 18:15; cf. 1:21; 4:19; 1 Macc. 4:46; 14:41). Surely Jesus would prove to them that he was the fulfillment of these expectations by supplying continuous bread from heaven, like the manna their ancestors had eaten in the wilderness (6:30–31). With him as their king (6:15), they would experience material prosperity and political liberation just as their ancestors had experienced them under Moses.

Throughout the discourse that interprets this incident, John shows how Jesus fulfills the symbols of deliverance in the story of the first Passover and the ensuing exodus. The Galilean crowd, however, plays the role of faithless Israel in the same story. Jesus is the fulfillment of biblical expectations about the eschatological age. Those who come to him, therefore, hear and learn from the Father and experience the long-awaited time when God himself would teach his people (Isa. 54:13; Jer. 31:33). This does not mean that Jesus meets the expectations of the crowd for the prophet like Moses. They want political deliverance (6:15) and perishable food for their bellies (6:26–27) from a charismatic leader. He, by contrast, is not so much Moses, the channel through whom God supplied bread and water to his people (Exod. 16:1–36; 17:6; Num. 20:7–11; Ps. 105:40–41; cf. 105:26), as he is the heavenly bread and divinely supplied water themselves (6:35). Like them, but unlike Moses, he is directly from God (6:32–33), and unlike even the miraculous bread and water of the exodus, Jesus does not supply the transient needs of mortal bodies, but eternal life. "I am the bread of life," he says, "the one who comes to me shall never hunger, and the one who believes in me shall never thirst" (6:35; cf. 6:38–40, 47–51, 58).

This bread, moreover, is Jesus' flesh, which he gives for the life of the world (6:51), and only those who eat his flesh and drink his blood will have life and experience the resurrection on the last day (6:53–54). Although the meaning of these statements is the subject of vigorous dispute, most interpreters agree that they refer forward to the symbolic representation of Jesus' sacrificial death in the Lord's Supper.[53] Perhaps they also look backward to the Passover sacrifice. John tells us that the Baptist gave Jesus the title "the Lamb of God" (1:29, 36). He also wants his readers to know that the events surrounding Jesus' crucifixion occurred during the day of preparation for the Passover feast, and that Jesus was sentenced to death at about the time of the slaughter of Passover lambs in the temple (19:14). After he died, like a sacrificial Passover lamb, his legs were not broken so that "the scripture might be fulfilled, 'not a bone of him shall be broken'" (19:36; cf. Exod. 12:46; Num. 9:12).

In 6:51–58, therefore, Jesus is probably claiming to be the Passover sacrifice. Like the Passover lamb, his blood will be shed and only those who consume him participate in the benefits of his sacrifice. For John, as the parallels between 6:35 (cf. 6:40) and 6:53–54 show, to eat Jesus' sacrificial flesh and blood means coming to and believing in him.[54] This is "real" food and drink, and those who participate in this sacrifice, by implication, participate in the fulfillment of the Passover sacrifice.[55]

The crowd to whom Jesus addresses these provocative remarks does not understand them, and in the end finds them so difficult that they turn away from Jesus. Their interest in doing the works of God (6:28), in believing in Jesus (6:29), and in heavenly bread (6:34) quickly chills when Jesus refuses to provide them with literal manna and instead offers himself as the bread of life that has come down from heaven (6:35–40). Their response grows even colder when Jesus begins to speak of consuming his flesh (6:52), and degenerates into outright rejection when Jesus refuses to make his language more palatable (6:66). Like the Israelites in the wilderness who murmured against Moses and Aaron, and therefore against God (Exod. 16:8; Num. 21:5, 7), the Galilean crowd "began murmuring because [Jesus] said, 'I am the bread that has come down from heaven'" (6:41; cf. 6:52). Likewise, they "were murmuring" about his claim that those who would live eternally must eat his flesh and drink his blood (6:61). Just as Jesus fulfills and surpasses the story of God's redeeming work at the first Passover and during the exodus, so the crowd to whom he speaks plays the role of the unbelieving wilderness generation.

Jesus Is the Source of Water and Light at Booths (7:37–39; 8:12)

John also shows how Jesus fulfills the two central rites of the feast of Booths. The descriptions of this festival in the Mosaic law are unadorned. It celebrated the autumn harvest of olives and grapes, much as the feast of Weeks celebrated the summer harvest of wheat (Exod. 23:16; Lev. 23:39; Deut. 16:13), and recalled the period of wandering in the wilderness when God "made the people of Israel live in booths" (Lev. 23:43). The festival was to last for seven days (Lev. 23:34), although the day after the formal feast had ended was to be a period of rest (Lev. 23:39), and could therefore be considered part of the festival itself. During the first day, the people were to gather "the fruit of majestic trees, branches of palm trees, boughs of leafy trees, and willows of the brook" and use these in ceremonies of rejoicing before the Lord (Lev. 23:40; Deut. 16:14).[56] They were also to live in booths for the seven days of the formal festival (Lev. 23:42; cf. Neh. 8:14–17).

This general description leaves much room for improvisation, and the Mishnah, compiled around A.D. 200, identifies two major ceremonies observed during the festival that are not found in the Mosaic law: the ceremony of water pouring (*Sukkah* 4:9–10) and the ceremony of lights (*Sukkah* 5:2–4). As the Mishnah describes it (*Sukkah* 4:9), the ceremony of water pouring occurred on each of the festival's seven days. A golden pitcher was filled with about one and a half pints of water from the Pool of Siloam. This water was carried in procession from the pool to the Water Gate on the temple's south side, where the procession was greeted with three blasts of the ram's horn. The priest on duty then carried the water into the temple, up the ramp of the altar, and turned east. There he faced two silver bowls, each with a spout in the bottom, one for wine and one for water. Into these the priest poured both the pitcher of water from Siloam and a pitcher of wine, and both liquids ran through the spouts in each bowl and onto the ground. Since Josephus seems to refer to the water-pouring ceremony during the reign of Alexander Jannaeus (103–76 B.C.), and the ceremony itself would fit well with the connection between the festival and future rain in Zechariah (14:16–19), it was probably firmly fixed in the festival's liturgy well before the first century.[57]

The ritual of illumination occurred only at the close of the first day of the feast (at least according to the Mishnah) and began with the lighting of four massive golden candlesticks in the Court of Women. Once they were lighted, "there was not a courtyard in Jerusalem that did not reflect the light . . ." (*Sukkah* 5:3).[58] Pious men danced with torches in hand, the temple orchestra played, and a festal procession marched from the Court of Israel to the temple's eastern gate accompanied continuously by blasts from the trumpets of two priests (*Sukkah* 5:4). It is more difficult to corroborate the Mishnah's record of this ceremony than it is to confirm the water-pouring ritual, but it is also difficult to see why such a detail would have been fabricated.[59]

John tells us that Jesus traveled from Galilee to Jerusalem to celebrate this festival (7:2, 10) and used the opportunity to engage in extensive teaching among the crowds in the temple (7:14, 28; 8:2, 20, 59). On the last and greatest day of the feast, John tells us, Jesus stood and cried out this:

> If anyone is thirsty, let him come to me and drink. The one who believes in me, as the scripture has said, rivers of living water shall flow from his belly. (7:38)

John comments that when Jesus said this he was referring to the coming of the Spirit to those who had believed in him (7:39). John points out that Jesus spoke these words on the last and greatest day of the feast—on the day, in other words, of the water-pouring ceremony's last

enactment. At this climactic point in the festival's celebrations, therefore, Jesus claims to fulfill one of its central events. Living water will
pour forth from those who come to Jesus, just as water and wine pour
forth from the festival's silver bowls.

John goes on to say that these words referred to the Spirit, which
those who had believed in Jesus would receive after his glorification
(7:39). Jesus has not only fulfilled the water-pouring ceremony, therefore, but from the later perspective of John and his community, has
replaced it by sending the Spirit.

At some point during the same feast, John tells us that Jesus spoke
these words:

> I am the light of the world. The one who follows me does not walk in
> darkness but will have the light of life. (8:12)

Here again, the imagery comes from a central event during the festival
and Jesus claims to be its fulfillment. His claim to be the light of the
world recalls the prophecy in Zechariah that in the eschatological age
"there shall be continuous day . . . , for at evening time there shall be
continuous light" (Zech. 14:7), a statement that appears only a few
paragraphs before the claim that eventually the nations would journey
to Jerusalem year by year to keep the feast of Booths (14:16).[60] Here
Jesus claims to be the fulfillment of these eschatological hopes and the
replacement for the light ceremony at the feast of Booths.

Jesus Issues a New Commandment and a New Covenant (13:34; 14:15, 21, 23–24; 15:10, 12, 14, and 17)

Finally, Jesus' replacement of the Mosaic law with a new commandment forms a critical theme of Jesus' farewell discourses in the second
half of the gospel. During the supper that Jesus ate with his disciples
on the night of his arrest, Jesus provided an example of humble service
for them by washing their feet (13:14–15). Later, he summarized the
significance of his action in a "new commandment": they were to love
one another just as he had loved them (13:34). On one level this commandment was not new, for the Mosaic law had also instructed God's
people to love one another (Lev. 19:18). On another level, however, the
commandment was entirely new, since Jesus was not telling his disciples to obey the Mosaic commandment, but was issuing the content of
the Mosaic commandment as his own. As he says later in the dis-

course, "This is my commandment, that you love one another just as I have loved you" (15:12; cf. 15:10, 12, 14, 17). The commandment is new because it now belongs not to Moses but to Jesus.[61]

In chapter 14, Jesus links this new command with love for himself in a way that recalls the Mosaic law's own summary of Israel's covenant obligations. In the Mosaic law, especially in the Deuteronomic literature, God promises "steadfast love to the thousandth generation of those who love me and keep my commandments" (Deut. 5:10; cf. Exod. 20:6). The echoes of this central covenant obligation reverberate through centuries of Jewish literature and into the teaching of Jesus himself as the Synoptic Gospels record it.[62] There Jesus cites love for God (Deut. 6:4) and love for neighbor (Lev. 19:18) as the greatest commandments of the Mosaic law, and the scribe to whom he is speaking heartily agrees with this concise statement of Jewish covenant obligations (Mark 12:28–33; cf. Matt. 22:34–40; Luke 10:25–28).

In John, the form of this central requirement is preserved, but now Jesus speaks of love for himself and of keeping his own commandments. Just as he issued an old commandment in a new christologically oriented form in 13:34, so in 14:15, 21, 23–24 he preserves the form of the Mosaic covenant's central requirement but issues it as his own, new covenant. In the words of 14:15, "If you love me, you will keep my commandments."[63]

Jesus Assumes the Place of the Law: A Summary

John, then, understands Jesus to be the fulfillment of and replacement for the Mosaic law. Jesus replaces the Mosaic law's purification rites with his own abundant wine. The law's focus on the worship of God in a single, divinely appointed shrine is replaced by the worship of God in Jesus, the new temple. Jesus replaces the central elements in the biblical narratives that give Passover and the feast of Unleavened Bread their meaning and himself becomes the Passover sacrifice. He replaces the central events at the feast of Booths. He reissues the central elements of the Mosaic covenant as his own.

Jesus has not simply replaced like with like, however—he offers something better than the Mosaic law. Those who have faith in Jesus receive spiritual satisfaction that surpasses the experience of Israel in the same way that vessels filled with abundant wine surpass empty vessels that once held water. Those who believe in Jesus worship in Spirit and in truth, and their feast never ends, for they never again hunger, thirst, or walk in darkness. Jesus has not merely replaced the Mosaic law, but his self-revelation has fulfilled it.

LAW AND TRUE GRACE (1:16–17)

We can now return to the prologue with its programmatic statement about the relationship between the Mosaic law and Jesus Christ. Since the information we have gleaned about that relationship in the rest of the Gospel is critical for understanding 1:17, we should summarize briefly what we have learned.

For John, the law stands on the side of Jesus. Moses, who gave the law to the Jews (7:19, 22), wrote about Jesus, and belief in Moses leads to belief in Jesus (1:45; 5:46–47). Jesus justifies both his deeds and his claims about himself by appeal to the law (7:21–24; 10:34–38) and argues that his opponents' lack of faith and attempts to kill him are violations of the law (5:45; 7:19). Even one of the Pharisees recognizes that the attempts of his colleagues to condemn Jesus without understanding what he does and says place them outside the law's boundaries (7:51). In the dispute between Jesus and his opponents, therefore, and despite his opponents' claims to the contrary (5:18; 8:59; 9:16, 28–29; 10:31, 33; 19:7), the law testifies to the innocence of Jesus and to the truth of his claims (5:45–47).

At the same time that John recognizes the law's positive relationship to Jesus, he argues unrelentingly that Jesus' own new revelation has overwhelmed and superseded the law. Thus Jesus works on the sabbath and leads others to do the same (5:1–18), not out of disrespect for the law but because of his equality with God (5:17) and his fulfillment of the law's deepest intention (7:23). He assumes the place allotted in the law to the temple, not out of disrespect for the temple—the temple is his Father's house (2:16), zeal for which led to his death (2:17)—but because his resurrected body (2:21) and the Spirit whom God gives (4:23; 7:39; 14:16, 26; 15:26; 16:7; 20:22) fulfill the prophetic expectation that in the final day God would dwell with his people. He fulfills the primary symbols of three great Jewish festivals—Booths, Passover, and Unleavened Bread—not because he stands against them but because he is the greater reality toward which they point. His flesh and blood are "real" (*alēthēs*) food and drink.[64] Similarly, he issues a new commandment in his own name and demands covenant loyalty to himself, not as a way of dishonoring the Mosaic covenant but to show that the time of the new covenant, when God's people would be taught by God himself (Jer. 31:31–34; Isa. 54:13) has now arrived (6:45; 13:34; 14:15, 21, 23–24; 15:10, 12, 14, 17). The sign at Cana, then, is an appropriate symbol of Jesus' relationship to the Mosaic law in John's Gospel. Jesus fills and overwhelms the Mosaic law with an abundance that can only signal the coming of the eschatological age.

If we bring this approach to the Mosaic law to John's first statement about the relationship between the law and Jesus, we can now understand what that statement means. In 1:16–17 John says this:

> From his fullness we have all received grace in place of grace. For the law was given through Moses, grace and truth came through Jesus Christ.

This statement does not contrast a graceless law with the grace that is available in Jesus Christ. The essence of grace is that it is given freely, and the law too was a gift, as the passive voice of the verb "was given" (*edothē*) reveals. God gave the law just as he gave Jesus Christ.

Nevertheless, 1:16–17 does describe a contrast between the law and Jesus Christ. Grace and truth have come in Jesus Christ to a degree that they were not available in the law. Thus, just as in the Old Testament Israel is the vine, so in John's Gospel Jesus is the true vine (15:1). Just as the law describes God's gift of bread to his people, so in John's Gospel Jesus is the true bread (6:32), the real food and drink of the Passover festival (6:55).[65] The Mosaic law was characterized by grace; but its measure of grace pales in comparison with what has become available with the appearance of Jesus Christ. Believers, John claims, have drunk deeply from the fullness of the incarnate Word and, in so doing, have replaced the grace of the law with the true grace of Jesus Christ.[66]

NOTES

1. The phrase "the Jews" in John's Gospel refers only to a group within the Jewish leadership who opposed Jesus. See D. Moody Smith, "John," in *Early Christian Thought in Its Jewish Context,* ed. John Barclay and John Sweet (Cambridge: Cambridge University Press, 1996), 96–111, here at 97.

2. C. H. Dodd, *The Interpretation of the Fourth Gospel* (Cambridge: Cam-

bridge University Press, 1953), 78–79; Rudolf Smend and Ulrich Luz, *Gesetz, Biblische Konfrontationen* (Stuttgart: Kohlhammer, 1981), 120. Jesus was arguing "from light to heavy," as the later rabbinic scholars would have put it.

3. Paul can also use the term "law" to cover more than the Pentateuch (Rom. 3:10–19; 1 Cor. 14:21). On the Jewish character of John's interpretive method here, see Raymond E. Brown, *The Gospel according to John I–XII,* AB 29 (New York: Doubleday, 1966), 409–10; Rudolf Schnackenburg, *The Gospel according to St. John,* 3 vols. (New York: Crossroad, 1982–87; orig. ed., 1965–75), 2:310–11; Barnabas Lindars, *The Gospel of John,* NCB (Grand Rapids, Mich.: Eerdmans, 1972), 373; F. F. Bruce, *The Gospel of John* (Grand Rapids, Mich.: Eerdmans, 1983), 234–35.

4. For the application of phrases within scripture to the historical circumstances of the Qumran community, see, e.g., the *Habakkuk Pesher* (1QpHab), found in Florentino García Martínez, *The Dead Sea Scrolls Translated: The Qumran Texts in English,* 2nd ed. (Leiden: E. J. Brill; Grand Rapids, Mich.: Eerdmans, 1996), 197–202.

5. Cf. Severino Pancaro, *The Law in the Fourth Gospel: The Torah and the Gospel, Moses and Jesus, Judaism and Christianity according to John,* NovTSup 42 (Leiden: E. J. Brill, 1975), 191–92. A similar problem arises, as we shall see below, in Jesus' use of the law of testimony (Deut. 17:6; 19:15) in 8:17.

6. Cf. Smith, "John," 96–111.

7. C. K. Barrett, *The Gospel according to St. John,* 2nd ed. (Philadelphia: Westminster, 1978), 168. Cf. Dodd, *Interpretation,* 86.

8. D. A. Carson, *The Gospel according to John* (Leicester, U.K.: Inter-Varsity; Grand Rapids, Mich.: Eerdmans, 1991), 132–34.

9. As Smith points out, for John, "'Jews' and 'Pharisees' seem to be interchangeable terms" ("John," 97).

10. Cf. Pancaro, *Law in the Fourth Gospel,* 114.

11. On this, see ibid., 14.

12. For the way in which the command to avoid "any work" was interpreted among some circles in the Second Temple period, see *Jub.* 2:17–23; 50:6–13; and CD 10:14–11:18.

13. Herold Weiss argues that both charges in 5:18 are false ("The Sabbath in the Fourth Gospel," *JBL* 110 [1991]: 311–21, here at 317). The subsequent narrative, says Weiss, demonstrates that Jesus, although he considered himself to be one with the Father, did not claim equality with him. Similarly, Jesus did not break the sabbath, but only claimed to be keeping it in the same way God keeps it. The distinction between equality and unity, however, seems too fine, and, whereas it may be true that Jesus is redefining the sabbath rather than abolishing it, he is clearly defining it in a way that violates it, from the perspective of the Mosaic law. Jesus is innocent, then, not because he actually keeps the Mosaic law but because the Mosaic law is no longer in force in the traditional way.

14. Cf. Deut. 13:5; 17:7; 19:13, 19; 21:9, 21; 22:21, 24; 24:7.

15. John implies that Jesus does not break the law, but abolishes it by fulfilling it. On this see Pancaro, *Law in the Fourth Gospel*, 160, 164–65.

16. The *kai* ("and") at the beginning of 5:37 probably does not introduce a new witness but refers epexegetically to the Father's witness through Jesus' works as described in 5:36. This is not the position of most commentators, but see Schnackenburg, *Gospel according to St. John*, 2:123–24.

17. See especially Exod. 19:9–10; 24:1–2, 9–12; 33:7–11, 18–23; Deut. 34:10. For the liveliness of this tradition in the Second Temple period, see Sir. 17:13; 45:5. I am indebted for these references to the thorough discussion of Pancaro, *Law in the Fourth Gospel*, 220–24.

18. Cf. Leon Morris, *The Gospel according to John: The English Text with Introduction, Exposition, and Notes*, 2nd ed., NICNT (Grand Rapids, Mich.: Eerdmans, 1995), 291; and Carson, *Gospel according to John*, 262–63.

19. See, e.g., Lev. 18:5; Deut. 4:1, 10; 5:33; 8:1, 3; 11:8–9; 12:1; 30:15–20; 32:46–47.

20. For this understanding of 5:42 and 44, see Johannes Beutler, "Das Hauptgebot im Johannesevangelium," in *Das Gesetz im Neuen Testament*, ed. Karl Kertelge, QD 108 (Freiburg: Herder, 1986), 222–36, here at 226–29.

21. The *Assumption of Moses*, written sometime between the second century B.C. and the mid-second century A.D., refers to Moses' role as intercessor (12.6), and *Jub.* 1:19–21, probably from the first century B.C., places a prayer of intercession for Israel on Moses' lips. First-century Jews probably believed that Moses continued to intercede for them before God. See J. Jeremias, "Μωυσῆς," *TDNT* 4:848–73, here at 853; and Charles H. Talbert, *Reading John: A Literary and Theological Commentary on the Fourth Gospel and the Johannine Epistles* (New York: Crossroad, 1992), 129–30.

22. Cf. Schnackenburg, who links Jesus' healing of the lame man with the Father's desire to forgive the man's sins (5:14, 17, 19) and so to give the man life "in the deepest sense" (*Gospel according to St. John*, 2:135). Since the giving of life is also the Mosaic law's intention, Jesus' sabbath healing fulfilled that intention.

23. The Jewish historian Josephus, who flourished at about the time of the Fourth Gospel's composition, also held that the Jewish law did not "permit execution without a trial" (*Jewish War* 1.209; cf. *Jewish Antiquities* 14.167 and Sus. 48). See Barrett, *Gospel according to St. John*, 332; and Pancaro, *Law in the Fourth Gospel*, 138.

24. See Pancaro, *Law in the Fourth Gospel*, 138–57, especially 145, 148, and 155. Pancaro sees only what we have called the deeper meaning in this passage; but it seems better to understand John's language here, as so often elsewhere, on two levels.

25. One of the earliest manuscripts of John's Gospel, the Bodmer Papyrus II (from about A.D. 200), places a definite article before the word "prophet" in

7:52. The Pharisees therefore urge Nicodemus, "Search and see that the prophet does not arise from Galilee." The early date of this reading, its possible confirmation in two other ancient witnesses, and its consistency with the context (cf. 7:40) make it likely to be correct. See Schnackenburg, *Gospel according to St. John*, 2:161.

26. Cf. Matt. 18:16; 2 Cor. 13:1; 1 Tim. 5:19; Heb. 6:18; 10:28; Rev. 11:3.

27. See Carson, *Gospel according to John*, 339.

28. Cf. John 12:34; 15:25; Rom. 3:19; 1 Cor. 14:21.

29. John 10:35 does not explicitly say that the people who are called gods receive that designation because they have received the word of God, but that reasoning seems to be implied.

30. On Jesus' argument "from the lesser to the greater" here, see especially Brown, *Gospel according to John I–XII*, 410.

31. Rudolf Bultmann offers this suggestion tentatively in *The Gospel of John: A Commentary* (Philadelphia: Westminster, 1971; orig. German ed., 1964), 389.

32. Brown, *Gospel according to John I–XII*, 409–10.

33. Carson, *Gospel according to John*, 399.

34. Pancaro believes that "those to whom the word of God came" refers to Christians who are now children of God (John 1:12) (*Law in the Fourth Gospel*, 190–91). The word that they received, he says, is the word of Jesus as described in the Fourth Gospel.

35. See, e.g., 2:19–20; 7:35; 8:19, 22, 27. Misunderstandings in the Gospel are certainly not limited to the opponents of Jesus; but those of Jesus' opponents take on a particularly hard, polemical edge.

36. On this element of the passage, see Pancaro, *Law in the Fourth Gospel*, 191.

37. See Shimon Gibson, "The Stone Vessel Industry at Ḥizma," *IEJ* 33 (1983): 176–88; he concludes that "it was their lack of susceptibility to defilement which caused the extensive use of stone vessels during the late Second Temple period" (p. 188).

38. See Leonard Goppelt, "ὕδωρ," *TDNT* 7:320. E. P. Sanders shows that impurity as defined by Leviticus 11 and 15 was often removed in the Second Temple period by full immersion in a special pool or *miqveh* (*Judaism: Practice and Belief 63 BCE–66 CE* [London: SCM; Philadelphia: Trinity Press International, 1992], 222–29). Clearly the stone jars of John 2:6 could not accommodate full immersions. Nevertheless, the mention of purification by hand washing in Lev. 15:11 shows that total immersion was not the invariable rule.

39. This suggestion comes from Robert H. Gundry, *Mark: A Commentary on His Apology for the Cross* (Grand Rapids, Mich.: Eerdmans, 1993), 358–59.

40. See BAGD, "μετρητής," 514.

41. See Gen. 49:11; Hos. 2:22; 14:7; Joel 3:18; Amos 9:13–14; Jer. 31:5, 12; *1 Enoch* 10:19; *2 Apoc. Bar.* 29:5; *Sib. Or.* 2.318, 320; 3.620–24, 744–45; and the

discussions of Schnackenburg, *Gospel according to St. John*, 1:338; and Brown, *Gospel according to John I–XII*, 105.

42. The translation is from ANF 1:563.

43. The verb is in the past tense also in the Hebrew text (Ps. 69:10).

44. Compare, for example, the Hebrew Bible and the Septuagint at Exodus 26–27.

45. In addition to the commentaries, see Wilhelm Michaelis, "σκηνή," *TDNT* 7:368–94, here at 386; J.-A. Bühner, "σκηνόω," *EDNT* 3:252–53; Hartmut Gese, *Essays on Biblical Theology* (Minneapolis, Minn.: Augsburg, 1981), 204; and Peter W. L. Walker, *Jesus and the Holy City: New Testament Perspectives on Jerusalem* (Grand Rapids, Mich.: Eerdmans, 1996), 164.

46. Cf. 2 Macc. 5:15–21; the discussions in F.-M. Braun, *Jean le théologien: Le grandes traditions d'Israël l'accord des Écritures d'après le Quatrième Évangile*, Ebib (Paris: Librairie Lecoffre, 1964), 91; and Brown, *Gospel according to John I–XII*, 172.

47. Cf. Carson, *Gospel according to John*, 224.

48. Cf. Braun, *Jean le théologien*, 91.

49. See Baruch M. Bokser, *The Origins of the Seder: The Passover Rite and Early Rabbinic Judaism* (Berkeley: University of California Press, 1984).

50. For the possibility that some slaughtered the Passover lamb in their own homes, see the discussion in Sanders, *Judaism: Practice and Belief*, 133–34.

51. See *Jub.* 49:6, which mentions the consumption of wine at the first Passover, and Wisd. 18:9, which mentions singing. See also Ezekiel's *Exagōgē*, lines 152–92, and the discussion in Bokser, *Origins of the Seder*, 19–25.

52. I am indebted to Sanders, *Judaism: Practice and Belief*, 138, for these references.

53. Morris, *Gospel according to John*, 333–37, is a notable exception. See also the hesitance of Carson, *Gospel according to John*, 277–80.

54. See Carson, *Gospel according to John*, 288, 297.

55. Cf. Edwyn Clement Hoskyns, *The Fourth Gospel*, ed. Francis Noel Davey, 2nd ed. (London: Faber & Faber, 1947), 281–82, 289; and Hermann Strathmann, *Das Evangelium nach Johannes*, NTD 4, 10th ed. (Göttingen: Vandenhoeck & Ruprecht, 1963), 108.

56. In Neh. 8:15 they are used to make the booths.

57. Cf. George Foot Moore, *Judaism in the First Centuries of the Christian Era: The Age of the Tannaim*, 3 vols. (Cambridge, Mass.: Harvard University Press, 1927–30), 2:45. Zech. 14:20 may refer to the Mishnah's two silver (or plaster) bowls located in front of the altar for use in the ceremony. See George W. MacRae, "The Meaning and Evolution of the Feast of Tabernacles," *CBQ* 22 (1960): 251–76, here at 273.

58. The translation is that of Herbert Danby, *The Mishnah* (Oxford: Oxford University Press, 1933), 179–80.

59. Perhaps Philo (20 B.C.–A.D. 45) reveals some knowledge of the ritual

when he explains the significance of the date on which the feast begins. This day, he says, falls on the autumn equinox and therefore at a time when there is no interval between the shining of sun and moon and thus no period of complete darkness (*Special Laws* 2.210).

60. See Brown, *Gospel according to John I–XII*, 343.

61. Cf. Raymond Brown, *The Gospel according to John XIII–XXI*, AB 29A (New York: Doubleday, 1970), 613–14; and George R. Beasley-Murray, *John*, WBC 36 (Waco, Tex.: Word Books, 1987), 247–48.

62. See, e.g., Josh. 22:5; 1 Kgs. 3:3; Neh. 1:5; Dan. 9:4; Sir. 2:15–16; Tob. 14:7–9; and *Jub.* 20:7.

63. I am indebted for these insights to Johannes Beutler, *Habt keine Angst: Die erste johanneische Abschiedsrede (Joh 14)*, SBS 116 (Stuttgart: Katholisches Bibelwerk, 1984), 55–62.

64. Cf. 15:1, where Jesus, calling upon biblical imagery for the nation of Israel, refers to himself as the "true" (*alēthinē*) vine. See Jer. 2:21; Isa. 5:1–7; 27:2–11; Ezek. 15:1–8; 17:5–10; 19:10–14; Ps. 80:8–16; and Barrett, *Gospel according to St. John*, 472.

65. Cf. Ruth B. Edwards, "ΧΑΡΙΝ ΑΝΤΙ ΧΑΡΙΤΟΣ (John 1.16): Grace and Law in the Johannine Prologue," *JSNT* 32 (1988): 3–15, here at 11.

66. The common translation of *charin anti charitos* in 1:16 as "grace upon grace" (RSV, NAS, REB, NRSV), as if the incarnate Word has lavished "one blessing after another" (NIV, CEV) upon us, is probably not correct. It assigns a meaning to the preposition *anti* that is unique in all known Greek literature. See Edwards, "ΧΑΡΙΝ ΑΝΤΙ ΧΑΡΙΤΟΣ," 5–6.

5

Correspondence and Contrast:
The Mosaic Law and the
New Covenant in Hebrews

THE BASIC ARGUMENT OF HEBREWS is among the most straightforward of the entire New Testament: the "new covenant" is
superior in every way to the "first covenant," and therefore
Christians should suffer hardship faithfully rather than revert to
Judaism. This simple point, however, is expressed in a sermon of such
rhetorical sophistication, structural complexity, and theological depth
that its detailed exposition is extraordinarily difficult.

Among the difficulties is the element of paradox in the sermon. At
the same time that Jesus appears as the cosmic Son through whom God
created the universe (1:2) and who occupies the throne of God himself
(1:8), he also appears as the suffering Son who learned obedience
through affliction (5:8). Alongside its picture of God as a consuming fire
(12:29) into whose hands it is a fearful thing to fall (10:31), the author of
Hebrews places the portrait of a merciful God sitting upon a throne of
grace and ready to help in time of need (4:16; cf. 6:10; 12:5–11).[1]

The author's use of the Mosaic law—"the first covenant" as it is
often called (8:7, 13; 9:1; 9:18)— constitutes one of the letter's difficult
paradoxical elements.[2] On one hand, the law made nothing perfect
(7:19; cf. 10:1), was not without fault (8:7), and has been changed (7:12;
cf. 8:13; 10:8–9). On the other hand, the Mosaic law provides the basis
for the author's understanding of Jesus' person and work. Jesus is a high
priest. He officiates over a sacrifice that involves the shedding of blood.
This sacrifice takes place in a tabernacle with a Holy of Holies, and it
effects expiation for and purification from sin. At the same time that
the author argues forcefully for the obsolescence of the Mosaic

covenant, therefore, that covenant itself appears to dictate the grand structure of his theology.[3]

This approach to the Mosaic covenant also reverberates outward to incorporate the narrative portions of the Pentateuch in which the record of the Mosaic covenant is embedded. Here too the author compares the faithfulness of Moses as a priest with the faithfulness of Jesus and believes that the communities over which each was appointed have received an invitation to enter God's eschatological rest. Abraham, similarly, received a promise confirmed with an oath and so stands parallel to the present people of God, whose hope is also confirmed with an oath. In all these instances, however, the present community of faith and their high priest, Jesus, stand at an immense eschatological advantage over their ancient counterparts.

We can analyze this delicately balanced approach to the Mosaic law under five points of correspondence and contrast, each carefully woven into the fabric of the author's argument:

1. Infractions against the Mosaic law were punished with exactitude. Rejection of the salvation available in Jesus will also be punished, but with greater precision.
2. Moses was an honorable and faithful priest. Jesus was honorable and faithful too, but in a greater sense.
3. The ancient people of God failed to heed the good news preached to them and so failed to enter God's rest. This leaves an eschatological sabbath rest for God's present people, and they dare not neglect to enter it.
4. The Mosaic law regulates a priesthood and sacrifices. The new covenant has its own version of these, but they are superior in every way to their ancient counterparts.
5. God's ancient people were punished for apostasy from the old covenant. Punishment of greater severity is reserved for those who fall away from the new covenant, and so faithfulness to it is that much more important.

THE DIVINE REVELATION AND SANCTIONS FOR ITS REJECTION (1:1–2:18)

The first paragraph of Hebrews (1:1–4) introduces the primary themes of the entire sermon in a grand rhetorical flourish designed to capture the readers' attention and propel them forward into the subsequent argument. Here the author contrasts the sporadic nature of God's revelation in the past and the many different modes in which it came with the definitive revelation of his glory and essence in God's Son (1:1–3a). He then articulates the paradox of the incarnation: none other than this Son, through whom God made the universe and who sustains all things, cleansed God's people from their sins (1:3b). He is, therefore, better than the angels (1:4).

The last line of this initial statement provides a link to the first major section of the argument (1:5–2:18). In this section the author offers first a series of seven scriptural proofs that the son is superior to the angels in his relationship to God (1:5–14) and then an exegetical argument that the Son is perfectly suited to the task of removing sin because of his human suffering (2:5–18). The angels continue to provide a foil for Christ in the second subsection (2:5, 16), but their role in the argument fades so that by the end the theme of Christ's merciful and faithful high priesthood takes precedence (2:17–18).[4]

Between his series of scriptural proofs (1:5–14) and his exegetical argument (2:5–18), the author places an exhortation to his readers in which he urges them, in light of the importance of the salvation he has just described (1:1–14), not to drift from their commitment to it (2:1–4). This exhortation contains the first clear reference to the Mosaic law in the letter:

> For if the message spoken by angels was valid and every transgression and disobedience received a just penalty, how shall we escape if we disregard salvation of such importance? (2:2–3a)

"The message spoken by angels" is the Mosaic law, which, according to a tradition alive in first-century Christian circles, was given to Moses on Mount Sinai through the mediation of angels (Gal. 3:19; Acts 7:53; cf. Acts 7:38; Deut. 33:2 LXX). It both corresponds to and stands in contrast to the more recent message of revelation.

Three correspondences emerge. First, in both cases the message was mediated. The Mosaic law was mediated through the angels. The message of salvation was mediated to the author's readers through the Lord and those who heard him (2:3b). Second, the message mediated in each case was "valid" or "authentic." The angels helped to confirm the validity of the Mosaic law (2:2). The message of salvation received confirmation from Jesus' first hearers (2:3b) and from God himself, who joined their witness by providing a chorus of "signs, wonders, various miracles, and impartations of the Holy Spirit, according to his will" (2:4).

Third, and most important for the author, the law contained sanctions for disobedience, and so, he concludes, must the message of salvation. His comment that "every transgression and disobedience received a just penalty" (2:2) appears to recall the detailed way in which the Mosaic law describes legal precepts and the punishments that should accompany their transgression. No sin goes unmentioned, he implies, and each sin carries an appropriate penalty. In the same way no one should treat the message of salvation with indifference and expect to escape punishment. The emphasis in both cases is not on the severity of the punishment but on the impossibility of escaping it.

This final point of parity between the Mosaic law and the message of salvation also reveals the critical point of contrast between the two. If Jesus is as superior to the angels as the author has shown him to be in the previous argument (1:4–14), then the message mediated by Jesus will also be superior to the Mosaic law.[5] If this is true, then the exactitude with which transgressors were punished under the Mosaic law can only be intensified under its far superior counterpart. Under Moses, every infraction received its just punishment. In a rhetorically effective move, the author leaves his readers to guess how uncompromising the punishment will be for those who lightly disregard the salvation mediated through God's own Son. The clear implication is that it will be considerably more exacting.

THE PRIESTLY ROLES OF JESUS AND MOSES (3:1–6)

In 2:17 the author had introduced the theme of Jesus' high priesthood and had commented that Jesus became a "merciful and faithful" high priest. The next major section of his argument (3:1–5:10) will explore these two qualities of Jesus' high priesthood in reverse order, first treating his faithfulness and the faithfulness to which his people are called (3:1–4:13), and then discussing his merciful demeanor (4:14–5:10).

In 3:1–6 the author begins this elaborate exposition of 2:17 by comparing the faithful priestly service of Jesus and Moses. He calls upon his readers to ponder Jesus in his role as "apostle and high priest of our confession" (3:1) and then compares his faithfulness to the faithfulness of Moses. Although he does not explicitly call Moses a priest in the passage, he could hardly be unaware that Moses was a Levite (Exod. 2:1), and he certainly knew that Moses offered sacrifice (9:19–22; cf.

Exod. 24:3–8). Probably he knew that Ps. 99:6 described Moses as a priest, and like other Jews of the Second Temple period, he probably regarded this aspect of Moses' career as evidence of his unique relationship with God.[6] In the background of 3:1–6, therefore, is not a comparison between Moses as mediator of the law and Jesus as mediator of the new covenant.[7] Here the author's use of the law is more subtle: he compares the priestly role of Moses, as described in the law, with the priestly role of Jesus.

As in 2:1–4, correspondence and contrast characterize the comparison. Both Moses and Jesus were faithful to God. Moses served faithfully as a servant in God's house, as God's own commendation of him in Num. 12:7 (LXX) demonstrates (3:2, 5). Christ was faithful to the one who appointed him apostle and high priest (3:2), and he was faithful over God's house as the son, who is the rightful heir of the house (3:6).

Yet Jesus stands in contrast to Moses in three ways. First, he receives greater honor, just as the builder of a house receives greater honor than the house itself (3:3). Second, if a three-way analogy is drawn between God's creation of the universe, the building of a house, and the respective roles of Jesus and Moses, then God and Jesus must be paired together and Moses must be paired with what they make (3:4).[8]

Third, Moses' faithfulness was limited to that displayed by a servant in the house (3:5); but Jesus' faithfulness occurred in his role as son over the house (3:6). Since the author finally defines the metaphor "house" as the faithful community in 3:6, his point is that Moses has no authority over the people of God. Instead, as with the angels (1:14), his role within the household of God was to serve a later generation, and he accomplished this service faithfully by testifying to the message of salvation, which still lay in the future (3:5b; cf. 11:13, 26, 39–40). Not Moses, but God's Son, therefore, stands over God's household as its final apostle and priest (3:6).

Although 3:1–6 focuses on the narrative portion of the law in which Moses' priestly role is described rather than, as in 2:1–4, on the Sinaitic legislation, the strategy of correspondence and contrast remains consistent. In 3:1–6 the priestly role of Moses as it is described in the law finds a parallel in the priestly role of Christ. Both were faithful in the roles to which they were appointed. Nevertheless, Moses' role was to testify to the far more glorious vocation of Jesus, who would come later and who would preside over the "house" in which Moses had only functioned as a servant. This same approach to the narrative material in which the Mosaic covenant is embedded reappears in the letter's next section.

THE WILDERNESS GENERATION
AND THE PRESENT PEOPLE OF GOD
(3:7–4:13)

In 3:7–4:13 the author continues to focus on faithfulness. Now, however, he turns from the faithfulness of Jesus and Moses (2:17–3:6) to the faithfulness of the respective communities they were appointed to lead.[9] His purpose in this section is hortatory: he wants to call his readers to faithfulness on the pilgrimage toward their eschatological rest with an exposition of Ps. 95(94 LXX):7–11.

His treatment falls into three paragraphs. The first (3:7–19) presents the rebellious wilderness generation of Israelites, described in vv. 8b–11 of the Psalm, as a negative example for the present-day people of God. The author urges his readers to avoid the unfaithfulness of God's ancient people and instead take advantage of "today" (Ps. 95:7b) to exhort each other to faithfulness. If they fail, they will suffer the same fate as the wilderness generation, whom God punished by forbidding them, on oath, from entering his "rest" (Ps. 95:11).

The second paragraph (4:1–11) links three biblical passages together (Ps. 95:7; 95:11; and Gen. 2:2) as a way of persuading the readers faithfully and obediently to pursue the eschatological rest that still awaits them. The author argues that if Ps. 95:11 and Gen. 2:2 are allowed to interpret each other, they mean that God has existed in a state of rest since the seventh day of creation and that entry into this rest has been available to his people from ancient times.[10] Because the wilderness generation failed to enter God's rest through their faithlessness, the offer of entry remains unfulfilled, as Ps. 95:7b shows. "Thus," the author concludes, "a sabbath celebration remains for the people of God, for the one who enters his rest also rests from his own labors, just as God rests from his" (4:9–10).[11] In light of this, the author urges his readers to "pursue with zeal entry to that rest" (4:11).

The third paragraph (4:12–13) concludes the section with a metaphorically rich description of the effectiveness of God's word. The author seems to be saying that his own exposition of the scriptures has shown the word of God to be both potent and incisive.

In 3:7–4:13, therefore, the author appeals again to the narrative portion of the Mosaic law, albeit through the interpretive lens of Psalm 95. And here again, his strategy is to show both the correspondence and the contrast between the events described in the Mosaic law and present circumstances.

Two areas of correspondence emerge between the law's wilderness generation and the present generation of God's people. First, both generations were "evangelized" (4:2, 6). By this the author means that both received the invitation to enter the heavenly rest that God has occupied since the seventh day of creation (4:4–6; cf. Gen. 2:2 LXX). Second, the danger of failing to heed this offer exists for the present generation of God's people just as it did for their ancient counterparts (3:12–13; 4:1, 11).

These areas of correspondence are overshadowed, however, by a critical point of contrast: the new people of God occupy a position on the timetable of God's redemptive work that is superior to the position of ancient Israel. The author makes this case by using Ps. 95:7–11 to unlock the meaning of the law's account of Israel's wilderness wandering. David's use of the term "today" in the Psalm implies that the political "rest" eventually granted to the ancient people of God was not the "rest" God refused to the wilderness generation (4:8). The rest of which the Psalm speaks, then, must be the heavenly rest of God (4:4–5). The "today" in the Psalm also implies that another, eschatological day remains during which God will once again offer to his people entry into his rest (4:7). The present people of God live within that day (3:13; 4:1, 9–10) and are on a pilgrimage toward God's eternal rest (4:3). This position, in the author's view, is one of immense privilege (3:6).

The same perspective reappears when the author links the "rest" (*katapausis*) that God promised to his people with the eschatological entry of God's people into his own heavenly "sabbath celebration" (*sabbatismos*) (4:6a, 9). By making this connection, the author transforms the celebration of the sabbath into an eschatological feast.[12] And when he claims that "those who have believed are entering the rest" (4:3), he implies that those who have been faithful to the gospel (4:2) have already in some sense started that eschatological celebration.[13]

As he had done in 3:1–6, the author here applies the hermeneutical strategy of correspondence and contrast to the narrative that surrounds the record of the Mosaic covenant. Although the wilderness generation and the faithful of the author's own generation constitute in some sense one people of God, the present people of God nevertheless have been given an eschatological advantage over their ancient counterparts. They stand at the threshold of entry into God's eschatological rest (4:3) and are in the process of experiencing the fulfillment of the offer of rest that, according to the Psalmist, he made to the wilderness generation.

JESUS AND THE HIGH PRIESTS OF THE MOSAIC LAW (4:14–10:18)

In 4:14–10:18 the writer again brings to the surface of his argument the theme of Jesus as the perfect high priest. He had announced this theme in 2:17–18, and it was the subtext of his treatment of faithfulness in 3:1–4:13. Jesus, he had said in 2:17, became both a "merciful and faithful high priest." Having explored the theme of faithfulness in 3:1–4:13, the author now turns in 4:13–5:10 to Jesus' merciful demeanor. He follows this in 5:11–6:20 with an extended exhortation to his readers not to regress in their commitment to "the Son of God." Then, in 7:1–10:18, he engages in a detailed comparison between the levitical priesthood and Jesus' priesthood.

In a way typical of the sermon's complex structure, the exposition of Jesus' merciful demeanor (4:14–5:10) also lays the groundwork for the longer comparison of Jesus with the high priests of the Mosaic cult (7:1–10:18). Thus, already in 4:14–5:10, the author mentions the divine call of Jesus according to the order of Melchizedek (5:1, 5–6, 10), a theme that will dominate 7:1–28, and he anticipates his argument in 7:27–10:18 that Jesus offered a sacrifice which effected "eternal salvation" (5:1, 9).[14]

Jesus, the Merciful High Priest (4:14–5:10)

In 4:14–5:10 the author describes in detail how Jesus qualifies as a "merciful high priest" (2:17). He is able to sympathize with human weakness since he has been tested by suffering just as other people are tested (4:15). He cried loudly, wept, suffered, and learned obedience from his suffering (5:7–8). In light of this, the faithful community can come to God's gracious throne with boldness for help in their effort to hold fast their confession (4:14, 16).

Along the way to this primary point, the author prepares the groundwork for his later detailed comparison between Jesus and the levitical high priest. He does this by discussing briefly the qualifications for a high priest and the way in which Jesus meets them. A high priest, he says, is to be appointed by a divine call (5:1b, 4), can commiserate with people in a way consistent with his own, weak human nature (*metriopatheō*, 5:2), and offers "gifts and sacrifices" to mediate between God and people (5:1a).[15] Jesus, similarly, was appointed by God (5:5–6), shared in human suffering (4:15; 5:7–10), and mediated between God and people (5:9). On these three critical points, then, Jesus qualifies as a high priest.

Already, however, the contrast between Jesus and the high priests begins subtly to emerge. Jesus is superior, the author argues, in each of the three qualifying characteristics. First, whereas the common high priest "is obligated to offer sacrifice for his own sins, just as he does for the people," Jesus is without sin (4:15; 5:3). Second, Jesus' priesthood after the order of Melchizedek, unlike that of the mortal levitical priests, is eternal (5:6, 8–10). Third, the sacrifice Jesus offered secured the eternal salvation that the work of the levitical priests only foreshadowed (5:9). Each of these points will receive further elaboration in 7:1–10:18.

Jesus, A Priest in the Order of Melchizedek (7:1–28)

The author begins in 7:1–28 by describing in greater detail the nature of Jesus' priestly order. He is a priest not because he belongs to the tribe of Levi but, according to Ps. 110:4, because God appointed him a priest after the order of Melchizedek (6:20; 7:1–17). The author first shows how magnificent Melchizedek is, and then, relying on the enigmatic account of Melchizedek in Gen. 14:18–20 and the brief interpretation of that account in Ps. 110:4, argues for four points of contrast between Jesus and the levitical high priests.

First, he focuses on the notion that Abraham paid a tithe to Melchizedek (7:4–10; Gen. 14:20b). This payment, the author comments, corresponds to the law's requirement that the levitical priests should receive tithes from the people (7:5). But it also demonstrates the superiority of Melchizedek to the levitical priests. The biblical text reveals the superiority of Melchizedek to Abraham when it says that Abraham tithed to the king and received a blessing from him, "and it is beyond all doubt that the lesser is blessed by the greater" (7:6–7). Since the Levites are descended from Abraham, they too are inferior to Melchizedek. Indeed, the author comments, one might even say that Levi, the patriarch of the law's priestly clan, paid tithes to Melchizedek through his ancestor Abraham, for at the time that Abraham met Melchizedek, "he was in the loins of his father" (7:5, 9–10).

Second, the author argues that, unlike the levitical priests, Jesus is qualified for the priesthood because of his eternal existence. The "forever" of Ps. 110:4 shows that Melchizedek "lives" (7:8). Jesus, because of his "indestructible life" also continues to live and therefore belongs to this eternal priestly order (7:15–16).[16] Psalm 110:4 recognizes this when it says of Jesus, "You are a priest forever according to the order of Melchizedek" (7:17). This means that Jesus never passes his priesthood along to another, but is always present to intercede for God's people, enabling them to approach God and be saved (7:24–25).[17]

In contrast, the levitical priests were appointed not because of any affinity with things eternal but simply because a "fleshy commandment" of the law mandated that it be so (7:16). They are, moreover, "men who die" (7:8) and who must therefore pass their priesthood along to successors after their death. This means that levitical priestly service must be accomplished through many priests rather than, as in the case of Jesus, through one only (7:23).

Third, the statement in Ps. 110:4 that "[t]he Lord has sworn and will not change his mind" shows that Jesus was appointed to his priesthood by means of a divine oath (7:20–22). A divine oath, as the author has already explained (6:13–20), demonstrates in the clearest way possible the immutability of God's will as it is expressed in the promise that accompanies the oath. God has promised with an oath that Jesus' priesthood would last forever. The levitical priests, however, assumed their duties without such an oath, and, although the author does not say so explicitly, the contrast with Jesus implies that the priestly order of which they were a part was not immutable.

Fourth, unlike the levitical high priests, Jesus was sinless and therefore did not have to offer sacrifice for his own sin before sacrificing on behalf of the people (7:26–27). The high priests, however, because they were appointed in their weakness were required to offer sacrifice for their own failings (7:27–28).

Since the Mosaic law mandates and regulates the levitical priesthood, these four points of contrast already imply that the salvation Christ effected (7:25) has superseded the Mosaic law.[18] For the first time in the letter, however, in this section of his argument the author makes this implication explicit by using the term "law" (*nomos,* 7:5, 12, 16, 19, 28) and its verbal cognate "legislate" (*nomotheteō,* 7:11).[19] The primary reason for the law's obsolescence is that it is unable to cope with a high priest outside the levitical tradition. Jesus descended from the patriarch Judah rather than from Levi and was therefore disqualified from the priesthood from the perspective of the Mosaic law. Yet, for the author, Ps. 110:4 certified with a divine oath that at some future time a priest would arise from the order of Melchizedek rather than from the order of Levi (7:11–14). Since this divine oath was uttered after the law itself was given, the author believes that it points toward the passing away of the law's regulative authority (7:28), for "when the priesthood changes, a change of law also happens by necessity" (7:12).

In addition to this primary reason, the law shares in the weak and provisional nature of the priests whom it regulated, for it appointed priests by means of a "fleshy commandment" (7:16). The term "fleshy" (*sarkinos*) appears in the New Testament only here and three times in the Pauline epistles. Occasionally it has positive connotations, as in 2 Cor. 3:3, where Paul contrasts "fleshy hearts" with "stone tablets," thus indicating that living, breathing people, upon whom the eschatological Spirit of God has been at work, are preferable to sterile letters of recommendation.[20] When the term is used in contrast with the divine realm, however, it most often carries a negative connotation. Thus, Paul says that whereas the law is spiritual, he is "fleshy, sold under sin" (Rom. 7:14) and tells the wayward Corinthians that he is not able to speak to them as "spiritual people" but only as "fleshy people" (1 Cor. 3:1). This holds true for texts outside the New Testament as well.[21] In Heb. 7:16 the author uses the term in this second, negative sense. The "fleshy commandment" that appoints the levitical priests stands in contrast to the "indestructible life" through which Jesus is appointed to the priestly order of Melchizedek. The contrast implies that just as the "indestructible life of Jesus" identifies him with the eternal world, so the "fleshy commandment" identifies the law with the transitory world of the priests. Thus, like the priests who could not bring "perfection," the law "could perfect nothing" (7:19). In a way that is consistent with its "fleshy" character, the law "appoints priests who have weakness" (7:28) and are therefore prone to sin (7:27).

In contrast to this law stands the "better covenant" of which Jesus is guarantor. Three characteristics of this covenant make it better

(7:27–28). First, this covenant is immutable and eternal, as God's sworn promise of Christ's eternal priesthood (Ps. 110:4) demonstrates. Second, this promise came after the law in time and (presumably) takes precedence over it. Third, the affiliation of the promise with God's eternally perfected Son rather than with sinful and weak priests demonstrates the superiority of this covenant to the Mosaic law.

In summary, 7:1–28 provides an elaboration and extension of the claim in 4:14–5:10 that Jesus meets the law's requirement for divinely appointed priests. By reading Gen. 14:18–20 through the lens of Ps. 110:4, the author is able to argue that although Jesus did not belong to the tribe of Levi, he was nevertheless appointed by God to be a priest. He occupies the priestly order of Melchizedek by virtue of his indestructible life and is therefore the priest of whom Ps. 110:4 spoke. His priesthood is better than a levitical priesthood for four reasons: it is a priesthood to which the levitical priests themselves paid homage by tithing through their ancestor Abraham; it is an eternal priesthood; it was confirmed with an oath; and its priest Jesus is sinless.

This better priesthood, and the covenant that its priest introduced, not only sweeps away its levitical predecessor, but the law that regulated the levitical priesthood as well. The temporal nature of that law is revealed in its "fleshy commandment" concerning priestly lineage, its affiliation with weak, sinful priests, its lack of confirmation with an oath, and the modification of its requirement for the priesthood by the later text, Ps. 110:4. Levitical priesthood and Mosaic law go together, and both have given way to the superior priesthood and the "better covenant" of Jesus.

A Better Sacrifice in a Better Sanctuary, Establishing a Better Covenant (8:1–10:18)

In 8:1–10:18 the author concentrates on another qualification for every high priest—that he must offer gifts and sacrifices to make possible a relationship between people and God (5:1; cf. 8:3). In this section, the author will maintain that Jesus meets and exceeds this expectation by offering better sacrifices (9:23) than the levitical high priests, and by doing so in a greater and more perfect tabernacle (9:11) than the one described in the Mosaic law. Because Jesus' sacrifice purifies the conscience (9:14) and effects ultimate forgiveness of sins (9:12, 25–28; 10:12–18), it fulfills the prophecy of Jer. 31:31–34 that God would one day write his laws upon the hearts of his people (8:10; cf. 10:16) and, in his mercy, remember their sins no more (8:12; cf. 10:17). Jeremiah calls this work of God a "new covenant," and the author of Hebrews believes that Jesus has inaugurated this covenant through the shedding of his blood (9:15–22).

Three areas of correspondence and contrast between the Mosaic law and the salvation effected by Christ emerge from this section. Each involves a sanctuary, sacrifices, and a covenant, but on each of these points the priesthood of Jesus is superior.

First, Jesus offers sacrifice in a superior sanctuary. Like the tabernacle described in the Mosaic law, it consists of two tents, an outer tent and an inner tent, separated from one another by a curtain (9:11–12, 24; cf. 9:1–10; 10:19–20). It is the "true tabernacle, which the Lord pitched, not a human being" (8:2), and is heavenly in nature (8:5; 9:23–24). It is the "greater and more perfect tabernacle," not handmade and not part of the visible, created world (9:11, 24). The Mosaic counterpart to this heavenly tabernacle, however, is only the shadowy outline of the real tabernacle in heaven (8:5a). It is the antitype of the heavenly building, and was constructed by Moses along the lines of the original, heavenly type that God allowed Moses to see on Mount Sinai (8:5b). It is the "first" tent (9:1, 8), and as long as it still "has standing," the way to final, ultimately effective atonement remained closed (9:8).[22] It is aligned with the present age, for which it serves as a figure (9:9).

Second, within this heavenly sanctuary Jesus offers a sacrifice superior to that of the high priests. He offered himself, completely unblemished by sin, as a sacrifice (9:14; cf. 9:12). The shedding of his own blood, moreover, effected the ultimate sacrifice to end all sacrifices—he offered it once and signaled its finality by sitting down at God's right hand, never to offer sacrifice of any sort again (9:12, 25–28; 10:12–18; cf. 1:3; 8:1; 12:2). This ultimate sacrifice secured eternal redemption, opened the way into the heavenly holy of holies, and provided unencumbered access to God (9:8, 12, 24; 10:19–21). It accomplished this through purifying the conscience from dead works (9:14) and redeeming God's people from the transgressions they had committed under the first covenant (9:15). The priests of the first covenant, however, were required to go continually, year after year, into their earthly holy of holies to offer sacrifice on the Day of Atonement (9:6, 25; 10:1–4, 11). Their sacrifices consisted of animals (9:12–13; cf. 9:19–20) and were bound up with a system of dietary regulations and ritual washing (9:10). Because of this, these sacrifices were useful only for cleansing the flesh and body (9:10, 13), and it was impossible for them to purify the conscience or to atone for sin (9:9; 10:2–4, 11).

Third, Jesus inaugurates a "better covenant" than the covenant God made with his people at Mount Sinai. Like the Sinaitic covenant, the covenant Jesus inaugurates is sealed with blood. Thus, at the inauguration of the "first covenant" (9:15) Moses sprinkled the blood of calves and goats on the book of the covenant, the covenant people, the tabernacle, and the vessels used in worship (9:18–22). In a similar way, the new covenant was inaugurated by the shedding of blood, but this blood was the priest's own and not merely that of calves and goats (9:25).

Why was a "better covenant" necessary? The careful way in which the author has structured the argument of 8:1–10:18 reveals the answer.[23] The author begins the section by introducing the two themes of Christ's superior priestly ministry and his ministry in a superior sanctuary (8:1–6a). At the end of this section, he introduces a third, overarching theme: Christ's superior priestly service is matched by his inauguration of a superior covenant, based on superior promises (8:6).

His next section introduces in a general way both the reasons why the first covenant had to be replaced and the content of the new covenant's superior promises (8:7–13). The first covenant had to give way to its better successor, the author explains, because God "found fault" with it (8:7–8). The author is not specific about the fault; but it clearly lies with the first covenant itself and not, as is often said among interpreters, with the people who transgressed the covenant. This is evident already both from 8:7, which says that the first covenant was not "blameless," and from the beginning of 8:8, which, in the most reliable manuscript tradition says, "For finding fault [with the first covenant] he says to them . . ." rather than, as in many translations, "Faulting them, he says . . . ."[24]

The promises of the new covenant are buried within the author's lengthy quotation of Jeremiah's prophecy (8:8–12; cf. Jer. 31:31–34). They are, first, that God will put his laws into the minds of his people and write them on their hearts (8:10) and, second, that he will be merciful toward them in spite of their iniquities and will remember their sin no more (8:12).

As the argument proceeds, the author makes clear that the fault of the first covenant lay in its inability to accomplish these two tasks. It could not reform the minds and hearts of God's people because its rituals operated only within the realm of the flesh. Under the Mosaic covenant, "gifts and sacrifices are offered that are not able to perfect the conscience of the worshiper, dealing only with food and drink and various washings, regulations of the flesh, laid down until the time of the new order" (9:10; cf. 9:13). The first covenant also could not bring forgiveness of sin (9:15; 10:3–4, 11) as the repetitiveness of the Mosaic Day of Atonement sacrifice shows. This sacrifice must occur year after year, and therefore serves only to remind people of their sin rather than to redeem them from it (9:15; 10:3–4).

Precisely on these two points, however, the priestly work of Jesus succeeds and therefore shows itself to be the fulfillment of God's promises through the prophet Jeremiah. Not only does the sacrifice of Jesus, which inaugurated the new covenant, "purify our conscience from dead works" (9:14; cf. 10:22), but it provides redemption from the transgressions committed under the first covenant (9:15). This sacrifice, moreover, has removed sin for all time (9:26; cf. 9:12).

At the end of the argument the author summarizes his case by returning to the prophecy of Jeremiah. Now, however, he limits his quotation to the two salient points:

> This is the covenant that I will make with them after those days, says the Lord: I will put my laws upon their hearts and write them upon their minds. (10:16; cf. Jer. 31:33)

> And their sins and their iniquities I will remember no longer. (10:17; cf. Jer. 31:34)

For the author, therefore, Jesus' death inaugurated a new and better covenant that answered the deficiencies of its Mosaic counterpart by providing both inward renewal and eternal forgiveness. This can only mean that God himself has made the first covenant obsolete (8:13).

It would be a mistake to conclude from this evaluation of the Mosaic covenant, however, that the author viewed it as an inept construction, unable to accomplish the purposes for which God had designed it. The author forestalls such conclusions by linking his thesis of the Mosaic covenant's obsolescence to the prophecy of Jeremiah (8:8–12; 10:16–17) and by using the figure of a "shadow" to describe the law's part in God's redemptive purposes (10:1). The Jeremiah passage shows that God had designed the first covenant to become obsolete upon the introduction of the new covenant (9:13). The figure of the shadow reveals that God's purpose for the law was never frustrated: it was intended to provide a faint, temporary outline of the real redemptive work of Christ—"the good things to come" (10:1). Although it could not accomplish God's ultimate redemptive purposes of purifying the consciences of his people and forgiving their sin, the Mosaic law could outline the sacrificial structure by which Jesus would eventually complete this task. Its fault, therefore, lay not in its inability to accomplish the purposes for which it was designed, but in its provisional and transitory nature.

COVENANT SANCTIONS AND COVENANT FAITHFULNESS (10:19–13:25)

The author devotes the final third of his sermon to a call to faithfulness among his readers. He urges them, in light of Christ's high priestly work on their behalf, to hold tightly and without wavering to their hope (10:23), even in the midst of hardship. He warns them of the disastrous consequences of failing to do so (10:26–31). He then encourages them to recall the example of their own former faithfulness (10:32–39), of the faithfulness of God's ancient people (11:1–40), and of the faithfulness of Jesus (12:1–3). All suffered, and yet all were faithful.

They should not forget that they are sons of God and that God, as a good Father, disciplines his beloved sons (12:4–11). To turn one's back on the new covenant, he continues, is to imitate the unfaithful people of old and to invite God's uncompromising judgment (12:12–29). The author's readers should live as Christians, obey their leaders, and pray for the author. He closes his sermon with a benediction recalling the benefits of living under the new covenant. A few pleasantries typical of ancient letter closings transform the whole sermon into an epistle and bring the document in its entirety to an end (13:1–25).

At three points in this lengthy admonition, the author turns to different parts of the Mosaic law to aid his plea. In all three instances, he continues to use the strategy of correspondence and contrast to make his case.

Apostasy, Old and New (10:26–31)

In 10:26–31, the author adds a stern warning against apostasy to his exhortation in 10:19–25 to draw near to God, to hold fast the Christian confession, and to provoke love and good works among Christians. The person who sins with full knowledge of what he or she is doing, says the author, can expect no further sacrifice for sin but instead only judgment (10:26–27). The reference to "no sacrifice for sin remaining any longer" (10:26) already hints that the author is not talking generally about any sin here, but specifically about the sin of apostasy—rejecting the great high priest who has offered his own blood as the final and perfect atoning sacrifice.

This becomes even clearer in 10:28–29, where the author compares the penalty for apostasy in the Mosaic law with the judgment that those who abandon the Christian confession can expect. The author describes the Mosaic penalty this way:

> Anyone who rejects the law of Moses dies on the [testimony of] two or three witnesses. (10:28)

The sentence is a paraphrase of the statement in Deut. 17:6 that one witness is not enough to convict someone of abandoning the worship of God, a capital crime in the Mosaic law. If the law demands death for apostasy, the author argues, "how much worse" will the punishment be for those who trample the Son of God underfoot, consider the blood of the covenant unclean, and insult the Spirit of grace (10:29)?

The argument is reminiscent of 2:2–3. In both passages the author recalls the law's penalty for transgression and then leaves his readers to guess how much more exacting the punishment will be for those who transgress God's ultimate redemptive provision in Christ. As with that argument, the argument here implies that God's redemptive work in Christ follows a pattern similar to that found in the Mosaic covenant, but is superior to it. Both covenants require faithfulness, and both carry severe penalties for willful abandonment of their precepts. Yet the new regime represents God's perfect and final provision for redemption. It is therefore far superior to the old system and, the author argues, demands a correspondingly more fearsome punishment of those wanton enough to abandon it.

An Earthly Covenant and Its Heavenly Counterpart (12:18–29)

In 12:18–29 the author appeals to the law's narrative of the Mosaic covenant's inauguration, and his argument follows a pattern similar to that of 10:26–31. Here he compares the giving of the first covenant with the giving of the new covenant. In each case the people of God have journeyed to a mountain and are gathered at its foot. Each covenant has a mediator.[25] The inauguration of each covenant was accompanied by astounding events. The possibility for refusal of God's covenant speech stood, or stands, open.

The new covenant, however, is in every way the eschatological superior of its ancient counterpart. The first covenant was made at Mount Sinai, and the tangible, earthly events of darkness, gloom, whirlwind, trumpet blast, and the voice of God accompanied its inauguration. The new covenant people of God have journeyed to the heavenly Jerusalem of first-century eschatological expectation, to the eschatological Mount Zion, the site of God's final work of restoration among his people according to the prophets.[26] They have joined the solemn, yet joyful celebration of the victory they have won.[27] They have entered the company of other firstborn children of God who have received their inheritance (cf. 12:16).[28] God is there; the perfected righteous are there; Jesus and his redemptive, sacrificial blood are there (12:23–24). This swirl of imagery draws a bold dividing line between the fear and gloom associated with the giving of the first covenant and the rich mood of celebration surrounding the establishment of its new, eschatological counterpart.

From this profound difference between the two covenants, the author draws the conclusion that his readers should not follow the example of the wilderness generation (cf. 3:7–19) and refuse God's word to them (12:25–29). He then bolsters this conclusion by again recalling the difference between the two covenants. God spoke to the wilderness generation on earth—a physical voice was heard amid a tangible display of God's power, and as a result the earth shook. But God has spoken to his more recent people from heaven, and, in accord with prophetic prediction (Hag. 2:6), has established a kingdom that is unshakable. Those who refused the warning of God in that earthly, shakable world of ancient times did not escape God's judgment. How much less, the author argues, will those escape who ungratefully repudiate the word of God during the time of his ultimate, unshakable kingdom.

As with 10:26–31, the new covenant follows the pattern of the Mosaic covenant, but with a vast eschatological difference. The call to obedience, sanctions for disobedience, a mediator, a people who have paused at a mountain on their journey, and a word from God are common to both. But at every level, the old covenant is aligned with what is tangible, earthly, shakable, and therefore provisional, whereas the new covenant constitutes the fulfillment of God's eschatological promises through the prophets.

Participation in a Superior Cult (13:9–16)

In his concluding section of specific ethical admonitions, the author briefly returns to the theme of Christ's superior sacrifice, which had formed the focus of his argument in 8:1–10:18. Here, however, he applies the theme to a specific admonition not to be "carried away by various and strange teachings" (13:9). The author's primary concern is with the notion that eating certain foods can strengthen the heart. This is not a reference to the distinction between clean and unclean foods but to laws concerning the consumption of sacrifices offered on the tabernacle altar (13:10).[29] The author probably has in mind the occasional provisions in the Mosaic law for the worshiper's participation in eating such sacrifices as the Passover lamb, the offering of well-being, and the thanksgiving offering (Exod. 16:5–7; Lev. 7:11–21; 22:29).[30]

Instead of eating from these sacrifices, the author argues, the Christian should seek a strengthened heart in "grace" (13:9), presumably "the grace of God" by which Jesus tasted death for everyone (2:9). This grace is available at the Christian altar, the place where Jesus died (13:10).[31] At this place Jesus' own high priestly work provided the means by which Christians could "come with confidence to the throne of grace" and there "receive mercy and find grace in time of need" (4:16). The author's point is that his readers should not resort to the ancient ways of Judaism as they are described in the Mosaic law but should hold tightly to God's gracious provision of atonement in the death of Christ.

For the author's readers, however, this means leaving the comfort of the familiar and socially acceptable and embracing the status of outcasts. The author urges them to shoulder this burden by comparing their own social ostracism to the death of Jesus outside the walls of Jerusalem. This death, says the author, corresponds to the burning of the bodies of the animals used in the Day of Atonement sacrifices "outside the camp" (13:11–12; cf. Lev. 16:27), and it is a sacrifice that Christians must emulate (13:13).

Perhaps the shift of thought from Jesus' sacrifice to the sacrifice of Christians "outside the camp" leads the author to think in terms of other Christian "sacrifices." He briefly mentions these in 13:15–16. The Christian now renders sacrifices of praise and good works, such as sharing possessions.

The author's allusions to the Mosaic law in these three passages (13:9–10; 13:11–13; and 13:15–16) arise from his conviction that the death of Jesus and the faithfulness of Christians fit within the framework of the Mosaic law's sacrificial system. At the same time, they presuppose the obsolescence of that system. The death of Jesus has replaced the sacrifices of the Day of Atonement. Those who follow Jesus participate in his sacrifice and benefit from the grace of God as a result. They offer their own sacrifices, but these consist of the intangible qualities of praise to God, the pursuit of good works, and faithfulness in spite of social ostracism.

FIRST COVENANT AND NEW COVENANT IN HEBREWS: A CONCLUDING SUMMARY

Nothing could be clearer from the argument of Hebrews than that the author believed the Mosaic law to be obsolete. Its obsolescence is revealed supremely in its inability to accomplish what Christ's death had effected. The death of Christ had provided the final atonement for sin and purified the consciences of those who came to God through him. The Mosaic law could not do this, and so, for the author, it must give way to its superior successor.

The author supports this dramatic claim by means of an elaborate comparison between Jesus' priesthood, sacrifice, sanctuary, and covenant with the priesthood, sacrifice, sanctuary, and covenant of the Mosaic law. Jesus' person and work are identified with unity, heaven, interior qualities, and the eschatological age. Thus, he offered one unrepeatable sacrifice in a heavenly sanctuary to cleanse the conscience, and in so doing ushered in the age for which all the ancient faithful longed. The Mosaic system is identified with diversity, the earthly, the fleshy, and the provisional. Thus, the ancient priests offered many sacrifices year after year. They did this in an earthly tabernacle in order to purify many fleshy and material things, and all of this provided a mere outline of the things that were to come.

As confirmation that his comparison runs in the right direction, the author quotes at the center of his argument a biblical prophecy that God would one day give his people a new covenant. This covenant would both place God's law inside his people and effect the forgiveness of their sins.

The entire law is obsolete, moreover, and not simply the portion of the law that regulates the priesthood and the sacrifices.[32] It is true that the author uses the term "law" (*nomos*) principally to refer to these sections of the Pentateuch, but he also provides unequivocal hints that his argument takes the entire Sinaitic covenant into its sweep. In 9:15–22 he makes the term "first covenant" synonymous with "every commandment spoken by Moses according to the law" (9:19). Similarly, in 10:28 the law whose penalties for disobedience have been superseded by greater penalties in the new covenant is the entire "law of Moses" (cf. 2:2–3). This is confirmed by the author's understanding of sabbath celebration in terms of participation in the eschatological rest of God (4:3–11). The entire Mosaic covenant, therefore, and not merely a part of it, has been superseded by the new covenant: the change in priesthood has required not merely a change in some laws pertaining to the priesthood, but a different law entirely (7:12).[33]

At the same time that the author argues intensely for the obsolescence of the Mosaic law in this sense, however, he makes it indispensable in another way for comprehending the significance of Jesus' saving work. Like the Mosaic tabernacle itself, it provides a "blueprint" (*hypodeigma*) for understanding what Christ's death accomplished.[34] Christ is a high priest who offered a blood sacrifice of such significance that it redeemed God's people from all the accumulated sins of ages past. The blood of this sacrifice also provided purification and inaugurated a covenant between God and his people. The present people of God, like their ancient counterparts described in the law, are on a journey and have gathered at the foot of a mountain for their covenant's inauguration. Both covenants carry sanctions for disobedience, and the consuming fire of God stands as a warning in the present just as it did in the past.

For the author of Hebrews, therefore, the Mosaic law occupies a firmly fixed place within Christian theology; but it is firmly fixed in both the positive and negative sense of that expression. It stands as the immovable framework upon which the Christian understanding of the person and work of Christ hangs. But it can never become the edifice itself. Without it, the death of Christ is only the crucifixion of a man named Jesus outside the walls of Jerusalem, who, like any other crucified man of his time, did not want to die. With it, Jesus' death represents the consummation of the redemptive purposes of God—the final goal for which patriarch, matriarch, lawgiver, prophet, and sage eagerly hoped. If the Mosaic law is allowed to rise out of its firmly fixed place and move into a position of prominence, the result is disaster. Those who allow this to happen, says the author, are trampling the Son of God underfoot, considering the blood of the covenant unclean, and insulting the Spirit of grace (10:29). On the basis of the Mosaic law itself, they can only expect the most severe judgment (10:28–31).

NOTES

1. On this feature of Hebrews, see John Dunnill, *Covenant and Sacrifice in the Letter to the Hebrews*, SNTSMS 75 (Cambridge: Cambridge University Press, 1992), 118–19.

2. The term "covenant" in the phrase "the first covenant" must always be supplied by the context. The author uses the term "law" only in chapters 7–10 and primarily to refer to the law's regulations concerning priesthood and sacrifice.

3. Cf. Rudolf Smend and Ulrich Luz, *Gesetz*, Biblische Konfrontationen (Stuttgart: Kohlhammer, 1981), 115–16; Susanne Lehne, *The New Covenant in Hebrews*, JSNTSup 44; Sheffield: Sheffield Academic Press, 1990), 22, 27, 54, 103; and Hans-Friedrich Weiß, *Der Brief an die Hebräer*, MeyerK 13 (Göttingen: Vandenhoeck & Ruprecht, 1991) 405–6.

4. In this summary of the argument, I have in most cases followed the exegetical decisions of Harold W. Attridge, *The Epistle to the Hebrews*, Hermeneia (Philadelphia: Fortress, 1989), 17–21, 35–103.

5. On the connection between the superiority of Christ to the angels and the superiority of Christ, as the latest revelation of God, to the law, see Graham Hughes, *Hebrews and Hermeneutics: The Epistle to the Hebrews as a New Testament Example of Biblical Interpretation*, SNTSMS 36 (Cambridge: Cambridge University Press, 1979), 7–8.

6. See, e.g., Philo, *Life of Moses* 2.66–186; Attridge, *Hebrews*, 105; and William L. Lane, *Hebrews 1–8*, WBC 47A (Dallas, Tex.: Word Books, 1991), 74.

7. As Mary Rose D'Angelo argues in *Moses in the Letter to the Hebrews*, SBLDS 42 (Missoula, Mont.: Scholars Press, 1979), 66–67, 93. Cf. Hughes, *Hebrews and Hermeneutics*, 9–12.

8. Here I follow Attridge's understanding of 3:4 in *Hebrews*, 104.

9. On the connection between the two sections, see especially C. Spicq, *L'Épître aux Hébreux*, 3rd ed., 2 vols., Ebib (Paris: Librairie Lecoffre, 1953), 1:71; Attridge, *Hebrews*, 114; and Weiß, *Der Brief an die Hebräer*, 254.

10. On this, see Gerhard von Rad, "A Rest Still Remains for the People of God: An Investigation of a Biblical Conception," in *The Problem of the Hexateuch and Other Essays* (New York: McGraw-Hill, 1966), 94–102; and

A. T. Lincoln, "Sabbath, Rest, and Eschatology in the New Testament," in *From Sabbath to Lord's Day: A Biblical, Historical and Theological Investigation* (ed. D. A. Carson; Grand Rapids, Mich.: Zondervan, 1982), 197–220, here at 209.

11. For the rendering of *sabbatismos* as "sabbath celebration," see Spicq, *L'Épître aux Hébreux*, 83–84; and especially Otfried Hofius, *Katapausis: Die Vorstellung vom endzeitlichen Ruheort im Hebräerbrief,* WUNT 11; (Tübingen: J. C. B. Mohr [Paul Siebeck], 1970), 102–10.

12. For the parallel between 4:6a and 4:9, see Hofius, *Katapausis,* 106; and idem, "σαββατισμός," *EDNT* 3:219.

13. See Lincoln, "Sabbath, Rest, and Eschatology in the New Testament," 213.

14. See the comments of Attridge, *Hebrews,* 138; and Lane, *Hebrews 1–8,* 110–12, on the structure of the section.

15. On the meaning of *metriopatheō,* see Spicq, *L'Épître aux Hébreux,* 108–9, and idem, *TLNT* 2:486–88; and on the three qualities of the priest in 5:1–4, see Attridge, *Hebrews,* 142–45.

16. The phrase "indestructible life" probably refers to the inability of the crucifixion to consign Jesus to the grave forever. See Lane, *Hebrews 1–8,* 184.

17. On the translation "nontransferable" for *aparabatos* in 7:24, see Ceslas Spicq, "ἀπαράβατος," *TLNT* 1:143–44.

18. On the importance of the close relationship between law and priesthood for the author's argument about the superiority of God's revelation in Christ, see Hughes, *Hebrews and Hermeneutics,* 15–20.

19. Some commentators believe that the ambiguous phrase *ho laos gar ep'autēs nenomothetētai* in 7:11 should be translated "for based upon it [the priesthood] the people has been given a law" (Attridge, *Hebrews,* 198). Philo, however, can use the verb *nomotheteō* with *epi* followed by the genitive, just as the author does here, to mean "it has been regulated concerning . . . [people, beasts, etc.]" (*Special Laws* 2.35). Thus, the phrase probably should be rendered, "For the people have received regulations concerning it [the priesthood]." Admittedly, this makes the phrase weak and redundant (Walter Gutbrod, "νόμος, κτλ.," *TDNT* 4:1090); but the parallels in Philo seem too close to take the phrase in Hebrews any other way. See Lane, *Hebrews 1–8,* 174 n. "b."

20. Cf. Ezek. 11:19 and 36:26, where "fleshy hearts" are preferable to unresponsive "stone hearts."

21. See, e.g., Pseudo-Democritus C,7; Aeschylus, Fragments 464,2; Epictetus, *Gnomologium Stobaei* 4; *Test. Job* 27, and the discussions in Eduard Schweizer, "σάρξ," *TDNT* 7:101–2, and Attridge, *Hebrews,* 202.

22. Since no noun is expressed for the adjective "first" in 9:1, it is often taken to refer to the "first covenant" (cf. 9:15) rather than to the "first tabernacle." The "first tent" of 9:8 is also often taken to mean the "outer tabernacle," referring only to the "first" and less sacred "tabernacle" of the two-tent

structure (cf. 9:2, 6) rather than to the entire two-tent structure itself. For the interpretation followed here, see L. D. Hurst, *The Epistle to the Hebrews: Its Background of Thought*, SNTSMS 65 (Cambridge: Cambridge University Press, 1990), 26–27. On the translation of the phrase *eti tēs prōtēs skēnēs echousēs stasin* (9:8) as "while the first tabernacle still has standing," see Attridge, *Hebrews*, 240.

23. On the importance of Jer. 31:33–34 to the structure of this section, see Attridge, *Hebrews*, 226.

24. Cf. Philip Edgcumbe Hughes, *A Commentary on the Epistle to the Hebrews* (Grand Rapids, Mich.: Eerdmans, 1977), 298–99; and Lane, *Hebrews 1–8*, 202 n. "S" and 209.

25. The author avoids explicitly calling anyone but Jesus a "mediator" (*mesitēs*); but in 12:24 he implies that Moses, like Jesus, was in some sense a mediator.

26. For the role of the heavenly Jerusalem in Jewish and Christian eschatological expectation of the late first century, see *2 Apoc. Bar.* 4:2–6; 4 Ezra 7:26; 13:36; and Revelation 21. For Mount Zion as the site of God's final work of restoration among his people, see, e.g., Isa. 2:2–4; 4:2–6; 24:23; 51:11; 52:8; Mic. 4:7–8; Zeph. 3:14–20. On both concepts, see Georg Fohrer and Eduard Lohse, "Ζιών, κτλ.," *TDNT* 7:292–338, here at 312–17 and 325–37.

27. This is all part of the meaning of the term "festal assembly" (*panēgyris*), which was sometimes used of the religious festivals celebrating athletic victories in the Greco-Roman world. See Spicq, "πανήγυρις," *TLNT* 3:4–8.

28. See Attridge, *Hebrews*, 375.

29. See Marie E. Isaacs, *Sacred Space: An Approach to the Theology of the Epistle to the Hebrews*, JSNTSup 73 (Sheffield: Sheffield Academic Press, 1992), 97, 217; and eadem, "Hebrews 13.9–16 Revisited," *NTS* 43 (1997): 268–84, here at 281.

30. Cf. Spicq, *L'Épître aux Hébreux*, 423.

31. Ibid., 425.

32. It is difficult to agree with Lehne (*New Covenant in Hebrews*, 23, 26) that "the writer reduces the law to its cultic prescriptions."

33. On 7:12, see Isaacs, *Sacred Space*, 115. It is true that the author preserves the comment in Jer. 31:31–34 that God would put his laws in the minds of his people and write them on his people's hearts, but as Smend and Luz point out, these references to the law are not developed (*Gesetz*, 114). *Contra* Lehne, *New Covenant in Hebrews*, 99–100.

34. On the meaning of *hypodeigma* in Hebrews, see Hurst, *Epistle to the Hebrews*, 13–17.

6

Principled Conformity, Radical Departure, and Sensible Compromise: The Law and the Believing Community in Luke-Acts

L UKE'S APPROACH TO THE MOSAIC LAW is puzzling. Those who greet Jesus' birth at the beginning of the Gospel and those who follow him at the Gospel's end piously conform to the requirements of the Mosaic law. They faithfully go to the temple, make the required sacrifices, undertake the pilgrimage to Jerusalem for Passover, and keep the sabbath (Luke 1:6, 22–24; 2:27, 37, 39, 41–42; 23:56; 24:53). In Luke's second volume also, both the beginning and end are marked by faithful, and apparently commendable, devotion to the Mosaic law. The early Christians observe the Jewish festivals, pray in the temple, assume Nazirite vows, and convincingly withstand accusations against their devotion to Moses (Acts 2:1; 3:1; 21:26; cf. 6:7; 22:12; 23:3; 25:8; 28:17).

Sandwiched between this record of piety in both books, however, stands a radical approach to the law. In the Gospel Jesus seems to advocate work on the sabbath, redefine cultic purity in terms of almsgiving, proclaim the proper standing before God of an uncircumcised Roman and an unorthodox Samaritan, keep the company of notoriously unrighteous Israelites, and reserve his sharpest criticism for those most punctilious about observing the law (Luke 5:29–30; 6:9; 7:9, 36–50; 11:37–12:1; 15:1–2; 17:18; 19:5–7).

In Acts, God himself tells Peter in a vision to rise from his sleep, kill, and eat from a motley group of clean and unclean animals (Acts 10:9–16; 10:44–11:18). The testimony of God's dramatic visitation to uncircumcised Gentiles leads the Jerusalem church to drop the requirement of circumcision for membership within the people of God. The Gentiles, it seems, are not obligated to accept the yoke of the law, a yoke that according to Peter neither the present generation of Jews nor their ancestors had been able to bear (Acts 15:1–29).

Interpreters have untangled this complicated knot of evidence in various ways. Many interpreters claim that Luke's approach to the law is consistently conservative. Jewish Christians are required to keep it, and Gentile Christians, although not obligated to become Jewish proselytes, are brought under the law's requirements by means of the Apostolic Decree in Acts 15.[1] Some interpreters think that for Luke the law was the divinely sanctioned way of life for God's people until the introduction of a new era with the coming of Christ. Luke faithfully records in his two volumes the gradual acceptance among Jesus' followers of the notion that a new age had dawned.[2] One interpreter thinks Luke is anti-Semitic, and that his account of the abandonment of the Jewish law among the early Christians serves his attempt to show that the separation of Christianity from Judaism was the fault of the Jews.[3]

Even in the controverted field of New Testament studies, this amount of disagreement over the interpretation of identical evidence is unusual. Indeed, the last position is almost the mirror image of the first.[4] When one is faced with such complex evidence and the wide interpretive spectrum it has produced, it is tempting to conclude that Luke had no view of the Mosaic law, or at least that his expression of his view is hopelessly ambiguous.[5] If we understand the kind of literature Luke chose to write and something about his goals for writing, however, we can see that he had a clear vision of the role of the Mosaic law within the purposes of God to save his people.

AN INTERPRETIVE FRAMEWORK
FOR LUKE'S APPROACH TO THE LAW

Luke wrote both as a historian and as an apologist for early Christianity. In order to understand his approach to the Mosaic law, we must grasp how his approach could help him accomplish the tasks appropriate to these two roles.

Luke Wrote as a Hellenistic Historian

If we want to understand Luke's approach to the Jewish law, we must keep in mind that he wrote self-consciously as a historian. We know this from the first sentence of his work. There he describes his task as the production of a "narrative" (*diēgēsis*) similar to other narratives that have attempted to describe "the things accomplished" among the early Christians (Luke 1:1). He has, he says, followed "everything meticulously" from the beginning and intends to write his narrative "in ordered sequence" (1:3).

These were precisely the qualities that, according to ancient literary critics, historians should cultivate. The second-century lecturer and litterateur Lucian of Samosata, in his essay *The Way to Write History*, says that once past the preface, "the body of the history which remains is nothing from beginning to end but a long narrative (*diēgēsin*)" (55). The history writer, moreover, must not draw the parts of his account together helter-skelter without careful attention to their order. Instead, they should be "attached like one link of a chain to another," each part complete in itself and its connection with the next part clearly revealed (55).[6]

If Luke was writing within this tradition, then interpreters of Luke should not expect that everything Christians say about the law in his narrative represents his own view of it. As a writer of history, Luke had the task of writing about "human accomplishments" (*praxeis*, Aristotle, *Rhetoric* 1.4.13, 1.1360A35), of describing developments as they unfolded rather than simply providing an essay on his own views. Lucian describes the historian's commitment to report what happened this way:

> He will consider very rightly that no man of sense will blame him for recounting the effects of misfortune or folly in their entirety; he is not the author, but only the reporter of them. If a fleet is destroyed, it is not he who sinks it; if there is a rout, he is not in pursuit. (38)

Certainly many would-be writers of history in antiquity did not accomplish this goal, least of all apparently in the late second century when Lucian penned these words, but those with axes to grind were easy to spot and widely despised.[7]

It should surprise no one, therefore, that Luke's understanding of the law will not appear on the surface of everything the followers of Jesus say or do concerning the law in his narrative.[8] By virtue of the lit-

erary genre in which he chose to write, his approach will be more subtle. His view will not go unexpressed, but to show that it was not
always triumphant in the Christian community is only to write good
history.

Luke Wrote as a Social Apologist

Luke also hoped to show, in the face of accusations to the contrary,
that Christianity posed no threat to the social stability of the Roman
Empire. By Luke's time, Christians had been defending themselves
against the charge of social and political sedition for many years.
Already in 1 Thessalonians, probably the earliest Christian writing
still in existence, Paul expresses concern that the Thessalonian Christians not disgrace the gospel in the public eye through socially unac-
ceptable conduct (1 Thess. 4:9–12). The theme reappears in the advice
of the Pastoral Epistles and 1 Peter. Whereas Christians should not be
surprised by persecution when it comes (2 Tim. 3:12; 1 Pet. 4:12), these
letters say, they should not provide society with a just cause for ill
treatment by unnecessarily violating its norms (1 Tim. 3:2–13; 6:1–2;
Titus 2:1–10, 14; 3:1, 8, 14; 1 Pet. 2:12, 15; 3:16). To do so would be to
endanger the appeal of the gospel (1 Tim. 6:1; Titus 2:10; 1 Pet. 3:1–2).

By the second century, many Roman officials and cultural elites
viewed Christianity as a strange eastern cult that undermined accepted
moral norms and threatened the social order.[9] Around 185, the phi-
losopher Celsus could say with a glee typical of his acerbic criticism of
Christianity, "The cult of Christ is a secret society whose members
huddle together in corners for fear of being brought to trial and punishment."[10] Among the many problems that he identified in the Christian movement, perhaps the most basic for Celsus was the threat that
Christians posed to the established societal order. They upset the firm
boundaries of social stratification by appealing to the socially
oppressed; they refused to recognize the gods of others; and they
encouraged people to abandon their ancestral ways of life. Celsus was
troubled, for example, that Christians asked Jews to "become strangers
to their heritage" and to leave "the [law] of their fathers," and he is
amazed that some are actually persuaded to do this. "How can you
despise the origins in which you yourselves claim to be rooted?" he
asks.[11]

Although Celsus wrote these remarks a full century after the composition of Luke-Acts, the concerns he raises were probably also in the air in Luke's day. Part of Luke's purpose was to refute them. Thus, before Jesus' ministry begins, John the Baptist advises the soldiers who respond to his preaching not to engage in the seditious and illegal activity of which they were sometimes accused (Luke 3:14).[12] Luke also tones down the politically provocative elements of Jesus' triumphal entry to Jerusalem and cleansing of the temple.[13] In the passion narrative the charges against Jesus are phrased in specifically political terms—he is perverting the nation, forbidding the payment of taxes to Caesar, claiming to be a king himself (Luke 23:2), and inciting trouble among the people from Galilee to Judea (Luke 23:5). Jesus is, however, innocent of all this. The Roman governor Pilate declares Jesus innocent three times (Luke 23:4; 14, 22), a verdict that the Jewish tetrarch Herod Antipas confirms (Luke 23:15). One of the troublemakers crucified with Jesus recognizes that, unlike himself, Jesus has done nothing improper (Luke 23:41), a sentiment with which both the Roman centurion and the crowd of common Jews ranged around the cross agree (Luke 23:47–48).

The theme receives even greater stress in Acts. Here, although Christians are often charged with overthrowing ethnic tradition and disturbing the social order (Acts 6:11, 13–14; 16:20–21; 17:6–7; 18:13; 19:25–27; 24:5–6), the ridiculous nature of the charges is also revealed. Not infrequently they are turned back upon the Christians' accusers (Acts 7:27, 38–39, 51–53; 16:35–39; 17:5; 18:17; 19:40), and honest representatives of both the Jewish people and the pagan government find Christians innocent of any wrongdoing (Acts 5:33–39; 19:37; 26:32). Rulers and governors who keep Christians imprisoned do so from corrupt motives (Acts 12:3; 24:26–27; cf. 25:2–3, 9). Even Paul's appeal to Caesar was formally unnecessary, for he was innocent of the charges leveled against him (Acts 26:32; cf. 23:29; 25:18; 26:31).

It should not be surprising, then, to find Luke eager to stress Christianity's willingness to coexist peacefully with other traditions, particularly with the one that gave it birth. Nor should we be surprised at his report that the town clerk at Ephesus, despite the charges against Paul and his companions, considered them guilty of neither sacrilege nor blasphemy against the goddess Artemis (Acts 19:37). Luke wants to show furthermore that Christians do not despise their Jewish roots, nor do they advocate that Jews abandon the essential elements of their ancestral customs.[14] Where they have parted ways with Jewish custom, they have been driven to do so against their own instincts and by the overpowering authority of God himself (Acts 10:1–11:18; 15:6–11).

Christians, moreover, are pious people, noted for their good works, their good sense, and their avoidance of common vices (Acts 9:36; 10:1–4; 20:18–35; 27:31, 33–34, 43). The proclamation of the gospel, as Paul puts it to the Ephesian elders, involves declaring "those things that are advantageous" (Acts 20:20). In his defense before Festus, Paul summarizes the position that Luke hopes his readers will attribute to Christianity generally, "Neither against the law of the Jews, nor against the temple, nor against Caesar have I committed any offense" (Acts 25:8).

The Mosaic Law in the Framework of Luke's Purposes

If we remember that Luke's reasons for writing and the genre in which he chose to write shaped what he would say, then we shall be less inclined to conclude that Luke's understanding of the law was simply ambiguous or that every comment on the law must fit into the framework of a single view. Luke writes self-consciously as a historian. Some of the views on the Mosaic law expressed within Luke-Acts fail to harmonize with others because of Luke's understanding of his task: he was to tell the story as it actually unfolded, not as he would have it unfold if he were spinning it from his imagination.

Luke also writes as an apologist in an age when Christianity was beginning to be viewed as a socially dangerous, politically seditious religion. To the extent that he is able to do so and still be faithful to his task as a historian, he intends to emphasize the conservative, socially affirming nature of Christianity.

If we read Luke's material on the Mosaic law in the light of these two aspects of his narrative, we discover that a coherent approach to the law emerges. It can be summarized in three propositions:

1. The Mosaic law was normative for God's people until the ministry of Jesus.
2. Despite some continuity between Jesus' ethical teaching and the Mosaic law, Jesus replaced the law with his own, more radical ethic.
3. The reluctance of the early Christians to understand this and their pragmatic approach to its implementation in their communities reveals their respect for traditional social customs.

In what follows, we shall examine the unfolding of these propositions within Luke's narrative.

THE PAST VALIDITY OF THE MOSAIC LAW

Until the beginning of Jesus' public ministry in Luke 4:14–15, the authority of the Mosaic law among God's people remains unquestioned. Those who prepare for the Savior's arrival and greet him when he comes conform to the law with exemplary exactitude and devotion. The strains of this leitmotif appear already in Luke's description of John's parents. Zechariah and Elizabeth are people of impeccable piety: "both were righteous before God, living by all the commandments and just requirements of the Lord with blamelessness" (1:6; cf. Deut. 4:40). Zechariah conscientiously fulfills the temple service required of him "according to the custom of the priesthood" (1:9).

While Zechariah faithfully completes his duties (cf. Acts 10:1–4), the angel Gabriel appears to him and announces that he and Elizabeth will have a son despite their advanced years (1:11–20). The angel announces that this child will conform to the law's requirements for someone of unusual dedication to God. Like the first of Israel's prophets, Samuel, he will drink neither wine nor beer as a sign of his special status (1:15; cf. 1 Sam. 1:11; Num. 6:3). After the birth of their son, Zechariah and Elizabeth present him for circumcision on the eighth day in conformity with the law (1:58). The parents of the prophet who would prepare Israel for the visitation of the Lord (1:17, 76) were faithful followers of their ancestral customs and of the Mosaic law.

The same is true of the parents of Jesus himself. They also circumcised Jesus on his eighth day (2:21). In addition, Luke points out that they waited the amount of time prescribed by the Mosaic law for purification before presenting Jesus in the temple (2:22). In presenting him there, Luke says, they acknowledged the law's special treatment of the firstborn son (2:23), and they offered the sacrifices that the law required (2:24). All of this was a faithful effort "to do the custom that the law required concerning him" (2:27), or, in the words of Luke's concluding summary, to perform "everything according to the law of the Lord" (2:39).[15]

The theme continues in Luke's succinct portrait of Jesus' childhood. As Jesus matures and prepares for his public ministry, he too reveals a pious devotion to the Mosaic law and to the temple.[16] With his parents, he journeys to Jerusalem for Passover "according to custom" (2:41–42). While in Jerusalem he lingers in the temple, which he calls "my Father's house" (2:49)—to learn from the teachers gathered there (2:46–47). He was obedient to his parents (2:51; cf. Exod. 20:12; Deut. 5:16) and, during his forty days of testing in the wilderness, answers the devil only with words from Deuteronomy.[17]

This narrative portrait of piety according to the standards of the Mosaic law accomplishes three tasks. First, it plants the roots of Jesus' ministry firmly in biblical soil. It therefore provides a link between Luke's story of earliest Christianity and the biblical accounts of God's dealings with his people. The air tingles with the expectation of the arrival of something new; but these expectations are voiced in the language and among the people of the Bible.

Second, Luke's stress on the piety of Elizabeth, Zechariah, Joseph, and Mary locates Jesus within a stable and admirably devout community. The people who await Jesus are not eager to overthrow tradition; they are devoted servants of their people's laws.

Third, Luke's frequent characterization of the Mosaic law as a body of ethnic customs subtly identifies the law itself with the Jewish people. Customs are, by definition, the laws of a certain group and are therefore neither universal nor eternal. When Luke speaks of Zechariah keeping the "custom of the priesthood" (Luke 1:9), of Jesus' parents doing "the customary requirement of the law" (2:27), and of their observing Passover "according to the custom of the Feast" (2:42), Luke is lending a subtle quaintness to the Mosaic law.[18] Already he is clearing a path for the inclusion of Gentiles within the people of God apart from the Mosaic law, and for the transfer of authority within the people of God from the Mosaic law to the teaching of Jesus.

JESUS' NEW ETHIC

In 4:14–9:50 Luke describes the public ministry of Jesus in Galilee prior to his journey to Jerusalem (9:51–19:44). This section of the Gospel focuses on Jesus' immense authority, the rise of opposition to him, and the call and training of Jesus' disciples. It also reveals much about Luke's understanding of Jesus' approach to the Mosaic law. Here Luke seems to structure his Gospel in part to show how Jesus authoritatively replaced the Mosaic law with his own teaching. Jesus first clashes with those committed to the observance of the Mosaic law and then explains to them that his new claims cannot be contained within their traditional framework (4:14–6:11). He follows this provocative proclamation with actions and teaching that both recall the original constitution of Israel under the Mosaic covenant and imply that he is the mediator of a new covenant with a newly constituted people and dominated by a new, more radical ethic (6:12–7:49).

The basic concerns of Jesus' new ethic find repeated emphasis in the central section of the Gospel (9:51–19:44). In this section the prophet like Moses begins his journey to Jerusalem where he will accomplish his own redemptive "exodus" (9:30–31). Here Jesus affirms portions of the Mosaic law but sovereignly reinterprets them on his own terms. Jesus accepts the law's command to love one's neighbor and to care for the poor; but he absorbs these Mosaic concerns into his own more radical ethic as he describes it in the Gospel's programmatic opening chapters (6:20–49; cf. 4:16–30). The result is a mixture of continuity with discontinuity; but the stress lies on the discontinuity between Jesus' teaching and the Mosaic law.

Jesus Breaks with the Old and Introduces the New (4:14–9:50)

Jesus Breaks with the Old (4:14–6:11)

In 4:14–5:26, for the first time, we discover an element of tension in Jesus' conformity to the customs of his people. He goes to the synagogue on the sabbath, "according to his custom," and takes an active role in the proceedings by reading and explaining the scripture (4:16–22). At first those who heard him marveled at "the gracious words" that he spoke. "This is the son of Joseph isn't it?" they asked in amazement (4:22). But as Jesus begins to speak of God's acceptance of foreigners, their amazement turns to anger so bitter that they try to kill him (4:23–30).

Similarly, Jesus bypasses the Mosaic ritual for purification for a leper by simply touching him and rendering him pure (5:12–13). To be sure, Jesus then instructs the man to show himself to the priest and make an offering for his "cleansing, just as Moses commanded"; but he appends to this command the critical interpretive statement "as a testimony to them" (5:14). Since Luke has just mentioned how those who heard Jesus preach "began testifying to him and marveling at his gracious words" (4:22), and since the notion of testifying to Jesus receives special emphasis in Acts, Luke probably understood Jesus' words to mean that this leper would testify not merely to the priest before whom he appears, but to all who might see him in the temple, of Jesus' authority and power.[19] Although the man would stand before the priest fully recovered and purified, he should appear before him with his offering so that others might see what Jesus has done.[20]

The tension between Jesus and his ancestral customs intensifies in the next three paragraphs (5:17–32). In the first paragraph, Jesus' authoritative pronouncement that the sins of a paralytic are forgiven meets with the disapproval of the scribes and Pharisees, the official interpreters of the law (5:17–21). Jesus answers their criticism by healing the paralytic (5:22–26). In the second paragraph (5:27–32), "the Pharisees and their scribes" criticize Jesus' preference for the company of tax collectors and sinners—those who are not scrupulous in keeping the law (5:30). Jesus responds by claiming that he has come to call precisely such people to repentance (5:31–32).

In the third paragraph these same scribes and Pharisees criticize Jesus for eating and drinking instead of fasting and praying as they and the disciples of John do (5:33). At this, Jesus throws down the gauntlet with three parables whose point is that in his teaching and deeds old ways are being forced to yield to new ways: a wedding feast has started, a new garment has appeared, new wine has arrived (5:34–39).[21] Trying to force Jesus' new ways into the old, traditional mold will only end in disaster: the bridegroom will be taken away, the garment ruined, the wineskins burst, and the self-deception that the old wine is better than the new will continue.

The next two paragraphs develop this theme by taking Jesus' departure from past tradition to new lengths. Both paragraphs describe how Jesus authoritatively contramanded the Mosaic instructions to avoid "any work" on the sabbath (Exod. 20:10; 31:15; 35:2; Deut. 5:14; Jer. 17:22). In the first paragraph (6:1–5), Jesus' disciples were making their way through the grainfields, picking the grain, rubbing it in their hands, and eating it. This activity showed that the disciples had not properly planned for the sabbath by preparing their food the previous day (cf. Exod. 16:22–30). This was work that might have been avoided, therefore, and it constituted a breech of the sabbath commandment.[22] Jesus does not defend the action of the disciples by trying to claim that it was not really a breech of the Mosaic law. Instead, he cites David's breech of another biblical commandment as a precedent for their action and claims that as the Son of Man he has authority over the sabbath.[23]

In the second paragraph (6:6–11) Jesus prefaces his healing of a man with a shriveled hand on the sabbath with the rhetorical question, "Is it permitted to do good or to do evil on the sabbath, to save or to destroy?" (6:9). The implication is that doing good on the sabbath, even if the good deed might easily have been done on another day, is permissible.[24]

The stress that Luke places on this notion is clear from his inclusion later in his Gospel of two other accounts of sabbath healings in which precisely the same issue reappears. In 13:10–17—a passage unique to Luke—Jesus heals a woman on the sabbath who had been crippled for eighteen years. The synagogue ruler frames the problem precisely: "There are six days on which one must work; therefore come and be healed on those days and not on the sabbath day" (13:14). The synagogue ruler is not against healing—only against healing on the sabbath and thus violating the Mosaic law's prohibition of work on that day. Jesus argues, however, that this healing could not wait any more than animals could wait until the next day to be watered (13:15). Indeed, the sabbath is the most appropriate day for such work: "Is it not necessary for this woman, a daughter of Abraham, whom Satan has bound for all of eighteen years, to be released from this bondage on the sabbath?" (13:16). In a similar account a few paragraphs later, Jesus insists on healing a man suffering from massive fluid retention on the sabbath (14:1-3).[25] If a son or ox can be pulled from a well on the sabbath, then this sick man, he reasons, can be healed (14:5).

Jesus' work of healing, then, takes precedence over the Mosaic command to rest on the sabbath for the same reason that the work of sustaining or rescuing life takes precedence over the sabbath command: both kinds of activities involve doing good (6:9).[26] Indeed, insofar as sabbath rest can symbolize release from bondage, no day could be more appropriate than the sabbath for accomplishing Jesus' work of proclaiming "freedom to captives" and loosing "the oppressed" (13:16; cf. 4:18). The effect of this approach to the sabbath is to make the ministry of Jesus one long sabbath day, a time in which good ought always to be accomplished, whatever the day of the week according to the Mosaic calendar.[27]

In 6:1–11, therefore, Jesus demonstrates in concrete terms what he means when he compares himself and his teaching to a bridegroom, a new garment, and new wine (5:33–39). The sabbath commandment, along with the entire Mosaic law, must bow to his eschatological authority. He takes up the sabbath commandment and radically transforms it by making it the best day symbolically for accomplishing the work that, for him, dominates every day—doing good and saving life (6:9).

Jesus Introduces the New (6:12–7:49)

In the next section of Luke's Gospel, Jesus' new agenda is revealed (6:12–7:49). Jesus begins by choosing twelve apostles from among his disciples (6:12–16). The number twelve is significant for Luke because it recalls the number of Israel's tribes and shows that Jesus' disciples are the leaders of a newly constituted Israel.[28]

Jesus descends the mountain with these leaders and issues to the "great crowd of his disciples" gathered on the plain below his own teaching on how God's eschatologically constituted people should conduct their lives (6:17–49). He calls for a radical departure from the common standards of society. He congratulates those who are poor, hungry, distraught, and persecuted because their reward will be great, and warns those who are rich, satisfied, care-free, and socially acceptable of coming doom (6:20–26). He commands love for enemies and explains at length and in concrete terms what this means. It means repaying hatred with love, cursing with blessing, mistreatment with prayer, violence and theft with pacifism, and begging and borrowing with a kind of giving that hopes "for nothing in return" (6:27–35). His followers should, in short, imitate the mercy of God (6:36). In addition, Jesus' disciples should be critical of themselves before criticizing others (6:37–42) and should recognize that the conduct of their lives and the words from their mouths reveal their true inner condition (6:43–45).

Jesus concludes his teaching with a blessing for those who hear and obey his words and a curse for those who hear but ignore them (6:46–49). Those who obey build on a sure foundation and will withstand the forces arrayed against them. Those who fail to obey are building without a foundation and, like a house with no footing, will fall before the winds of adversity.

The setting and shape of the sermon inevitably recall the giving of the Mosaic law. Like Moses, Jesus descends the mountain to issue the law to God's people assembled on the plain (Exod. 34:29–35:1; cf. Deut. 1:1). Like the Mosaic law, these words are not advice but commands for the people of God, and thus they end by pronouncing a blessing on those who heed them and a curse on those who do not (Lev. 26:3–39; Deut. 27:11–30:20).

Yet the teaching itself is far from a reinterpretation of the Mosaic law for a new day. It is something new. Jesus never quotes directly from the law or any other portion of the Bible. Even allusions to the law are faint.[29] Moreover, Jesus' teaching in this passage is much shorter, more radical, and less casuistic than the law of Moses. Having broken with the Mosaic law in the two sabbath controversies that precede this passage (6:1–11), here Jesus seems to issue his own law for the newly constituted people of God.

Love for Enemies and Almsgiving: Jesus' Radical Ethic Emphasized (9:51–16:31)

After all this, the reader is not wholly unprepared for Luke's reference a few paragraphs later to Jesus' "exodus" that he will fulfill in Jerusalem (9:31). This comment stands near the beginning of the next major section of Luke's Gospel just as Jesus' own reference to the link between his death and the "new covenant" (22:20) stands near its end. Jesus is the prophet like Moses (Acts 3:22–23; 7:37) whose saving work follows the redemptive pattern of the ancient exodus, and whose rejection stands in historical continuity with Israel's rejection of Moses (Acts 7:27, 39) and all the prophets (Luke 4:24; 6:23, 26; 11:47–51; 13:33–34; Acts 7:52). Within these boundaries of structural continuity with biblical tradition, Luke's central section (9:51–19:44) continues to reveal clear discontinuities between Jesus' teaching and the Mosaic law. Jesus fulfills the expectations of Moses and the prophets and resembles them in broadly conceived ways, but his teaching is not merely a reinterpretation of the Mosaic covenant. It is a new covenant altogether.

Love for Enemies (10:25–37 and 15:11–32)

In Luke's central section (9:51–19:44) he again describes Jesus' annulment of the Mosaic law and replacement of it with his own radical ethic of love for enemies, generosity to the poor, and inner purity. Jesus' insistence on love for enemies receives emphasis in two passages. In the first, Jesus answers the question of a hostile lawyer about what he can do to inherit eternal life (10:25–37). When Jesus asks what answer the law gives to this question, the lawyer answers his own question, the lawyer summarizes the requirements for eternal life in the words of Deut. 6:5 and Lev. 19:18—one must love God completely, and one's neighbor as oneself. Jesus agrees with the lawyer; but when the lawyer wonders who his neighbor is (10:29), Jesus tells the famous parable of the Good Samaritan (10:30–35).

 In this parable, the Samaritan goes beyond the law's requirement to love one's neighbor (Lev. 19:18) or even to love the resident alien (Lev. 19:34), and shows love for his enemy. He loves one who would not love him, does good to one who would seek his harm, and pays out money for the care of his enemy with no hope of repayment (cf. Luke 6:27–36). Despite his initial affirmation of the law in his dialogue with the lawyer (10:25–28), in the parable Jesus goes beyond the law by including one's enemies within the circle of one's neighbors.[30]

Similarly, Jesus tells the parable of the Prodigal Son (15:11–32) to a group of Pharisees and scribes who are dismayed that he does not join them in shunning "tax collectors and sinners" (15:1–2, 11–32). In the parable, a younger son rejects his father's authority over him and demands his inheritance prior to his father's death. He then squanders the money on debauched living, is reduced to utter destitution, and returns to the father, not for acceptance but for a position among his servants. According to Deut. 21:18–21, such a son should be stoned, but in Jesus' parable, the father has compassion on him, runs to meet him, embraces him, kisses him, and holds a feast in his honor. Jesus expects his followers to do the same with their enemies. Like God himself, they are to be "kind to those who are ungrateful and evil" (Luke 6:35).

In the central section of the Gospel, then, Jesus affirms that those who follow the law's commands to love God and neighbor will have eternal life. This implies that at least these parts of the Mosaic law continue to carry the same authority they have always had. On the other hand, Jesus defines love for one's neighbor in terms of his own radical ethic articulated in the Sermon on the Plain. His followers are to love their enemies and to be kind to those who do not reciprocate their kindness (6:35). They are to be merciful, unjudging, uncondemning, and forgiving (6:36). They are to do this in imitation of the mercy of God himself (6:36). These themes are not absent from the Mosaic law, for the law also mandates care for the dispossessed, and even the enemy, on the basis of God's own unmerited care for Israel (as in, e.g.,

Exod. 22:22–27; 23:4–9); but Jesus pushes them to the center of his ethic and presents them as his own newly issued law.[31]

Almsgiving and Inner Purity
(11:37–52; 16:1–13, 19–31)

Jesus' concern with giving away wealth to the poor (6:20–21, 24–25, 30, 34) and his concern with inner purity (6:43–45) also find frequent expression in Luke's central section and, unlike their appearance in the Sermon on the Plain, are closely linked. In 11:37–41 Jesus does not wash before he eats, to the astonishment of the Pharisee who had invited him to dinner. His host's surprise prompts Jesus to criticize the Pharisees generally for placing more emphasis on outer cleanliness than on inner purity: "You Pharisees purify the outside of cup and dish, but your inside is full of greed and evil" (11:39). Jesus then exclaims, "Fools! Did not the one who made the outside also make the inside?" (11:40). Jesus is not speaking here of the potter who made the cup but of the great Potter who makes people and is sovereign over them (cf. Isa. 29:16; 45:9; 64:8; Jer. 18:4–6). His focus, therefore, has shifted from the cleanliness of cups and plates back to the issue of personal purity: God did not merely make the outer person; he also made the inner person, and therefore attention to the inner person is necessary. In light of Jesus' failure in the story to attend to his own outer purity (11:38), his rhetorical question carries the nuance that inner purity is not merely as important as outer purity, but is more important. "Is it more important to wash before eating," he seems to be saying, "or to purify one's inner self of greed and evil?"

If this is correct, then the basic meaning of Jesus' next statement, despite some minor ambiguities, is clear. "But give the things inside as alms," Jesus says, "and, behold, everything is clean for you" (11:41). Interpreters of this statement are undecided about whether it means to give to the poor what is within the cup (11:39–40), to give alms from the heart, to give careful attention to one's inner being, or to give whatever lies close at hand.[32] Since Jesus has already linked the Pharisees' inner impurity with greed (11:39), however, he probably refers here to almsgiving as a sign of inner purity. Within its context, then, the statement is a claim that Jesus' own failure to attend to the details of outer purification is insignificant since inner purity purifies everything. Just as the Pharisees' inner impurity is revealed particularly in their greed, despite their concern with outer cleanliness (11:39), so inner purity is revealed in almsgiving and makes outward cleansing irrelevant.[33]

The link between inner purity and almsgiving reemerges in the parable of the Unjust Steward (16:1–9) and the parable of the Rich Man and Lazarus (16:19–31). Jesus concludes the parable of the Unjust Steward with the command to "make for yourselves friends from unrighteous mammon so that when it gives out they might receive you into eternal dwellings" (16:9). This command forges a conceptual connection between this parable and the parable of the Rich Man and Lazarus a few paragraphs later. In the second parable, the angels escort the poor man Lazarus to the "eternal dwellings" of Abraham's bosom, while the rich man, who failed in his duty to give alms to Lazarus, dwells after his death in the torment of Hades (16:22–23). In light of this second parable, Jesus' command to use unrighteous mammon for making friends means to give alms to the poor. Those whose purity of heart is revealed in such generosity, he implies, will dwell eternally with Abraham. Failure to give alms, on the other hand, reveals the kind of inner impurity that characterizes the Pharisees (16:14; cf. 11:39) and eventually leads to the torments of Hades (16:22–23).

This also seems to be the point of Jesus' interaction with the rich ruler (18:18–27) and Zacchaeus (19:1–9). Although the rich ruler has kept the second table of the law (18:20–21), he lacks one critical quality for receiving eternal life: the willingness to sell his possessions, distribute them to the poor, and follow Jesus (18:22–23). Like the Pharisees, who are full of greed and evil on the inside (11:39) and who are lovers of money (16:14), his desire to cling to his possessions reveals the true state of his relationship with God. In contrast, Zacchaeus gives half his possessions to the poor and, because he has been guilty of fraud, announces that he will repay his victims fourfold (19:8).[34] The close connection between this pronouncement and Jesus' proclamation that salvation has come to Zacchaeus's house (19:9) shows the intimate link in Luke's thinking between almsgiving and salvation.

This stress on the fundamental importance of care for the poor does not represent a departure from the Mosaic law. Indeed, as Abraham says to the rich man, one need only hear Moses and the prophets to discover the significance of the poor and oppressed to God (16:29). Jesus clearly affirms this part of the Mosaic law and takes it up into his own ethical teaching. Nevertheless, even here Jesus gives the law's teaching a new twist. He claims that almsgiving reveals inner purity, and inner purity renders the Mosaic rituals of physical purity unnecessary.

Thus, for the person who gives alms everything is clean (11:41), and even sinners such as Zacchaeus reveal their full membership within the people of God by their willingness to give away their material possessions (19:8).

The Mosaic Law and Jesus' New Ethic:
A Summary Statement (16:16–18)

Luke's stress on Jesus' radical ethic of love for the enemy, inner purity as the only purity that matters, and purely motivated almsgiving as the sign of this inner purity helps to explain the most difficult passage in Luke's two volumes on the law, and the only place in which Luke directly addresses the role of the law in God's unfolding historical plan. Unfortunately, the passage is notoriously obscure. In Luke 16:16–18, Jesus makes four statements:

v. 16a   The law and the prophets were until John.

v. 16b   From that time, the kingdom of God is being preached and everyone is urgently invited into it.

v. 17   But it is easier for heaven and earth to pass away than for a single pen-stroke within the law to fail.

v. 18   Anyone who divorces his wife and marries another commits adultery, and anyone who marries a woman divorced from her husband commits adultery.[35]

The connection between the first two statements is readily intelligible. Together they unfold the timetable of God's plan for the salvation of his people: the law and the prophets were the authoritative witnesses to God's will and designs until John (v. 16a), and from the time of John a new phase of God's saving purposes has been in effect (v. 16b). During this new phase, John (3:18), Jesus (4:18, 43; 7:22; 8:1; 20:1), and the Twelve (9:6) all preach the coming of the kingdom and urgently invite everyone to enter it. The statement seems to relegate the law and the prophets to a past era.[36]

How, then, should we understand v. 17, which seems to proclaim the continuing validity of the law down to its smallest detail? The conjunction "but" (*de*) supplies the answer. This next statement qualifies its predecessor so that no one will draw the conclusion from it that God's purposes moved beyond the law because of some inadequacy in the law itself. The statement does not therefore mean that every detail of the law remains in force as a guide to the conduct of the people of

God. It means instead that the law's purposes reach their fulfillment in the proclamation of the kingdom and in the urgent invitation to join it.[37]

With v. 18, however, there is not even a connecting particle to help the reader understand the logical flow of the argument. Does the saying simply have no connection with its context?[38] Did Luke put it here because his sources forced him into an arrangement of his material that was not entirely satisfactory from the standpoint of his readers?[39] Probably neither of these explanations is correct. If we understand vv. 16–17 as a statement of the law's fulfillment in the proclamation of the gospel, then in v. 18 Luke gives an example of kingdom ethics.[40]

As with the ethics of Jesus in the Sermon on the Plain, Jesus' statement on divorce is proclaimed without reference to the Mosaic law.[41] Jesus is teaching something new. Instead of following Deut. 24:1–4 and permitting remarriage after divorce, Jesus says that no man may remarry after divorce, and no unmarried man may marry a divorced woman. Although the Qumran covenanters took a similar position, they made every effort to show that it was the correct interpretation of the law.[42] Jesus makes no such effort. The role of the Mosaic law as a guide to the conduct of God's people has been fulfilled and has expired with the coming of Jesus.[43] He proclaims a new and more radical ethic.

The Fate of Jesus' Ethic in the Early Church

In his record of Jesus' ministry, Luke places no emphasis on the response of Jesus' disciples to their Lord's proclamation of a new ethic. After Jesus' death, however, Luke emphasizes the faithfulness of Jesus' followers to the Mosaic law. Suddenly the storm over the law, which thundered so loudly during Jesus' proclamation of the kingdom, dissipates, and we return to the serene world of Mosaic piety familiar from the infancy narratives. Jesus' followers observe the commandment to rest on the sabbath (Luke 23:56) and remain continually in the temple, where they bless God and pray at the appropriate hour (Luke 24:53; Acts 3:1). They observe the feast of Weeks (Acts 2:1), are defended by a famous legal scholar (Acts 5:34), and attract a great many priests to the faith (Acts 6:7).

What has happened? Has Luke contradicted himself? Does he believe that the law remains permanently valid for Jewish Christians, if not for others? Is this picture of faithfulness to the law a sign that Jesus' own approach to the law in the gospel is not so radical after all?

We can achieve clarity on this issue if we remember the constraints of the historical genre in which Luke has chosen to write and Luke's concern to point out the peaceful, tradition-affirming characteristics of early Christianity. As a writer of history, Luke was expected to record what happened even when it deviated from his own position. In the words of Lucian,

> The historian's one task is to tell the thing as it happened (*hōs eprachthē eipein*). . . . He may nurse some private dislikes, but he will attach far more importance to the public good, and set the truth high above his hate; he may have his favourites, but he will not spare their errors. (*The Way to Write History*, 39)

With this standard in mind, Luke's readers did not expect to see a univocal position on the law within his narrative, even among Christians. They might bring such expectations to a letter-essay or a homily, but as historical narrative Luke's work was supposed to reveal the vicissitudes of life.

If this is so, however, why does Luke seem to emphasize early Christian conformity to the law? A conscientious historian might report a viewpoint contrary to his or her own, but why underline it? In answering this question we must keep in mind Luke's apologetic purpose. He was writing in part to defend early Christians against charges that they advocated the overthrow of ethnic tradition and endangered the stability of the societies in which they lived. The early Christians' reluctance to adopt Jesus' departures from custom and their attempts at practical compromise once they had grasped them were boons for Luke. These elements of the story demonstrated that Christians were not a revolutionary rabble but a sensible people who valued tradition and understood that a pragmatic respect for ethnic custom could prevent dissension.

The constraints of his genre and his apologetic concerns, therefore, merged nicely on the issue of the law. Luke could trace the origins of his own understanding of the law back to Jesus himself, but he could also show to his cultured readers the conservative nature of the early church.

This perspective is critical for understanding Luke's approach to the Mosaic law in the central and concluding portions of Acts. Here we find the record of the infant church's first halting steps away from the law. This record is characterized not by clear, aesthetically pleasing linear development but by the unpredictable shifts between enthusiasm for the new and defense of the old that accompany any major cultural change, a principle not unknown to ancient observers of society. By recounting the early church's struggle with the law in this way, Luke both remained true to the expectations of his readers and advanced his defense of Christianity. Four sections of Acts are particularly important: Stephen's arrest and speech (6:8–7:53), Cornelius's conversion (10:1–11:18), the Jerusalem council (15:1–29), and Paul's later ministry (16:1–26:32).

Stephen's Arrest and Speech (6:8–7:53)

The charges against Stephen get to the heart of the matter: his accusers claim that he has blasphemed Moses and God (6:11), that he has spoken against the temple and the law (6:13), and that he has said that Jesus would destroy the temple and "change the customs that Moses handed down to us" (6:14). The speech is often thought to be Stephen's defense against these charges, but it actually functions as the final speech of the condemned in other accounts of martyrdom: it does not so much claim that the charges are wrong as it defiantly proclaims the truth.[44] The burden of Stephen's speech, therefore, is that Stephen's accusers are direct ideological descendants of those who spurned Moses and the prophets (7:9, 23–29, 35–40). Their rejection of the prophet like Moses demonstrates this (7:37, 52) and also shows that they have deviated from the prophetic insight that God does not dwell in a temple made with human hands (7:44, 49; cf. Isa. 66:1–2).

Along the way to these points, Stephen shows by positive references to circumcision (7:8), Moses (7:20–22, 36, 38), the law (7:38, 53), and the tabernacle (7:44–45), that he has blasphemed neither the law nor the cult. Luke wants his readers to notice this subtheme, and he therefore observes that the charges against Stephen are advanced by "false witnesses" (6:14; cf. 6:11).[45] None of this means, however, that in Luke's view Jesus did not advocate changes to the Mosaic law or teach the demise of the temple. The charge of blasphemy and the claim that Jesus personally would destroy the temple make the testimony false, but, as so often with false testimony, it is not spun from thin air. Stephen's refusal to meet the charges against him head-on, therefore, marks the early Christian community's first faltering step away from the Mosaic law in the Acts narrative.

Cornelius's Conversion (10:1–11:18)

The second step is bolder. In the Cornelius episode God himself instructs Peter to "kill and eat" from a visionary collection of all kinds of animals (10:13; 11:7). Peter assumes that God is instructing him to eat unclean food and strongly refuses to do so: "Most certainly not, Lord, because I have never eaten anything common and unclean" (10:14; cf. 11:8). God rebukes Peter for this reply with the dictum, "What God has purified, do not call common" (10:15; 11:9).[46]

Peter wonders what all this means, and the matter is clarified when Gentile emissaries of the centurion Cornelius arrive to see Peter. They explain that their pious master has had a vision of his own (10:17–22). A "holy angel" instructed him to send for Peter so that he might hear what Peter has to say (10:22). Upon his arrival at Cornelius's house, Peter proclaims that he has learned from God that, despite Jewish custom, it is not unlawful (*athemitos*) to associate with or visit a foreigner and that no person is common or unclean in God's eyes (10:28; cf. 10:20; 11:12). Luke's ponderous narration both of the story itself and of Peter's account of it to the skeptical Jewish Christians in Jerusalem reveals the immense significance it had for him.

Interpreters commonly point out problems in the passage:

1. The vision itself declares that no food is unclean, but Peter seems to interpret it in a less radical way to mean that he can associate with all kinds of people.
2. It is true that Peter eats with the Gentile Cornelius, but Luke has portrayed Cornelius as so pious that it is hard to imagine him setting unclean food before his Jewish guests.
3. At the subsequent Jerusalem council, thought of the purity of all foods seems to be forgotten as the Jerusalem apostles require Gentile believers to abstain from meat offered to idols, meat from strangled animals, and blood (15:20, 29; 21:25).

Such difficulties have been taken to mean that Luke has, none too successfully, tried to shape a legally radical tradition that he inherited to fit his own more conservative convictions on the Mosaic law.[47]

This understanding of the passage, however, does not carry conviction. It is difficult to imagine Luke editing his source so clumsily that he failed to deal with the twice-repeated divine directive that cleansed all foods. It is none other than God himself, after all, who tells Peter not to consider unclean what he has cleansed. Moreover, the issue of eating clean food and responding to an invitation for hospitality from a Gentile are intimately related, as Peter's astonished naysayers in Jerusalem recognize: "You went to men who have a foreskin and ate with them!" (11:3). Their fear was not unfounded, since although Luke notes that Cornelius is God-fearing and pious and therefore probably sympathetic to Judaism, nothing in the narrative hints that he would have understood the intricacies of Jewish law well enough to entertain observant Jews "for some days" (11:48) in purity.

The narrative must be left to stand as an account of God's own intervention into the affairs of the early Jewish Christian community for the astonishing purpose of abrogating the Mosaic food laws. Only divine intervention, Luke makes clear, forced this pious, tradition-affirming group to accept such a development. Lest any miss this point, Luke recounts the vision twice, says each time that in the vision God made the declaration three times, and records the amazed refusal of both Peter and the Jerusalem church at first to accept it.[48] The customs that Moses handed down had indeed been changed.

The Jerusalem Council (15:1–29)

If all of this is true, however, then why the need for a Jerusalem council, and why did the council decide to impose food restrictions on Gentiles? Luke says that the problems that led to the council arose because "some people" came from Judea to Antioch and told the Gentile Christians there that they must accept circumcision "according to the custom of Moses" in order to be saved (15:1). A group of Jerusalem-based Pharisaic believers expressed much the same sentiment at the time of the council, adding only by way of clarification that Gentiles should also keep the law of Moses (15:5).

Neither of these groups can be identified with "those from the circumcision" who in 11:2 were at first critical of Peter's visit to Cornelius but later admitted that he was right. The phrase "those from the circumcision" in 11:2 simply identifies the group as Jewish and does not refer, as in the RSV's rendering of the verse, to "the circumcision party." The group in 15:1 is not even specifically from Jerusalem, but from Judea, and Luke carefully dissociates them from the "apostles and elders" who comprise the Jerusalem council (15:24). Similarly, the group in 15:5 is a special-interest party of Pharisaic believers within the Jerusalem church. Thus, the reemergence of questions over the status of Gentiles within the church will not surprise the careful reader of Luke's narrative. Other, less compliant believers than those who changed their minds in 11:18 have entered the picture.

That the issue is the continuing validity of the Mosaic law and that the advocates of tradition lose the argument Luke also makes clear. The believing Pharisees in 15:5 formulate the question before the council precisely: Gentile believers must be circumcised and instructed to keep the Mosaic law. Peter and James express the council's opinion with equal precision: God himself has called the Gentiles to be part of his people without requiring them to accept the yoke of the law, and not to recognize this is to put God to the test (15:9–11, 13–21; cf. Deut. 6:16).

Peter's statement makes adherence to the law irrelevant for salvation, both for Jews and for Gentiles. Jews put their faith in the Lord Jesus for salvation and do this through his grace, just as the Gentiles do (15:11). God has cleansed the hearts of both groups, leaving no difference between them (15:9). The law, on the other hand, has been a yoke that no generation of Israelites from ancient times to the present has been able to bear (15:10). This statement echoes Paul's claim a few paragraphs earlier that through Jesus "everyone who believes is justified from everything from which you were not able to be justified by the law of Moses" (13:38–39). Both statements are difficult, but they probably mean that Israel has not kept the law, a familiar theme from Stephen's speech and from the Deuteronomic history, which has left such a definite stamp on both Luke and Acts (Acts 7:23–29, 35–40, 51–53).[49] For Peter, therefore, the imposition of the Mosaic law upon Gentiles is inappropriate because even Jews have not kept it and because salvation comes through grace and faith for both groups.[50]

James too rejects the thesis of the conservative group. God has already included the Gentiles within his people apart from the law, he argues, and this represents a fulfillment of prophecy. Jewish Christians should, therefore, not trouble Gentile believers (15:13–19).

James's next words, however, have created a storm of interpretive controversy. Instead of troubling the Gentiles, James says, the apostles and elders ought to write to them "to avoid pollution by idols, sexual immorality, what has been strangled, and blood" (15:20). Many interpreters believe that with these words, repeated in almost the same form on two other occasions (15:29; 21:25), Luke is recommending that Gentile Christians conform to the requirements listed in Leviticus 17–18 for aliens who live within the land of Israel.[51] Luke, it is then supposed, believed in the eternal validity of the Mosaic law: Jews would keep all of it, and Gentiles would keep the portion of it required for uncircumcised people who live among the Israelites.[52]

The link between these few requirements and the law's instructions for resident aliens, however, is not close. First, the correspondence between the four items in the Apostolic Decree and the requirements for the resident alien in Lev. 17:8–18:30 is far from exact. Although avoidance of blood, strangled animals, and sexual immorality find counterparts in the passage, it does not mention meat offered to idols or even idolatry.[53] Second, the law's requirements for resident aliens are not limited to the regulations covered in Lev. 17:8–18:30. Other parts of the law instruct resident aliens to participate in the feast of Unleavened Bread (Exod. 12:19), to keep the sabbath (Exod. 20:10; 23:12; Deut. 5:14), to observe the Day of Atonement (Lev. 16:29; cf. Num. 15:22–26), to offer only unblemished sacrifices (Lev. 22:18; cf. Num. 15:14), and to avoid blasphemy against the Lord's name (Lev. 24:16). It is difficult to see, therefore, how the several requirements listed by James could bring Gentile Christians into conformity with the Mosaic law.[54]

Instead, the Apostolic Decree more naturally plays the role of a pragmatic compromise. The strict Judean Jews and the believing Pharisees have suffered a sound defeat, but in the decree the apostles and elders offer a few guidelines for softening the practical implications of this defeat. By advising the Gentiles to abstain from meat offered to idols, from the consumption of blood, from strangled animals, and from sexual immorality, the apostles and elders have made it easier for the most conservative Jewish Christians to associate with Gentile believers.[55] Adherence to these rules would allow scrupulous Jewish Christians to mingle with Gentile Christians around a common table without fear of compromising basic Jewish dietary rules. It would also put to rest fears that mixing with Gentiles might lead to sexual immorality and idolatry as it had in ancient times (Num. 25:1–18).[56]

This pragmatic nature of the decree explains why its stipulations are offered not as law but as the better part of wisdom: "If you keep yourselves from these," the apostolic letter concludes, "you will prosper" (15:29).[57] The theological principle contained in Peter's vision of clean and unclean animals, therefore, remains uncompromised; but some of the shock of its implementation within the churches has been absorbed in the Apostolic Decree. Thus, Luke wants his readers to see that the church has acted with both principle and prudence to preserve its unity (cf. 6:1–7).[58]

Paul's Later Ministry (16:1–26:32)

This same notion of pragmatic compromise explains Paul's relationship to the Jewish law in the concluding portion of Luke's work. The first reference sets the tone for the others. In 16:1–5 Luke says that at the beginning of his extensive later ministry, Paul circumcised his new companion Timothy. Luke also carefully explains Paul's reasons for this action. He circumcised Timothy "because of the Jews who were in those regions, for they all knew that his Father was a Greek" (16:3). Luke does not say that Paul believed Timothy should be circumcised since Timothy was a Jew and Jews, even if they were Christians, should continue to keep the law. The way Luke puts the matter implies instead that Paul himself did not believe this, but knew that some Jews who did believe it would make trouble for him if Timothy remained uncircumcised. For Luke, Paul's sensible pragmatism, not his theological convictions, led to the circumcision of Timothy. The same celebration of peaceful compromise lies beneath Luke's reference in the next sentence to the Apostolic Decree. Paul, Timothy, and Silas, "as they traveled through the cities, handed over to them for observance the decrees decided by the apostles and elders in Jerusalem" (16:4). "Therefore," Luke continues, "the churches were strengthened in the faith and increased in number day by day" (16:5). Just as the apostolic letter had promised, the triumph of good sense and a generous spirit within the early church had brought with it prosperity.

The theological principle that Gentiles are included within God's people apart from the Mosaic law (10:28, 34–35, 47; 11:17–18; 15:9, 11, 14–19) remains uncompromised in all this; but it is not Luke's emphasis. Luke focuses instead on the prudence with which Christian leaders approached the implementation of this theological principle as they preached the gospel. He wants to show his readers that, although accused of doing so, the early Christians had no desire to upset unnecessarily the social structures and ethnic customs of those to whom they preached, whether Jewish or Gentile (16:21, 35–39; 18:13–15).

This concern comes especially to the fore in Luke's account of Paul's visit to Jerusalem, his arrest, and the official hearings about his case (21:17–26:32). When Paul arrives in Jerusalem, James expresses deep concern over rumors that have circulated among Jewish believers in the area about Paul's view of the law. Many thousands of Jewish believers, he says, think that Paul teaches diaspora Jews to abandon circumcision and the customs Moses gave to them (21:20–21). James wants Paul to put these notions to rest and to demonstrate his own fidelity to the law by undertaking a Nazirite vow and paying the expenses of four others who have done the same (21:23–24). Paul complies with the request (21:26), but again Luke's emphasis lies on the pragmatic value of Paul's complicity. Luke portrays a Paul who believes that Jews, including himself (cf. 18:18), are free to observe their traditional customs. This helps Luke's case that Christians do not carelessly trample on the ancient ethnic traditions of any people; but it is a long way from affirming that Paul believed Jewish Christians must, or even should, keep the Mosaic law.

In the same way, when Paul defends himself against the charges that he speaks against the Jewish people, their law, and their temple (21:28; 24:6), he stresses his respect for Jewish custom. Ananias, the believer who befriended him after his conversion, was "devout according to the law" and "of good repute among all the Jews who dwell" in Jerusalem (22:12). Paul was praying in the temple when God sent him to the Gentiles (22:21). He urges the high priest not to violate the law, and apologizes to him for in ignorance breaking the law's command not to speak evil of the people's ruler (23:3, 5). He affirms that he worships the God of his ancestors and believes everything written in the law and the prophets (24:14; cf. 26:6–7). He appeals to King Agrippa, who knows the "customs and controversies of the Jews," to recognize that he has not offended their ancestral ways (26:3).

None of this implies, however, that for Luke Jewish Christians must remain committed to the Mosaic law. Luke's real concern is revealed in Paul's defense before the governor Festus. "Neither against the law of the Jews, nor against the temple, nor against Caesar," he says, "have I committed any sin" (25:8; cf. 19:37). Paul is innocent of sedition not because he believes that the customs outlined in the Mosaic law remain in force by theological necessity but because the gospel does not overturn societal custom, whether Jewish or Roman.[59]

THE ROLE OF THE MOSAIC LAW
IN LUKE'S NARRATIVE: A SUMMARY

In his two-volume "narrative" Luke's approach to the Mosaic law becomes an important tool for accomplishing his purposes. He writes both as a historian and as an apologist. As a historian he hopes to entertain and instruct his readers with a faithful account of Christian origins. As an apologist, he hopes to show that Christianity affirms the tradition from which it came and respects the customs of the societies in which it exists. With these goals before him, Luke traces the relationship of the believing community to the Mosaic law from pious conformity to its standards as a matter of principle, to the amazed realization that its standards were no longer in effect, to a willingness to engage in pragmatic compromise for the sake of peace and prosperity.

Luke especially wants his readers to see that the early Christians continued to live piously within the boundaries marked out by their ancestral customs until God himself drove them to welcome people from other cultures into their communities. The process by which this happened, he hopes to show, was slow and halting. It was marked by astonishment among some and opposition among others. In the end, however, both Jesus' approach to the law and the church's unity were preserved through sensible compromise, a strategy that the apostle to the Gentiles adopted no less enthusiastically than the apostles and elders in Jerusalem.

By tracing the fate of Jesus' approach to the law in this way, Luke provided his "narrative about the deeds accomplished among us" with a realism appropriate to the genre in which he wrote. He also demonstrated for his cultured readers that the early church affirmed tradition, respected its Jewish origins, and acted sensibly to avoid unnecessary offense to the societies in which it flourished.

NOTES

1. See Jacob Jervell, "The Law in Luke-Acts," *HTR* 64 (1971): 21–36; Matthias Klinghardt, *Gesetz und Volk Gottes: Das lukanische Verständnis des Gesetzes nach Herkunft, Funktion und seinem Ort in der Geschichte des Urchristentums,* WUNT 2.32 (Tübingen: J. C. B. Mohr [Paul Siebeck], 1988); Michael Pettem, "Luke's Great Omission and His View of the Law," *NTS* 42 (1996) 35–54. Philip Francis Esler believes that Luke argued for the complete faithfulness of Christianity to the Mosaic law (*Community and Gospel in Luke-Acts: The Social and Political Motivations of Lucan Theology,* SNTSMS 57 [Cambridge: Cambridge University Press, 1987], 110–30). Since neither Luke's inherited traditions nor his own community exhibited such faithfulness, argues Esler, his Gospel contains generous amounts of material inconsistent with this argument.

2. See Max M. B. Turner, "The Sabbath, Sunday, and the Law in Luke/ Acts," in *From Sabbath to Lord's Day: A Biblical, Historical, and Theological*

Investigation, ed. D. A. Carson (Grand Rapids, Mich.: Zondervan, 1982), 99–158; Craig Blomberg, "The Law in Luke-Acts," *JSNT* 22 (1984): 53–80; and M. A. Seifrid, "Jesus and the Law in Acts," *JSNT* 30 (1987): 39–57.

3. See Jack T. Sanders, *The Jews in Luke-Acts* (Philadelphia: Fortress, 1987), 124–28.

4. As Pettem comments ("Luke's Great Omission and His View of the Law," 38).

5. So S. G. Wilson, *Luke and the Law*, SNTSMS 50 (Cambridge: Cambridge University Press, 1983).

6. Cf. Josephus's use of the term *diēgēsis* in *Antiquities* 11.68; 20.157. Translations of Lucian here and elsewhere belong to H. W. Fowler and F. G. Fowler. For their lively rendering of *The Way to Write History*, see *The Works of Lucian of Samosata*, 4 vols. (Oxford: Oxford University Press, 1905), 2:109–36.

7. See Charles William Fornara, *The Nature of History in Ancient Greece and Rome* (Berkeley, Calif.: University of California Press, 1983), 103–4. On the literary genre of Luke-Acts I follow the conclusions of Gregory E. Sterling, *Historiography and Self-Definition: Josephos, Luke-Acts and Apologetic Historiography*, NovTSup 64 (Leiden: E. J. Brill, 1992), 313–21, 331–89, rather than those of Richard A. Burridge, *What are the Gospels? A Comparison with Graeco-Roman Biography*, SNTSMS 70 (Cambridge: Cambridge University Press, 1992), 103, 202, 244–46; and Charles Talbert, *Reading Acts: A Literary and Theological Commentary on the Acts of the Apostles* (New York: Crossroad, 1997), 6–14.

8. See Seifrid, "Jesus and the Law in Acts," 53.

9. See the references to rumors about Christians and the responses to them in such second-century documents as the *Letter to Diognetus*, Justin Martyr's *First Apology*, and Athenagoras's *Plea Regarding Christians*.

10. *On the True Doctrine: A Discourse against the Christians* (Oxford: Oxford University Press, 1987) 53. This document is R. Joseph Hoffmann's attempt to piece together as much of Celsus's original anti-Christian tractate as possible from quotations in Origen's *Against Celsus*.

11. *On the True Doctrine*, 60–61. F. Gerald Downing has shown that belief in the obligation to observe ancestral customs was ubiquitous in antiquity ("Freedom from the Law in Luke-Acts," *JSNT* 26 [1986] 49–52) .

12. See Brent Kinman, "Luke's Exoneration of John the Baptist," *JTS* 44 (1993): 595–98.

13. Brent Kinman, *Jesus' Entry into Jerusalem in the Context of Lukan Theology and the Politics of His Day*, AGJU 28 (Leiden: E. J. Brill, 1995).

14. Thus, the testimony against Stephen that he claims Jesus "will tear down this place and change the customs that Moses handed down to us" (Acts 6:14) is the product of "false witnesses" (Acts 6:13), and Luke shows that the rumors about Paul teaching Jews to forsake Moses, abandon circumcision, and give up their ethnic customs are false (Acts 21:20–26). Cf. Acts 22:12.

15. Most interpreters of 2:22–39 point out the differences between Luke's

description of the actions of Jesus' parents and what the law actually required, and some have concluded from this that Luke had only a passing acquaintance with the law. The differences between the actions of Jesus' parents and the law's requirements, however, all lie in the direction of going beyond the law's requirements. Luke probably intended for his readers to notice this and to conclude from it that Jesus' parents were people of unusually commendable piety. Cf. Darrell L. Bock, *Luke 1:1–9:50*, BECNT 3A (Grand Rapids, Mich.: Baker, 1994), 235.

16. Cf. the devotion of Anna to the temple in 2:36–37.

17. "One shall not live by bread alone" (4:4; Deut. 8:3); "You shall worship the Lord your God, and him only shall you serve" (4:8; Deut. 6:13; 10:20; cf. 5:9); "You shall not put the Lord your God to the test" (4:12; Deut. 6:16).

18. Josephus and Philo, both roughly contemporaneous with Luke, identified the Mosaic law with Jewish custom for their Gentile readers as a way of gaining acceptance for it. This was a subtle way of persuading their readers that the Mosaic law, as the embodiment of Jewish "custom," should be protected by Rome along with other ancient and distinguished bodies of law. On this see Wilson, *Luke and the Law*, 3–11.

19. On the importance of witnessing to the gospel in Acts, see Hermann Strathmann, "μάρτυς, κτλ.," *TDNT* 4:474–514, here at 492–93; and for the notion that Jesus is asking the leper to testify that God is at work in Jesus, see I. Howard Marshall, *The Gospel of Luke: A Commentary on the Greek Text*, NIGTC (Grand Rapids, Mich.: Eerdmans, 1978), 210.

20. In 17:14 Jesus also tells ten lepers whom he has healed to show themselves to the priests and does not add "as a testimony to them." It is significant, however, that the one leper who gives glory to God by thanking Jesus, and therefore does what God requires, is a Samaritan, who would not have gone to a Jewish priest.

21. These parables all employ biblical symbols of Israel's eschatological deliverance. For the wedding banquet, see Isa. 62:4–5; Hos. 2:14–23. For the garment, see Isa. 51:6, 8; Heb. 1:11. For wine, see Gen. 49:11; Hos. 2:22; 14:7; Joel 3:18; Amos 9:13–14; and Jer. 31:5.

22. Unlike Matthew, who stresses the disciples' hunger, David's hunger, and the need to elevate mercy above sacrifice, Luke offers no humanitarian reasons for this violation of the sabbath. Instead, he only stresses Jesus' authority as the Son of Man to permit this violation of the literal sabbath commandment.

23. Cf. G. B. Caird, *The Gospel of St. Luke*, Pelican Gospel Commentaries (New York: Seabury, 1963), 98–99; Marshall, *Commentary on Luke*, 232; Wilson, *Luke and the Law*, 32–33; C. F. Evans, *Saint Luke*, TPINTC (London: SCM; Philadelphia: Trinity Press International, 1990), 314–15. John Nolland cites Deut. 23:24–25 as support for the activity of Jesus' disciples on the sabbath (*Luke 1–9:20*, WBC 35A [Dallas, Tex.: Word Books, 1989]); but that text only legitimates gleaning from a neighbor's field, which is not the issue.

24. Cf. Klinghardt, *Gesetz und Volk Gottes*, 225, 231.

25. For the definition of "dropsy" (*hydrōpikos*) as massive fluid retention, see John Nolland, *Luke 9:21–18:34*, WBC 35B (Dallas, Tex.: Word Books, 1993), 746.

26. The point of comparison, then, is not, as is sometimes thought, that allowing the chronically ill to suffer for another day is as tragic as allowing an animal to die of thirst or a son to languish in the bottom of a well.

27. See especially Caird, *Gospel of St. Luke*, 17–71; but also François Bovon, *Das Evangelium nach Lukas*, 3 vols., EKK 3 (Zurich: Benziger Verlag; Neukirchen-Vluyn: Neukirchener Verlag, 1989–), 1:271, 2:403; and Darrell L. Bock, *Luke 9:51–24:53*, BECNT 3B (Grand Rapids, Mich.: Baker, 1996), 1218–19.

28. See especially Luke 22:30 and the discussions in Caird, *Gospel of St. Luke*, 100–101; and Bovon, *Evangelium nach Lukas*, 1:280.

29. The only clear echo of the Mosaic law is 6:36, where Jesus adopts the form, if not the content, of Lev. 11:45.

30. Wilson believes that Jesus only affirms the law in the parable and does not supplement it (*Luke and the Law*, 14–17, 28–29). This attitude toward the law, he argues, stands in tension with the attitude expressed in Luke 18:18–23 where Jesus adds to the law his own, more stringent requirement. If my understanding of 10:25–36 is correct, however, no tension exists between the two stories.

31. On the law's concern for the poor and oppressed as a consequence of God's gracious redemption of Israel from bondage, see Paul D. Hanson, *The People Called: The Growth of Community in the Bible* (San Francisco: Harper & Row, 1986), 46–48.

32. For the first option, see Joseph A. Fitzmyer, *The Gospel according to Luke X–XXIV*, AB 28A (New York: Doubleday, 1985), 947; for the second, see the comments of Nigel Turner in J. H. Moulton, W. F. Howard, and Nigel Turner, *A Grammar of New Testament Greek*, 3 vols., 3rd ed. (Edinburgh: T & T Clark, 1908–63), 3:247; for the third, see Bock, *Luke 9:51–24:53*, 1114–15; and for the fourth, see Theodor Zahn, *Das Evangelium Lucas* (Wuppertal: R. Brockhaus Verlag, 1988; orig. ed., 1920), 480.

33. Jesus' statement in 11:42 that the Pharisees ought to have both tithed their herbs and attended to justice and the love of God does not mean that Jesus affirmed the continuing validity of the Mosaic law. Since Jesus has just identified purity with inward rather than outward matters (11:41), effectively nullifying the purity regulations of the Mosaic law, it is more likely that he simply intends to criticize the Pharisees for missing the really central elements of God's requirements: love for neighbor and God (cf. Luke 10:25–28).

34. Bock (*Luke 9:51-24:53*, 1520) comments that Zacchaeus may be following the law's requirement for repayment of a stolen animal (Exod. 22:1; 2 Sam. 12:6). This is possible; but since Zacchaeus could have fulfilled his obligation with only the repayment of the original sum plus an additional 20

percent (Lev. 5:16; Num. 5:7), he has gone beyond the law's requirements. This willingness to go beyond the law is reminiscent of Jesus' claim that the rich ruler, in addition to keeping the commandments, must sell everything he has and distribute it to the poor (18:22).

35. For the fourfold division of the passage, see Marshall, *Gospel of Luke*, 626. For the translation of the hotly disputed word *biazetai* as "urgently invited," see the definitive discussion by Philippe H. Menoud, "Le sens du verbe *biazetai* dans Lc 16,16," in *Mélanges Bibliques en hommage au R.P. Béda Rigaux*, ed. Albert Descamps and André de Halleux (Gembloux: Éditions J. Duculot, 1970), 207–12.

36. On Luke's division of salvation history into two periods, see Bock, *Luke 9:51–24:53*, 1351.

37. Cf. Zahn, *Evangelium des Lucas*, 580–81; Marshall, *Gospel of Luke*, 627; Fitzmyer, *Gospel according to Luke X–XXIV*, 1116; Bock, *Luke 9:51–24:53*, 1354–56.

38. Fitzmyer, *Gospel according to Luke X–XXIV*, 1119.

39. Marshall, *Gospel of Luke*, 631; cf. Wilson, *Luke and the Law*, 51.

40. Bock, *Luke 9:51–24:53*, 1356–57.

41. Nolland argues that 16:17 announces the eternal validity of the moral norms of the Mosaic law and that 16:18 intensifies rather than relaxes the law (*Luke 9:21–18:34*, 821–23). This understanding of 16:18, however, does not sufficiently account for (1) the relegation in 16:16 of the law and the prophets to a past era, (2) the difference between 16:18 and the implied permission to divorce in Deut. 24:1–4, and (3) the absence from 16:18 of any argument that it is somehow a legitimate interpretation of the law.

42. CD 4:19–5:6 attempts to explain its prohibition of taking more than one wife during a lifetime by reference to Mic. 2:6; Gen. 1:27; 7:19; and Deut. 17:17. 11QTemple[a] 57:15–19 envisions Israel's ideal king as married to only one woman as long as they both shall live, an ideal that the Qumran community may have also applied to the king's subjects. See Joseph A. Fitzmyer, "Divorce among First Century Palestinian Jews," in *H. L. Ginsberg Volume*, ErIsr 14 (Jerusalem: Israel Exploration Society, 1978), 103–10.

43. Cf. M. Turner, "Sabbath, Sunday, and the Law in Luke/Acts," 110–11.

44. C. K. Barrett, *A Critical and Exegetical Commentary on the Acts of the Apostles*, 2 vols., ICC (Edinburgh: T & T Clark, 1994–99), 1:335.

45. Cf. Craig C. Hill, *Hellenists and Hebrews: Reappraising Division within the Earliest Church* (Minneapolis: Fortress, 1992), 67–81.

46. Against the interpretation of Jürgen Roloff (*Die Apostelgeschichte*, NTD 5 [Göttingen: Vandenhoeck & Ruprecht, 1988] 170) and Pettem ("Luke's Great Omission and His View of the Law," 42–43), the critical issue is food rather than fellowship. Acts 10:13–14, 11:7–8, and the comment of the circumcised people in 11:3 show this clearly.

47. See Hans Conzelmann, *Acts of the Apostles*, Hermeneia (Philadelphia: Fortress, 1987), 80; and Barrett, *Acts*, 491–98.

48. It is true that since Jesus had already moved in this direction when he traced true purity to inner purity in Luke 11:41, God's intervention should have been less surprising than it was. But Luke's ancient readers would have found no problem with this: such are the oddities of life that the faithful historian will inevitably record. Cf. Seifrid, "Jesus and the Law in Acts," 43.

49. See David P. Moessner, *Lord of the Banquet: The Literary and Theological Significance of the Lukan Travel Narrative* (Minneapolis: Fortress, 1989), 294–307.

50. C. K. Barrett claims that Jews did not view the law as an "intolerable load" but as a "privilege" and a "joy" ("Apostles in Council and Conflict," *AusBR* 31 [1983]: 14–32, here at 18). Cf. Conzelmann, *Acts of the Apostles*, 117. This is true but misses the point of Peter's comment. He is not denying that individual Jews enjoyed doing God's will but that, as the biblical story of Israel reveals, the nation's history has been characterized by stiff-necked disobedience to the law. See, e.g., Deut. 10:16; Jer. 7:36; 17:23; and the discussion in Rudolf Pesch, *Die Apostelgeschichte*, 2 vols., EKK 5 (Zurich: Benziger Verlag; Neukirchen-Vluyn: Neukirchener Verlag, 1986), 2:78.

51. The list in Acts 15:20 differs slightly from the lists in 15:29 and 21:25. In the last two occurrences of the list, "food offered to idols" replaces "pollution by idols," and the other items appear in the order, "blood, what is strangled, and sexual immorality."

52. See, e.g., Conzelmann, *Acts of the Apostles*, 118–19; Jervell, "Law in Luke-Acts," 32–33; Pesch, *Apostelgeschichte*, 2:81; Roloff, *Apostelgeschichte*, 232–33. Klinghardt believes that the decree corresponds in a general way to the Mosaic law's prescriptions concerning resident aliens (*Gesetz und Volk Gottes*, 205).

53. Lev. 17:8–9 (cf. 17:3, 5) instructs both "the house of Israel" and "aliens" to bring their sacrifices to the priest rather than offer them on their own in the field, but the relationship between this and the first item in the decree is not close (Acts 15:29; 21:25). As Wilson points out (*Luke and the Law*, 88–99), the meaning of the rare term translated here "what is strangled" (*pniktos*) is not clear. It may refer to food prepared by stewing rather than to meat from a strangled animal.

54. Some interpreters believe that James is issuing a form of the "Noachic rules"—a list of minimal ethical norms against which Gentiles would be judged. Although such lists apparently circulated in the Second Temple period, they do not closely resemble the Apostolic Decree. See, e.g., *Jub.* 7:20–21; *Sib. Or.* 4:24–39; and the discussion in Alan F. Segal, *Paul the Convert: The Apostolate and Apostasy of Saul the Pharisee* (New Haven, Conn.: Yale University Press, 1990), 194–201.

55. See Seifrid, "Jesus and the Law in Acts," 47–51.

56. For an example of the fascination that the story of Israel's seduction by the Midianite women held for some first-century Jews, see Josephus's elaborate retelling of it in *Jewish Antiquities* 4.126–55.

57. See Blomberg, "Law in Luke-Acts," 66; and, on the translation "you will prosper" for *eu praxete* see Seifrid, "Jesus and the Law in Luke-Acts," 56 n. 41.

58. If this interpretation of the decree is correct, then the notoriously diffi-cult statement in 15:21 probably refers not to the locations at which Gentiles can find out more about the Mosaic law but to the widespread knowledge of the Mosaic law among Jews and the necessity in light of it to avoid offense to them. For the interpretive options, see I. Howard Marshall, *The Acts of the Apostles*, TNTC (Grand Rapids, Mich.: Eerdmans, 1980), 254; and for this choice among them, see M. Turner, "Sabbath, Sunday, and the Law in Luke/Acts," 117; and Blomberg, "Law in Luke-Acts," 66.

59. Cf. M. Turner, "Sabbath, Sunday, and the Law in Luke/Acts," 123.

7

The Law in the New Testament:
A Comparison of Five Voices

WE HAVE NOW HEARD FIVE NEW TESTAMENT VOICES speak on the role of the Mosaic law in Christian theology and practice. We must next hear the voices together to discover their distinct emphases and whether on some issues all five speak in unison.

THREE DISTINCTIVE EMPHASES

In their approach to the Mosaic law, the authors we have studied can be placed in three categories:

1. Paul and Matthew stand together in their interest in the ethical use of the Mosaic law.
2. John and the author of Hebrews stand together in their symbolic use of the law.
3. Luke stands by himself in his use of the law not only in ethical and symbolic ways but also to construct the story of God's saving purposes.

Paul, Matthew, and the Ethical Use of the Law

Both Paul and Matthew seem to be interested in what we can call the ethical significance of the Mosaic law. Each in his own way tackles the question of why Christians do not live by the Mosaic law, and each fills the vacuum left by the absence of the Mosaic law with an alternative means of regulating Christian life.

For Paul, believers are not obligated to the Mosaic law for two basic reasons. First, since the Mosaic law is a specifically Jewish law, a requirement that Christians live by the Mosaic law is equivalent to the exclusion of Gentiles from the people of God (Gal. 2:15–16; 5:2–4; Rom. 3:27–30; 4:13–17). God has shown that he welcomes Gentiles among his people apart from their acceptance of the Jewish law by sending his Spirit to them after they have responded in faith to the preaching of the gospel (Gal. 3:2–5). Second, the law's term of service within God's redemptive purposes has expired. God's people were not faithful to the law's requirements because, like all people, they are indelibly tainted with sin (Gal. 2:15–16; 3:10–11; Rom. 1:18–3:20; 5:12–21). The law demonstrates their sinfulness, is used by sin to increase evil, and pronounces the just sentence of condemnation upon the sinner (1 Cor. 15:56; Gal. 3:19; 2 Cor. 3:6–11; Rom. 3:19–20; 4:15; 5:20; 7:7–25). These circumstances nevertheless serve God's redemptive purposes by preparing the way for the atoning death of Christ (Gal. 3:19, 22; Rom. 3:9–19). Now that the era of God's redeeming work has dawned, the law's role in salvation history has come to an end (Gal. 3:19; 2 Cor. 3:7, 11, 14; Rom. 7:6; 10:4).

Some people misunderstood this approach to the Mosaic law as a claim that the Christian was subject to no external moral authority. Within Paul's churches some began claiming, "All things are permissible" (1 Cor. 6:12; 10:23), and Paul's opponents spread the rumor that he encouraged people to sin (Rom. 3:8; cf. 6:1, 15). Paul considered it important, therefore, to fill the ethical void left by the absence of the Mosaic law. He refers to this element of his teaching variously as his "ways in Christ Jesus," "the law of Christ," the "tradition," "the fruit of the Spirit," and the received "pattern of teaching" (2 Thess. 2:15; 3:6; 1 Cor. 4:17; 9:21; 11:2; Gal. 5:22–23; 6:2; Rom. 6:17).[1] It intersects with the Mosaic law at several places, most notably at the Decalogue and the love command (Gal. 5:14; Rom. 13:8–10), but excludes circumcision, traditional sabbath keeping, and dietary observance (1 Cor. 7:19; Gal. 5:6; 6:15; Rom. 14:5–6, 14). In addition, Paul's spiritualizing of the temple and sacrificial cult (1 Cor. 3:9–17; 6:19; Phil. 2:17; 4:18; 2 Cor 6:14–7:1; Rom. 12:1), his belief that Jesus' death atoned for all past human sin (Rom. 3:25–26), and his admonitions to submit to the Roman government (Rom. 13:1–7) imply the abrogation of the cultic and civil parts of the law.

Matthew answers the question of why Christians do not regulate their lives by the Mosaic law in a different way. For Matthew, Christians do not follow the details of the Mosaic law because Jesus, their authoritative teacher, did not do so. Jesus permitted his disciples to harvest grain on the sabbath to satisfy their hunger although they could have made meal preparations the day before (12:1–8). He pursued his vocation as a healer on the sabbath, even when the healings could easily have taken place on another day (12:9–14). He taught that "it is not what enters the mouth that makes the person unclean" (15:11), implying that the Mosaic dietary restrictions were no longer in force, and he authoritatively revised the Mosaic law's implied permission to divorce (5:31–32; 19:3–12). If this is the path Jesus followed, then his disciples must join him on the way.

Why did Jesus deviate from the Mosaic law? Matthew answers this question both in the antitheses (5:17–48) and in Jesus' interaction with the rich young man (19:16–22). The Mosaic law was a provisional statement of God's moral standard designed to accommodate the social and political conditions of a theocracy. It pushed God's ultimate ethical concerns as far as they could go among a hard-hearted people; but it was limited by the sinfulness of those to whom it was given. In Jesus' ethical teaching, however, God's ultimate ethical standard is expressed with unmistakable clarity and is required of everyone inside the boundaries of God's new, eschatologically constituted people. In Jesus' teaching, therefore, the Mosaic law has reached fulfillment (5:17).

It is sometimes said that Matthew had a more optimistic view of the human ability to fulfill the law than did Paul. Thus, Matthew stresses obedience as the path to righteousness, whereas Paul proclaims that since obedience is impossible, the believer must rely solely on God's grace to attain a righteous status before him. This reading of Matthew occasionally provides the foundation for claiming that Matthew stands opposed to Paul on the issue of the law.[2]

It is true that Matthew, unlike Paul, never refers to righteousness as a status but always as an ethical quality, and that Matthew makes no use of the notion, so common in Paul, that the Spirit enables believers to do the will of God. But if we are careful to take into account the wider context of each author's comments on the human ability to keep the law, we discover that they are not far apart on the relationship between human sinfulness and God's ethical standards. When Paul speaks of the human inability to fulfill the law, he is describing those who do not "live according to the Spirit"—those whose minds are ensnared by the flesh, who are hostile to God, and who are, therefore, unable to please him (Rom. 8:5–8). Although the point is not uncontroversial, it is difficult to see how these terms can describe believers. On the other hand, when in Matthew's Gospel Jesus calls for a righteousness that exceeds the righteousness of the scribes and Pharisees (5:20), and when he advocates a perfection that imitates the perfection of the Father (5:48), he is speaking to "his disciples" (5:1), not to humanity generally.

Once we understand this contextual difference, we discover that Matthew and Paul are in harmony at this point. Thus they agree with each other, and with the biblical prophets, that the hearts of those who are estranged from God are hopelessly hard. Paul often ascribes the inability of unbelievers to please God to their foolish, lustful, hard, impenitent, and veiled hearts (Rom. 1:21, 24; 2:5; 2 Cor. 3:15). Matthew too believes that the unwillingness of people to conform to God's standard of perfection lies in the hardness of their hearts. Adultery through divorce and other violations of the Decalogue, he says, derive from hard and evil hearts (15:18–19; 19:3–9; cf. 5:28). Similarly, evil words come from evil hearts (12:34; 15:18), and a heart devoted to material treasure leads to rejection of Jesus' call to perfection (6:21; 19:21–22).

On the other hand, Paul stresses as clearly as Matthew the need for Christians to submit to what Paul calls "the law of God" or "the law of Christ." Christians should keep the commandments of God (1 Cor. 7:19), fulfill the law of Christ (Gal. 6:2), and submit to the law of God (implied by Rom. 8:7). For Matthew as much as for Paul, therefore, the unbelieving human heart is too corrupt to obey fully God's moral requirements, and for Paul as much as for Matthew, faith in Jesus bears the fruit of conformity to God's ethical standards.[3]

John, Hebrews, and the Symbolic Use of the Law

John and the author of Hebrews show only a marginal interest in what we have called the ethical use of the Mosaic law. John speaks of a new commandment (13:34), and the author of Hebrews composes a few paragraphs of ethical exhortation, some of which may echo the Mosaic law (13:4–5; cf. Exod. 20:14; Deut. 5:18; 31:6–8). Both imply that the literal observance of the sabbath is no longer necessary (John 5:8, 18; 9:14; Heb. 4:9–10). But these matters do not reach the heart of either author's approach to the Mosaic law. For John and the author of

Hebrews, the central institutions of the Mosaic law point ahead to Christ. Moses wrote of him (John 1:45; 5:39, 46) and suffered for him (Heb. 11:26). Jesus absorbs the significance of the temple, the heavenly bread of the wilderness wandering, the paschal lamb, and the central rituals of the feast of Booths (John 1:29; 2:19–21; 6:31–51; 7:37–39; 8:12; 19:36). He is the ultimate high priest who offers the perfect and final sacrifice in heaven's ideal sanctuary (Heb. 2:17–3:1; 4:14–5:10; 6:20–10:18). For both authors then, the Mosaic law is viewed primarily as a collection of symbols whose full significance is revealed in Jesus.

This means that for both John and the author of Hebrews, those who have opposed or deviated from Christianity have settled for an impoverished understanding of the Mosaic law. Jesus' unbelieving Jewish opponents in John's Gospel have become mired in the details of conformity to the Mosaic law and have missed the grand scale on which the law points to Jesus (5:9b–18; 9:16; 7:45–52; 18:28; 19:31). The Christians for whom Hebrews was written, by casting a wistful glance at the synagogue, have turned away from the ultimate atoning sacrifice to the law's slight and provisional outline of that sacrifice (8:5; 10:1). For both John and the author of Hebrews the entire system by which Jews govern their lives has been overwhelmed and carried away by Christian revelation.

Despite this large amount of common ground, the specific use to which the author of Hebrews puts the law in his argument differs from the way in which John uses it. For the author of Hebrews, the law is primarily an instrument through which the priesthood and the sacrifices, particularly the Day of Atonement sacrifice, are regulated. Every aspect of Jesus' priesthood, sacrifice, and tabernacle is superior to its counterpart in the Mosaic law; but the law nevertheless provides the theological structure for making sense of Christ's death. Without the theological concept of atonement provided by the Mosaic law, Jesus' death is simply another human death. This results in a detailed symmetry of correspondence between Jesus and his work on one side and the high priests and their work on the other.

The way in which Jesus fulfills the Mosaic law in John's Gospel, on the other hand, is more general. The point of John's association between Jesus and the temple, the bread from heaven, light and water ceremonies at the feast of Booths, and the paschal lamb is to show that all the fundamental institutions of Judaism point to Jesus on a massive scale. It is true that Jesus is the bread from heaven for those who eat his flesh and drink his blood, that the water he provides is the Holy Spirit, and that, like the paschal lamb, he was slain; but in each case the correspondence is only briefly mentioned, or, as with eating Jesus' flesh and drinking his blood, its meaning remains ambiguous. Thus, whereas the author of Hebrews is interested in arguing for a detailed correspondence between Jesus and a single section of the law, John is primarily interested in showing that the law as a whole points to Jesus.

Luke-Acts and the Law in Salvation History

Luke uses the Mosaic law in ways reminiscent of the other four authors, but adds to their approaches his own distinctive understanding of the law. Like Matthew, Luke is interested in the inner connection between Jesus' ethical teaching and the Mosaic law. This inner connection is not explored in the Sermon on the Plain, as it is in Matthew's Sermon on the Mount; it is set forth in the parables Jesus tells during his journey to Jerusalem. Thus, the connection appears in the extension of the law's command of love for neighbor to include love for the enemy in the parable of the Good Samaritan (Luke 10:25–37). It is subtly present in the parable of the Prodigal Son, where the Father, rather than stoning his rebellious son, treats him mercifully (Luke 15:11–32). It becomes explicit in the claim of the parable of the Rich Man and Lazarus that Moses and the prophets agree with Jesus on the issue of caring for the poor (Luke 16:19–31). Luke's interest in the inner theological connection between Jesus' teaching and the Mosaic law is not as prominent as it is in Matthew; but it is present nevertheless.

Like Paul, Luke is interested in whether Christians must keep the Mosaic law. Gentile Christians do not have to be circumcised in order "to be saved" (Acts 15:1, 6–11, 19), and, if our understanding of the relevant passages is correct, dietary restrictions are not binding on Gentile Christians (Luke 11:41; Acts 10:1–11:18).

On the continued observance of the law among Jewish Christians, Paul and Luke have a different emphasis; but there is no difference between them on the substance of the matter. Paul could hardly be clearer about his convictions. Jews and Gentiles stand on the same ground before God: they share a common plight of violation of God's law, and they are included within God's people on the same gracious basis (Gal. 2:15–16; Rom. 1:18–3:30). If observance of the Mosaic law is not necessary for the Gentile, it is also not necessary for the Jew. Observance of the law is therefore neither here nor there—it can be observed or neglected for purposes of expediency, and the church should avoid offense either to those with scruples about its observance or to those who view observance as unnecessary (1 Cor. 7:19; 9:20–21; Gal. 5:6; 6:15; Rom. 2:28–29; 14:1–15:13). It is critical, on one hand, not to neglect the essential ethical commands of God (1 Cor. 7:19) and, on the other, not to compromise the principle of justification by faith alone (Gal. 6:15).

Luke hopes to show that the early Christians did not forbid the continued observance of the law among Jews. Thus, it is important to Luke that many priests joined the faith, that "many thousands" of zealously observant Jews embraced the gospel, and that Paul himself agreed to demonstrate his piety by undertaking a public display of his appreciation for the Mosaic law (Acts 6:7; 21:17–26). Luke has underlined all this to prove that the early Christians did not advocate cultural sedition, but, as far as possible, sought to accommodate traditional ethnic customs. On the critical issue of whether such conformity to the law is necessary for the salvation of the Jews, however, Luke and Paul are united. Luke's two great protagonists, Paul and Peter, agree that the law of Moses cannot justify (Acts 13:38) and that both Jew and Gentile are saved from the plight of universal sin by God's grace through faith (Acts 15:8–11). It is often said that Luke and Paul diverge on the continuing validity of the law for Jewish Christianity and the universal need for justification.[4] In light of these texts, however, it is difficult to see how this claim can be correct.

Luke's approach also has affinities with the approach of John and the author of Hebrews. Their symbolic use of the Mosaic law closely identified its literal observance with the Jewish people. Whereas neither would have conceded that the law belongs to the Jews (for both believed that Christ fulfilled the law), neither John nor the author of Hebrews attempts to deny that at the level of its literal observance the Mosaic law is intertwined with the Jewish people. In John the Jews are the champions of sabbath observance (5:18; 9:16; 19:31), testimony by means of two witnesses (8:13), executing blasphemers by stoning (8:59; 10:31), and cultic purity (18:28). The law is clearly "their law" (15:25). Similarly in Hebrews unbelieving Jews participate in the literal sacrifices, based on matters of food and drink and various washings (9:10; 13:9–10). Christians have a new commandment and an altar from which those who serve in the tabernacle have no right to eat; but the literal observance of the law belongs to the Jews (13:9–11).

For Luke too, the Mosaic law is the special possession of the Jewish people. He communicates this in the Gospel by using the term "custom" to define the law. Priests serve in the temple according to "custom"; pious parents redeem their firstborn son "according to the custom of the law"; and people converge on Jerusalem for Passover according to "custom" (1:49; 2:22, 47). In Acts, Christian Jews continue to observe the Mosaic law zealously (21:20), while Gentile Christians would do well merely to keep a few Jewish conventions and thus make social contact between the two groups easier (15:29).

Despite all this common ground between Luke-Acts and the other four documents, elements of Luke's approach to the law are distinctive. Only Luke has teased a defense of Christianity out of the conservative approach to the law among early Christians. He shows that despite the radical approach of Jesus to the Mosaic law during his ministry, the early church often piously conformed to the requirements of the law. Along with most Greeks, Romans, and Jews, they too believed that ancient and divinely revealed ethnic customs should not be changed lightly. Luke wants his readers to see that despite the tendency of the early church to take this principle too far (Acts 11:2; 15:1), it is a commendable instinct and refutes the notion that Christianity is bent on corrupting the fabric of Roman society.

The Differences among the Five Voices: A Summary

Paul, Matthew, John, the author of Hebrews, and Luke, therefore, each make a distinctive contribution to the canonical understanding of the law of Moses. Paul and Matthew stand together in their use of the law to discuss Christian ethics. Paul emphasizes the discontinuity between the age of the Spirit, in which righteousness is given to those who have faith apart from anything they do, and the time of condemnation, in which people were justly condemned for transgressing the law. Matthew emphasizes the requirement that Jesus' followers obey the teaching of Jesus and thereby fulfill the ultimate will of God toward which the law of Moses pointed. These emphases are different, but Paul and Matthew agree on the fundamental matters of the hardness of the human heart among those who do not accept Jesus and the expectation for obedience to God's will among those who do.

John and Hebrews stand together in their attempt to demonstrate the full-scale fulfillment of the law in the Christian dispensation. Neither shows much interest in the ethical use of the law; but both demonstrate Jesus' complete fulfillment of the law. John does this by claiming that Jesus has fulfilled the law on a broad scale. The author of Hebrews focuses more narrowly on Jesus' detailed fulfillment of the law's regulations concerning priesthood and sacrifice.

Luke-Acts has affinities with both pairs but stands apart from them in its positive use of the Mosaic law for apologetic purposes. Like Matthew and Paul, Luke is interested in the ethical use of the law. Like John and the author of Hebrews, he has a special interest in identifying the law with the Jewish people. Unlike any of the others, however, Luke used historical information about the conservative attitude of the early Christians toward the Mosaic law to defend Christians generally against the charge of sedition.

THE COMMON CONTRIBUTION

We now turn to the common ground among all five authors. On three basic issues, all are united:

1. The Mosaic law no longer regulates the lives of God's people.
2. A new "law" has taken its place.
3. The Mosaic law remains valid, but in a new way.

The Temporal Role of the Mosaic Law

All five authors agree that the Mosaic law is no longer the authoritative norm by which God's people should live. The arguments of Paul and the author of Hebrews are clearest on this point and are so similar that a literary connection between the two seems likely.[5] Both authors argue for the temporal nature of the Mosaic law by associating it with angelic mediation (Gal. 3:19; Heb. 2:2) and with the flesh (Gal. 4:23–26; Heb. 7:16; cf. 7:5, 15–18, 28).[6] Both also claim that since the law was incapable of providing a way out of the plight of sin, God provided the way through the death of Christ (Gal. 2:21; 3:10–14; Rom. 3:20; 8:2–4; Heb. 9:9–10, 15). The two authors recognize the divine origin and glorious nature of the Mosaic covenant (2 Cor. 3:11; Rom. 9:4; Heb. 2:1–4; 12:18–29), but both also claim that the death of Jesus inaugurates a new covenant (1 Cor. 11:25; Rom. 3:21–26; Heb. 9:15–10:18), rendering the old covenant inoperative and fulfilling the prophecy of Jer. 31:31–34 (2 Cor. 3:6–11, 14; Heb. 8:6–13; 10:16–17). The sweeping nature of the argument in each case makes it impossible to claim that the two authors describe the obsolescence of only certain parts of the Mosaic law or merely criticize the law's misuse: the entire Mosaic dispensation has reached its divinely appointed end (2 Cor. 3:13; Rom. 10:4; Heb. 7:12).

John is less explicit about the law's end, but the implications of his handling of the law are clear. John implies that since Jesus is the temple, literal worship in the temple will cease for believers (2:19–21; 4:20–24). It is only a short step from this to the thought that if Jesus sums up the significance of Passover (1:29; 19:36) and the feast of Booths (7:37–39; 8:12), literal observance of those festivals will also cease for believers. Similarly, if Jesus works on the sabbath in imitation of God and tells others to do the same (5:8, 18; 9:11, 14), then literal sabbath observance has disappeared. In addition, Jesus' new commandment (13:34) implies that the old commandment is no longer in force.

Matthew and Luke present the difficult cases. Each author includes a passage that affirms the continuing validity of the Mosaic law in every particular (Matt. 5:17–20; Luke 16:17), and each includes another passage that, at least on first reading, appears to confirm this stance (Matt. 23:1–3, 23; Luke 11:42). In addition, a number of scholars have observed that each author edits his sources in ways that play down Jesus' radical stance toward the law.[7]

All of this, however, must be placed alongside elements of a radical approach to the law in each work. Although Matthew softens the blow of Jesus' radical stance toward the sabbath and forbidden food, the blow still hits its mark. Matthew shows that Jesus pursued his vocation of healing on the sabbath, even when he might have healed on another day (12:9–14). Similarly, despite Matthew's changes to his Markan source, the substance of Jesus' comments on real defilement remains the same: if one is defiled only by what comes out of the mouth and heart, then what goes in does not matter (Mark 7:18–23; Matt. 15:17–20).[8] On divorce, the taking of oaths, and retaliation Jesus also nullifies the letter of the law (5:31–48; 19:3–9).

The situation is similar with Luke. Although the task of locating his

view of the law is complicated by the historical and apologetic purposes of his two volumes, it seems reasonable to assume that Luke's
own understanding of the Mosaic law can be found in Jesus' approach
to it in the Gospel and in the approach of God himself in Acts. In the
Gospel Jesus underlines the newness of his teaching with three programmatic parables and then demonstrates this newness in action by
working on the sabbath and allowing his disciples to do so (5:33–6:11).
He then issues his own law in the Sermon on the Plain to his own
newly constituted people (6:12–49). In the teaching that follows he
identifies real purity with inner purity and claims that the evidence of
such purity is almsgiving (11:37–41). In Acts God himself urges Peter
to disregard the dietary stipulations of the Mosaic law and to accept
the hospitality of Gentiles (10:13; 11:7). It is difficult to see how Luke
could have taken a different view of the food laws.

For all five authors, then, the authority of the Mosaic law to regulate the lives of God's people has passed away. In this sense, Jesus'
proclamation, ministry, death, and resurrection represent a break with
the past.

The Advent of a New Covenant and a New "Law"

In place of the Mosaic covenant, all five authors put something new.
The author of Hebrews speaks of a new covenant in which transgression finds atonement and the conscience finds cleansing (Heb. 8:8–13;
9:15; 10:11–18). Matthew and John imply that Jesus' ethical teaching
has replaced the Mosaic law (Matt. 5:1–7:29; John 13:34; 14:15, 21,
23–24; 15:10–17). Paul and Luke embrace both notions (1 Cor. 9:21;
11:25; Gal 6:2; 2 Cor 3:6–11; Rom 3:21–30; Luke 22:20; 6:12–49).

Three authors describe Jesus' death as the inauguration of a new
covenant. Luke and Paul both use the phrase "the new covenant" in
their record of Jesus' words at his final Passover meal with his disciples
(1 Cor. 11:25; Luke 22:20). As the definite article shows, the phrase is
a deliberate echo of the one passage in the scriptures of Israel that
speaks explicitly of "a new covenant": Jer. 31:31–34. Jeremiah claims
that when this new situation comes, God will forgive the iniquity of
his people and remember their sins no more (31:34). Luke links Jesus'
death to this element of the new covenant when he records Jesus'
statement that the wine within the cup at his last Passover meal is the
new covenant in Jesus' blood and that this blood is being poured out

"for you" (Luke 22:20). Paul appears to have in mind the same connection between the new covenant and the forgiveness of sins when he contrasts the new covenant with "the letter" that "kills" (2 Cor. 3:6). In Hebrews, this becomes a major theme. Jesus' death constitutes a sacrifice of atonement and a blood sacrifice for purification. It therefore effects both the forgiveness of sins and the purification of the conscience (9:9, 14–15). To the author of Hebrews, these two elements of Jesus' sacrificial death answer precisely to the promises in Jeremiah's prophecy of the new covenant that God would write his laws on the hearts of his people and would forgive their sins (10:14–18). For Luke, Paul, and the author of Hebrews, therefore, the old Mosaic covenant has been replaced with a new covenant, and this turn of events was anticipated by scripture itself.

Four of the five authors appear to claim that Jesus has established a new "law" for his disciples. This is perhaps clearest in Matthew and Luke. Both tell the story of Jesus in a way that implies a comparison between Jesus and Moses and between Jesus' ethical teaching and the Mosaic law. In Matthew, Jesus gives a summary of his ethical teaching from a mountain, just as Moses received the law from God on Mount Sinai (5:1). Jesus demonstrates in this summary how his ethical teaching both contrasts with parts of the Mosaic law and develops from themes implicit within it (5:21–48). Luke too portrays Jesus as a prophet like Moses (Luke 4:24; 7:16; 13:33; 24:19; Acts 3:22–23; 7:37) and compares his redemptive work to the exodus (Luke 9:31). As in Matthew, the Lukan Jesus delivers a summary of his ethical teaching in a geographical setting that recalls both Sinai, where Moses received the law, and the plains of Moab, where he delivered it for a second time to Israel (Luke 6:12, 17). Both Matthew and Luke end their summaries of Jesus' ethical teaching just as the Mosaic law concludes, by pronouncing a blessing on those who keep it and a curse on those who disobey (Matt. 7:24-27; Luke 6:46-49).

John too portrays Jesus as a new Moses. Moses rescued the people by lifting up a serpent; God does the same through Jesus by lifting him up on the cross (3:14–15). God provided bread for the people in the wilderness through the hand of Moses; Jesus too supplies bread from heaven, but of a kind that gives eternal life to those who eat it (6:31–51). Unlike Matthew and Luke, John does not connect this theme with Jesus' ethical teaching. Still, Jesus issues a "new commandment" to his disciples—they are to love one another (13:34; cf. 15:10–17)—and claims that if his disciples love him they will keep his "commandments" (14:15, 21; cf. 15:10, 14). The newness of the commandment probably lies in the recognition that it replaces the old commandments found in the Mosaic law.[9]

It is often said that Paul believed the Mosaic law had been replaced in the new era by the leading of the Spirit. Unlike the Mosaic law, it is thought, Pauline ethics lacks specificity. Instead, on this view, Paul draws from a wide range of ethical principles current in his time, both Jewish and Greco-Roman, to show how the basic principle of love for others is to be put into practice within the Spirit-directed community. Thus, Paul claims that those who are led by the Spirit are not under law (Gal. 5:18) and speaks of believers fulfilling the law (Gal. 5:14; Rom. 8:4; 13:8) rather than doing it. By walking in step with the Spirit, believers fulfill the law as a matter of course (Gal. 5:23) and so they do not "do" the law as if it were a list of obligatory good deeds. The thought that Paul's ethical advice arose from a "new law" is to these interpreters anathema.[10]

Yet evidence exists for just such a concrete body of ethical demands. Paul speaks explicitly of "the law of Christ" (Gal. 6:2; cf. 1 Cor. 9:21), a phrase that apparently refers to the law's command, renewed and strengthened by Jesus, to love others, even one's enemy. In addition, he refers to authoritative bodies of ethical tradition that he hands on to his churches (1 Cor. 4:17; 1 Thess. 4:1–2; 2 Thess. 3:6; cf. 1 Cor. 11:2, 17; 2 Thess. 2:15). It is certainly true that the love command holds the most important place in Paul's ethical teaching, that the Spirit's leading plays a critical role, and that Paul's ethical advice is far less comprehensive than the many concrete laws of the Sinaitic covenant. Nevertheless, Paul apparently handed on a body of ethical instructions to his churches to give them specific ethical guidance, and he considered them so generally authoritative that he issued them "everywhere in every church" (1 Cor. 4:17).[11]

Thus, a concrete body of ethical teaching replaces the instructions of the Mosaic law in Matthew, Luke-Acts, John, and the Pauline epistles.[12] If by the term "law" we mean detailed legislation in which, to paraphrase Hebrews, every transgression and infraction receives a commensurate penalty, then we cannot properly call this teaching a new law. But if we use the term more broadly to refer to specific ethical guidelines backed up by a general promise of blessing for obedience and woe for disobedience, the phrase "new law" seems to be an appropriate way of describing this material.[13]

The Continuing Validity of the Mosaic Law

Despite the replacement of the Mosaic covenant with a new covenant and a new "law," all five authors agree that the Mosaic law continues in some sense to be valid. It is valid both because it provides the theological structure for the gospel and because it constitutes a rich repository of specific ethical material for the newly constituted people of God.

The gospel matches the structure of the Mosaic law in various ways in the thinking of all five authors. The gospel and the Mosaic law are each constituent parts of a covenant (2 Cor. 3:6; Matt. 26:28; Heb. 7:22; 8:6, 8–10, 13; 9:15–17; 10:16; 12:24; 13:20), and both entail ethical obligations (1 Cor. 7:19; 9:21; Gal. 6:2; Matt. 5:1–7:27; Heb. 12:14–17; 13:1–19; John 13:34; 14:15, 21, 23–24; 15:10–17; Luke 6:20–49). These obligations are backed up by blessings for obedience and curses for disobedience (1 Cor. 3:12–17; 2 Cor. 5:10; Rom. 14:10; Matt. 7:24–27; Heb. 2:1–4; Luke 6:46–49). Just as obedience was a response to God's gracious and unmerited acts of redemption in the Mosaic covenant (Exod. 20:2; Deut. 5:6; 7:7–8; 9:5), so in the gospel obedience is a result of God's gracious work of redemption, not the reason for it.[14] For Paul and the author of Hebrews, each covenant has a sacrifice (1 Cor. 11:25; Rom. 3:21–26; Heb. 2:17–18; 4:14–5:10; 6:20– 10:18), and each has a people with a story (1 Cor. 10:1–11; Heb. 2:1–4; 12:18–24). For all five authors, therefore, the gospel imitates the broad structure of the Mosaic covenant in which the Mosaic law is imbedded.

The Mosaic law also continues to be authoritative for at least four authors at the level of specific content. Matthew and Luke affirm the continuing authority of the Decalogue, although the sabbath commandment no longer remains valid in its traditional sense (Matt. 19:18–19; Luke 18:20). In addition, they affirm the authority of the two great commandments of love for God and neighbor (Matt. 19:19; 22:37–40; Luke 10:27). John affirms the two great commandments, but does so in his own distinctive way, linking love for neighbor with love for Jesus, who is in turn one with God (10:30; 13:34; 14:15, 21, 23–24; 17:22). Paul not only considers authoritative the Decalogue (again, except for traditional sabbath rest) and the command to love one's neighbor (Gal. 5:14; Rom. 13:8–10; 14:5–6; Eph. 6:2–3), but he uses Deut. 25:4 to claim the right of financial support from the communities in which he ministers (1 Cor. 9:8–9) and relies on the Mosaic law to define the sanctity of these communities (1 Thess. 4:3–6; 1 Cor.

5:1–13; cf. Lev. 18:1–30; 19:20–22, 29; Deut. 17:7; 19:19; 22:21, 24; 24:7). Only Hebrews is silent about the continuing authority of the Mosaic law's ethical commandments.[15]

For all five authors, therefore, the new covenant has absorbed critical aspects of the old covenant. This is not an embarrassment, as it was for Marcion in a later age, but a boon, for it gives to the new covenant all the dignity of its ancient counterpart at the same time that it allows the new to surpass the glory of the old.

CONCLUSION

The answer to the question with which our study began is now clear. The five New Testament authors who explicitly address the issue of the law's continuing validity raise the question in different ways and provide correspondingly different answers. Paul and Matthew grapple with the role of the Mosaic law in governing Christian conduct. John and the author of Hebrews argue that the law points to Jesus, who fulfills it on a massive scale. Luke defends Christians against the charge of sedition in part by demonstrating their reluctance to venture outside the "impregnable palisades," as Pseudo-Aristeas calls them, of the Jewish laws (*Ep. Arist.* 139).

Despite these differences in the way the five authors use the Mosaic law, all are unified in the conviction that it has been overwhelmed and swept away in the eschatological current unleashed by the life, death, and resurrection of Jesus. Much of the Mosaic law, both at the level of structure and specific commands, has been creatively appropriated in this new, eschatological situation. Still, too much of the law has been omitted or radically reinterpreted for the emphasis to fall on the continuity between law and gospel. Continuity is present, but the gospel is something new.

NOTES

1. Cf. D. A. Hagner, "Balancing the Old and the New: The Law of Moses in Matthew and Paul," *Int* 51 (1997): 20–30, here at 27.

2. Roger Mohrlang, *Matthew and Paul: A Comparison of Ethical Perspectives*, SNTSMS 48 (Cambridge: Cambridge University Press, 1984), 43–44. Cf. Peter Stuhlmacher, *Reconciliation, Law, and Righteousness: Essays in Biblical Theology* (Philadelphia: Fortress, 1986), 122–26; and Ulrich Luz, *The The-*

ology of the Gospel of Matthew (Cambridge: Cambridge University Press, 1995), 146–50, although Luz qualifies this position on pp. 150–53.

3. Luz comments insightfully, "Matthew knew full well about the breadth of grace, for he had before his eyes the constant weakness and failure of human beings, Christian and otherwise" (*Theology of the Gospel of Matthew*, 150–51).

4. See, e.g., Philipp Vielhauer, "On the 'Paulinism' of Acts," in *Studies in Luke-Acts*, ed. Leander E. Keck and J. Louis Martyn (Philadelphia: Fortress, 1980), 41–42; and Eduard Verhoef, "(Eternal) Life and Following the Commandments: Lev 18,5 and Luke 10,28," in *The Scriptures in the Gospels*, BETL 131 (Leuven: Leuven University Press/Peeters, 1997), 571–77.

5. For a suggestive survey of the possible literary connections, see Ben Witherington, "The Influence of Galatians on Hebrews," *NTS* 37 (1991): 146–52.

6. On the way in which the angels of Heb. 2:2 demonstrate the provisional nature of the Mosaic law, see Graham Hughes, *Hebrews and Hermeneutics: The Epistle to the Hebrews as a New Testament Example of Biblical Interpretation*, SNTSMS 36 (Cambridge: Cambridge University Press, 1979), 7–8.

7. Cf., e.g., Mark 2:22 with Matt. 9:17 and Luke's omission of Mark 7:1–23. For the view that the redactional activity reflected in these passages betrays a conservative approach to the law, see the comments of Hagner, "Balancing the Old and the New," 24; and Michael Pettem, "Luke's Great Omission and His View of the Law," *NTS* 42 (1996): 35–54.

8. Cf. Hagner, "Balancing the Old and the New," 22–23. Hagner does not believe, however, that Jesus deviates from the law. Jesus only interprets it in ways that deviate radically from the interpretations of his contemporaries.

9. Cf. D. Moody Smith, "The Love Command: John and Paul?" in *Theology and Ethics in Paul and His Interpreters: Essays in Honor of Victor Paul Furnish*, ed. Eugene H. Lovering, Jr., and Jerry L. Sumney (Nashville: Abingdon, 1996), 207–17; he observes that the love command in John "is new eschatologically, but not historically" (p. 208).

10. See, among many others, Rudolf Bultmann, *The Theology of the New Testament*, 2 vols. (New York: Charles Scribner's Sons, 1951–55), 2:340–45; Eduard Lohse, "The Church in Everyday Life: Considerations of the Theological Basis of Ethics in the New Testament," in *Understanding Paul's Ethics: Twentieth Century Approaches*, ed. Brian S. Rosner (Grand Rapids, Mich.: Eerdmans, 1995), 251–65; Stephen Westerholm, *Israel's Law and the Church's Faith: Paul and His Recent Interpreters* (Grand Rapids, Mich.: Eerdmans, 1988), 198–218; idem, *Preface to the Study of Paul* (Grand Rapids, Mich.: Eerdmans, 1997), 90–93; and Colin G. Kruse, *Paul, the Law, and Justification* (Peabody, Mass.: Hendrickson, 1996), 104–6, 114, 292.

11. Cf. Alfred Seeberg, "Moral Teaching: The Existence and Contents of 'the Ways,'" in *Understanding Paul's Ethics: Twentieth Century Approaches*, ed. Brian S. Rosner (Grand Rapids, Mich.: Eerdmans, 1995; orig. pub., 1903), 155–76, here at 155–63; and Eckhard J. Schnabel, "How Paul Developed His

Ethics: Motivations, Norms and Criteria of Pauline Ethics," ibid., 267–97, especially 294–95.

12. Does the same idea lie behind the reference in Heb. 7:12 to "a change of law"? See Marie E. Isaacs, *Sacred Space: An Approach to the Theology of the Epistle to the Hebrews*, JSNTSup 73 (Sheffield: Sheffield Academic Press, 1992), 116.

13. The phrase "new law" first appears in the Christian tradition in *Barnabas* 2.6, where it is used to distinguish between the "yoke of Christ, which is free from compulsion," and the law of Moses with its sacrificial ritual (cf. "the ordinances of the Lord" in 2.1; 10.11; and 21.1). Justin uses the phrase frequently in his *Dialogue with Trypho the Jew* to refer to Jesus himself and the demands of the gospel (see 11.4; 12.3; 24.1 ["another law"]; and 34.1).

14. This is clearest in Paul where obedience arises from a transformed life (as in Rom. 6:1–8:17 and Gal. 5:16–26); but it is present in Matthew, John, and Luke also where the response to Jesus and his words precedes the requirement for obedience (Matt. 4:18–22; 9:13; Luke 5:8, 32; John 1:35–2:11).

15. The author may allude to Deut. 31:6–8 as a warrant for his admonition not to be greedy in 13:7, but his allusion could just as easily be to Josh. 1:5 or 1 Chr. 28:20 (cf. Gen. 28:15).

Indexes

Modern Authors

185

Ancient Sources